Network Performance Open Source Toolkit

Using Netperf, tcptrace, NIST Net, and SSFNet

Richard Blum

WILEY

Wiley Publishing, Inc.

Executive Publisher: Robert Ipsen
Executive Editor: Carol Long
Assistant Developmental Editor: Adaobi Obi Tulton
Editorial Manager: Kathryn Malm
Managing Editor: Pamela M. Hanley
Text Design & Composition: Wiley Composition Services

This book is printed on acid-free paper. ∞

Published by Wiley Publishing, Inc., Indianapolis, Indiana
Published simultaneously in Canada

For general information on our other products and services please contact our Customer Care Department within the United States at (800) 762-2974, outside the United States at (317) 572-3993 or fax (317) 572-4002.

Wiley also publishes its books in a variety of electronic formats. Some content that appears in print may not be available in electronic books.

Library of Congress Cataloging-in-Publication Data:

ISBN: 0-471-43301-2

Printed in the United States of America

10 9 8 7 6 5 4 3 2 1

*This book is dedicated to my grandmother, Margaret Gordon.
Sorry, grandma, it's not a mystery novel—but then again,
in a way, maybe it is.*

*"Trust in the Lord with all your heart and lean not on your own
understanding; in all your ways acknowledge him,
and he will make your paths straight."*

Prov. 3:5-6 (NIV)

Contents

Acknowledgments

First, all glory, honor, and praise go to God, who through His Son makes all things possible, and who gives us the gift of eternal life.

I would like to thank all the great people at Wiley Publishing, Inc. for their help, guidance, and professionalism. Thanks to Carol Long, the Acquisitions Editor, for offering me the opportunity to write this book, and to Adaobi Obi Tulton, the Assistant Developmental Editor, for both helping guide this book along, and working to help make the paragraphs make sense. Also many thanks to Carole McClendon at Waterside Productions for her help in arranging this opportunity for me.

Finally, I would like to thank my parents, Mike and Joyce Blum, for their dedication and support, and my wife Barbara and daughters Katie Jane and Jessica for their faith, love, and understanding, especially while I was writing this book.

Introduction

The job of the network administrator is complicated. If you are a network administrator, not only are you responsible for installing and maintaining the wires, hubs, switches, and possibly routers and firewalls, but you must also ensure that they all work efficiently together. Of course, this all must be done within the constraints of a budget, which these days is often smaller than what you really need to accomplish the job. The goal of this book is to show you some freely available tools that can be used to help monitor and troubleshoot a network, providing you with a toolkit of programs to use when problems arise.

The network administrator is often the first line of defense whenever anything behaves oddly on the network. Even when there is no clear-cut culprit, the network administrator has to prove that the network is not at fault. Network performance is often a difficult thing to measure. What is fast performance for one application can often be slow for another. It is your job to ensure that the network and the network applications are performing properly for your environment. This book is intended to help you with this task.

Overview

Network performance has been studied for many years, which has produced lots of theoretical work on how network traffic is affected by network load. Unfortunately, for the average network administrator in charge of the company network, equations and theories do not help solve real-world problems, such as slow network application performance. Instead, what is required is real-world tools that can monitor and analyze network behavior, to identify the cause of network performance problems and determine how to quickly (and usually, cheaply) fix them.

With the explosion of Open Source software in recent years, many free applications are becoming available that can help the average network administrator. Usually these applications can be easily downloaded, configured, and used to help determine both network performance and network application performance. Money that companies used to have to spend on network performance tools can now be used to purchase equipment to actually solve network problems.

Most Open Source applications are written for the Unix platform. In the past, this was a huge restriction, especially for network administrators who didn't happen to have a big Unix box lying around. However, with the popularity of free Unix distributions such as Linux and FreeBSD, anyone can have a Unix platform for Open Source applications. Now, for little or no money, network administrators can have a fully functional network monitoring and analysis toolkit at their fingertips. This provides opportunities for network troubleshooting that previously were only available with expensive high-end systems.

How This Book Is Organized

This book is divided into three sections. The first section presents a network performance primer, showing some of the basic elements that affect network performance, and explaining how to use some simple Open Source tools to monitor them.

Chapter 1, "Defining Network Performance," describes the techniques used by the Open Source tools to monitor network performance. Understanding how the tools work makes it easier to understand the output, and to determine what solutions can be used to solve any problems detected.

Chapter 2, "Watching Network Traffic," presents some Open Source tools used for monitoring network traffic, in both the Unix and Windows environments. Monitoring network traffic is often an excellent troubleshooting tool when looking for network performance problems.

Chapter 3, "Network Device Utilization," discusses how to use the Simple Network Management Protocol (SNMP) to query existing network devices for performance data. The Open Source tool net-snmp can be used to monitor real-time network performance data straight from the network devices themselves.

The second section of the book presents tools used for monitoring network performance. Determining network performance is done by sending a known stream of data between two endpoints located on the network. By measuring the delays in the data stream, the performance tool can determine what network problems may be present.

Chapter 4, "netperf," describes the netperf network performance tool, developed by Hewlett-Packard. The netperf application can be used to send different types of data streams across a network, and monitor the performance of each type of data stream.

Chapter 5, "dbs," discusses the dbs performance tool, developed at the Nara Institute of Science and Technology, in Japan. The dbs application can be used to perform network tests between two remote hosts on the network, without being connected to either one.

Chapter 6, "Iperf," presents the Iperf application, which was developed at the National Laboratory for Applied Network Research (NLANR), and is currently maintained at the University of Illinois. The Iperf application focuses on how TCP parameters can affect network application performance, and how fine-tuning TCP host parameters can increase the performance of many network applications.

Chapter 7, "Pathrate," discusses both the Pathrate and Pathload applications, developed and maintained by Constantinos Dovrolis, who is currently working at Georgia Tech. Both applications rely on advanced network statistical calculations, involving the delays present in transferring packets across network devices along the path between the two endpoints.

Chapter 8, "Nettest," describes the Nettest application, developed at the Lawrence Berkeley Labs as a secure shell for performing network tests between hosts. The Nettest application uses the OpenSSL security application to encrypt network performance sessions, and to control who is allowed to run network tests.

Chapter 9, "NetLogger," presents a slightly different technique used for monitoring network application performance. The NetLogger application provides a set of APIs that is used within network applications for logging network events, such as writing data to the network and reading data from the network. Once the network log is created, a graphical interface allows you to monitor each of the network events and determine which events have poor performance.

Chapter 10, "tcptrace," discusses the tcptrace application, developed at Ohio University. The tcptrace application analyzes data captured by the tcpdump application, quickly displaying information about each TCP session in the trace.

Chapter 11, "ntop," introduces you to the ntop application, developed at the University of Pisa, in Italy, to produce graphical Web pages showing network utilization by each device on the network. This helps you determine which devices are consuming the most resources on the network.

Chapter 12, "Comparing Network Performance Tools," wraps up the network performance tool section by presenting a sample network environment, and showing how each tool can be used to monitor network performance on the sample network.

The third section of the book describes how to use network application performance tools to analyze how network applications behave in different network environments. By analyzing the applications in a test network, you can often see potential problems before the application is released in the production network.

Chapter 13, "Measuring Application Performance," discusses how network application performance testing tools—both network emulators and network simulators—can help you determine how applications will perform in the production network.

Chapter 14, "dummynet," describes the dummynet application, which is available on FreeBSD systems to emulate network behavior using a FreeBSD host. This enables a single FreeBSD host to be used within a test network to emulate the network delay, bandwidth limitations, and packet loss of a full production network.

Chapter 15, "NIST Net," discusses the NIST Net application, developed at the U.S. National Institute of Standards and Technology to simulate network behavior using a Linux system. This application provides the network emulation functions to use a Linux system to model the production network.

Chapter 16, "Network Traffic Generator," presents the traffic application, which is used to generate specific data traffic patterns on the network. This can be used to artificially emulate production network traffic on a test network using a single host.

Chapter 17, "ns," describes the Network Simulator application, developed at the University of California Berkeley as a method to simulate network behavior without having to actually have a test network available.

Chapter 18, "SSFNet," discusses the Scaleable Simulation Framework (SSF), and how it is used to model network behavior, using either C++ or Java.

Chapter 19, "Comparing Application Performance Tools," wraps up the final section by showing how to model production networks, and how to use the emulation and simulation tools presented to predict network application performance.

Who Should Read This Book

The primary focus of this book is to help network administrators and technicians monitor and analyze network performance. Often it is not easy to determine what causes network performance problems. The tools presented in the first two sections of the book can be used in the production network to help identify the cause of network performance issues. The text explains how to install and configure each tool, and describes how to use the tool in the production network.

Because network applications go hand in hand with networks, the secondary focus of the book is to help in the analysis of network application performance. Both network application developers and network administrators must test network applications within a test network before deploying them to the production network. For this to be done properly, the production network environment must be accurately duplicated within the test network. Open Source network emulators and simulators make this possible. The book presents each emulator and simulator tool, showing how it can be used to duplicate the production network environment.

Tools That Are Needed

This book uses mainly Open Source tools intended for the Unix platforms. Some type of Unix platform is required to install, compile, and operate each of the tools. The use of Open Source Unix distributions, such as FreeBSD or Linux, is highly encouraged. All of the tools presented were installed, compiled, and tested on a Mandrake Linux 8.0 system (with the exception of dummynet, which requires a FreeBSD system).

All of the tools are available for download from their respective Internet Web sites. Some type of Internet access is required to access the tools' distribution packages. Of course, the faster the Internet connection, the quicker the downloads will proceed. Some of the distribution packages are fairly large, so using a slow-speed modem connection may take a while.

Summary

Trying to troubleshoot network performance issues while customers are complaining is not a fun job. Hopefully this book will present some ideas and options to help you identify and fix network problems before your customers notice them. Nothing takes the place of experience. Monitoring and analyzing network performance when there are no problems often helps in times when there are problems. Knowing what a healthy network looks like helps in identifying problems in a sick network.

In today's environment, there are constant advances in network technology. One advantage of using Open Source network performance tools is that they are often updated or replaced to accommodate newer features. You should always monitor the Internet and network performance newsgroups for new tools, and advances in the old tools. This will ensure that you will maintain an efficient and effective network performance toolkit.

PART

One

Network Performance Primer

Defining Network Performance

Before you dive into detailed discussions of network performance tools, it is a good idea to first understand what network performance is, and how it can be measured. This chapter defines network performance, describes the elements involved in measuring it, and shows techniques many network performance tools use to measure it

The words that network administrators hate to hear are "The network seems slow today." What exactly is a slow network, and how can you tell? Who determines when the network is slow, and how do they do it? There are usually more questions than answers when you're dealing with network performance in a production network environment.

It would be great if there were standard answers to these questions, along with a standard way to solve slow network performance. The open source network performance tools presented in this book can help the network administrator determine the status of the network, and identify the areas of the network that could be improved to increase performance. Often, network bottlenecks can be found, and simply reallocating the resources on a network can greatly improve performance, without the addition of expensive new network equipment.

Knowing the elements of network performance will help you better understand how the network performance tools work, and how to interpret the vast amount of information the tools provide. The first section of this chapter describes the elements involved in determining network performance.

The Elements of Network Performance

Much work has been devoted to the attempt to define network performance exactly. It is not the intention of this book to bore you with numerous equations that describe theoretical network philosophy about how packets traverse networks. Network performance is a complex issue, with lots of independent variables that affect how clients access servers across a network. However, most of the elements involved in the performance of networks can be boiled down to a few simple network principles that can be measured, monitored, and controlled by the network administrator with simple—often free—software.

Most network performance tools use a combination of five separate elements to measure network performance:

- Availability
- Response time
- Network utilization
- Network throughput
- Network bandwidth capacity

This section describes each of these elements, and explains how network performance tools use each element to measure network performance.

Availability

The first step in measuring network performance is to determine if the network is even working. If traffic cannot traverse the network, you have bigger problems than just network performance issues. The simplest test for network availability is the ping program. By attempting to ping remote servers from a client device on the network, you can easily determine the state of your network.

Just about all Unix implementations include the ping program to query remote hosts for availability. The ping program sends an Internet Control Message Protocol (ICMP) echo request packet to the destination host. When the echo request packet is received, the remote host immediately returns an echo reply packet to the sending device.

While most network administrators know what the ping program is, few know that there are lots of fancy options that can be used to perform advanced testing using the ping program. The format of the ping command is:

```
ping [-dfnqrvR] [-c count] [-i wait] [-l preload] [-p pattern] [-s
packetsize]
```

You can use different combinations of options and parameters to create the ping test that best suits your network environment. Often, just using the default options and parameters provides enough information about a network link to satisfy availability questions.

Receiving an echo reply packet from the remote host means that there is an available network path between the client and server devices. If no echo reply packet is received, there is a problem with either a network device or a link along the path (assuming the remote server is available and answering pings).

By selecting different remote hosts on the network, you can determine if all of the segments on your network are available for traffic. If multiple hosts do not respond to a ping request, a common network device is most likely down. Determining the faulty network device takes some detective work on your part.

While sending a single ping packet to a remote host can determine the availability of a network path, performing a single ping by itself is not a good indicator of network performance. You often need to gather more information to determine the performance of any connections between the client and the server. A better way to determine basic network performance is to send a string of multiple ping request packets.

Using Availability Statistics

When multiple ping packets are sent to a remote host, the ping program tracks how many responses are received. The result is displayed as the percentage of the packets that were not received. A network performance tool can use the ping statistics to obtain basic information regarding the status of the network between the two endpoints.

By default the Unix ping program continually sends ping requests to the designated remote host until the operator stops the operation by pressing a Ctrl-C key combination. Alternately, you can use the -c option in the ping command to specify a specific number of ping requests to send. Each ping request is tracked separately using the ICMP sequence field.

A sample ping session that uses multiple ping packets looks like this:

```
$ ping 192.168.1.100
PING 192.168.1.100 (192.168.1.100): 56 data bytes
64 bytes from 192.168.1.100: icmp_seq=0 ttl=255 time=0.712 ms
64 bytes from 192.168.1.100: icmp_seq=1 ttl=255 time=0.620 ms
64 bytes from 192.168.1.100: icmp_seq=2 ttl=255 time=0.698 ms
64 bytes from 192.168.1.100: icmp_seq=3 ttl=255 time=0.662 ms
64 bytes from 192.168.1.100: icmp_seq=4 ttl=255 time=0.649 ms
^C
--- 192.168.1.100 ping statistics ---
5 packets transmitted, 5 packets received, 0% packet loss
round-trip min/avg/max/stddev = 0.620/0.668/0.712/0.033 ms
$
```

In this example, a response was received for all of the packets that were sent, indicating no problems on the network. If any of the ping packets do not solicit a response, it can be assumed that either the echo request packet did not make it to the remote server, or the remote server's echo response packet did not make it back to the pinging client. In either case, something on the network caused a packet to be lost.

Once you establish that there are lost packets in the ping sequence, you must determine what caused the packet losses. The two biggest causes of lost packets are:

- Collisions on a network segment
- Packets dropped by a network device

Within an Ethernet segment, only one station is allowed to transmit at a time. When more than one station attempts to transmit at the same time, a collision occurs. Having collisions is normal for an Ethernet network, and not something that should cause panic for the network administrator.

However, as an Ethernet segment gets overloaded, excessive collisions will begin to take over the network. As more traffic is generated on the network, more collisions occur. For each collision, the affected senders must retransmit the packets that caused the collision. As more packets are retransmitted, more network traffic is generated, and more collisions can occur. This event is called a *collision storm*, and can severely affect the performance of a network segment.

Dropped packets can also result in packet losses. All network devices contain packet buffers. As packets are received from the network, they are placed in a packet buffer, waiting for their turn to be transmitted. This is demonstrated in Figure 1.1.

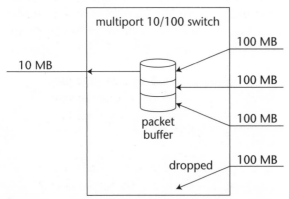

Figure 1.1   Dropping packets in a network device.

Each port on a router or switch device contains an individual buffer area that accepts packets destined to go out the interface. If excessive network traffic occurs, preventing the timely emptying of the buffer, or if more packets arrive than the port can transmit, the buffer will fill up.

If a network device's packet buffer gets filled up, it has no choice but to drop incoming packets. This scenario happens frequently on network devices that connect to networks running at different speeds, such as a 10/100 switch or router. If lots of traffic arrives on a high-speed 100-MB connection destined for a lower-speed 10-MB connection, packets will be backed up in the buffers, and often overflow, causing dropped packets and retransmissions from the sending devices.

To minimize this effect, most network devices are configured to allocate ample memory space for handling packet buffers. However, it is impossible to predict all network conditions, and dropped packets still may occur.

Using Large Ping Packets

Another problem with measuring availability is the size of the packets used in the ping request. Many network devices handle packets with multiple packet buffers, based on average packet sizes. Different buffer pools handle different-sized packets. Too many of one particular size of packet can cause dropped packets for that size category, while packets of other sizes are passed without a problem.

For example, switches often have three classes of packet buffers—one for small packets, one for medium-sized packets, and one for large packets. To accurately test these network devices, you must be able to send different-sized packets to test the different packet buffers.

To accommodate this, most network performance tools allow you to alter the size of the packets used in the testing. When testing networks that utilize routers or switches, you must ensure that a wide variety of packet sizes are used to traverse the network.

> **TIP** There have been many instances of security problems with large ping packets. As a result, most Unix systems only allow the root account to send large ping packets. You should be careful when sending larger packets to remote servers, so as to not adversely affect the remote server.

By default, the packet size used in the ping utility is 64 bytes (56 bytes of data and the 8-byte ICMP header). You can use the -s option to change the packet size, up to the maximum that is allowed on the network segment (1,500 for Ethernet networks).

After altering the packet size of the ping packets, you can see how this affects the ping statistics by observing the output from the ping command:

```
# ping -s 1000 192.168.1.100
PING 192.168.1.100 (192.168.1.100):1000 data bytes
1008 bytes from 192.168.1.100: icmp_seq=0 ttl=127 time=2.994 ms
1008 bytes from 192.168.1.100: icmp_seq=1 ttl=127 time=2.952 ms
1008 bytes from 192.168.1.100: icmp_seq=2 ttl=127 time=2.975 ms
1008 bytes from 192.168.1.100: icmp_seq=3 ttl=127 time=2.940 ms
1008 bytes from 192.168.1.100: icmp_seq=4 ttl=127 time=3.133 ms
1008 bytes from 192.168.1.100: icmp_seq=5 ttl=127 time=2.960 ms
1008 bytes from 192.168.1.100: icmp_seq=6 ttl=127 time=2.988 ms
^C
--- 192.168.1.100 ping statistics ---
7 packets transmitted, 7 packets received, 0% packet loss
round-trip min/avg/max/stddev = 2.940/2.992/3.133/0.060 ms
#
```

In this example, all of the large ping packets were still successful, indicating that all of the segments between the host and the client were processing the larger packets without any problems. If you experience packet loss with larger packets, but not with smaller packets, this often indicates a problem with a router or switch buffer somewhere in the network. Most router and switch devices allow the administrator to change the packet buffer allocations to allot more buffers for a particular packet-size range.

Response Time

As seen in the ping example, while network availability is one element of network performance, it cannot accurately reflect the overall performance of the network. The network customers' perception of the network is not limited to whether or not they can get to an individual server. It also includes how long it takes to process data with the server.

To obtain a more accurate picture of the network performance, you must observe how long it takes packets to traverse the network. The time that it takes a packet to travel between two points on the network is called the *response time*.

The response time affects how quickly network applications appear to be working. Slow response times are often magnified by network applications that need to send and receive lots of information across the network, or applications that produce immediate results from a customer entry. Applications such as TELNET, which require the customer to wait for a keystroke to be echoed from the remote host, are extremely vulnerable to slow network response times.

While network response time is often obvious to customers, trying to measure the response time between two separate hosts can be a difficult thing to do. Determining the time it takes for a packet to leave one network device and arrive at a remote network device is not easy. There must be some mechanism to time the leaving and arriving events, independent of the two systems on the network.

When using network performance tools that utilize round-trip response times, it is always wise to incorporate the remote system's CPU utilization in the data taken, to ensure that you are comparing response times run at similar system loads, eliminating the system-loading factor.

Response-Time Factors

In large networks, there are many factors that can affect response times between a client and a server. As the network administrator, you can control some of these factors, but others are completely out of your control. These factors can include:

- Overloaded network segments
- Network errors
- Faulty network wiring
- Broadcast storms
- Faulty network devices
- Overloaded network hosts

Any one or combination of these factors can contribute to slow network response time. Measuring the individual factors can be difficult, but the network performance tools presented in this book can measure the overall effect each factor has on network response times by sending known network traffic samples and determining how the data traverses the network

Determining Response Time from Ping Packets

As seen in the sample outputs for the ping program, the round-trip response time values for each ping packet sent are shown in the ping packet statistics:

```
64 bytes from 192.168.1.100: icmp_seq=0 ttl=255 time=0.712 ms
```

The response time is shown in milliseconds. For internal LAN connections, the response times should be well within 1 or 2 milliseconds. For WAN connections, the response times can often be over 200 or 300 milliseconds, depending on WAN connectivity speeds.

WARNING Remember that the ping response time values are round-trip response times. The current load on the remote system affects these values.

When multiple ping packets are sent, an average of their response times is calculated and displayed:

```
round-trip min/avg/max/stddev = 2.940/2.992/3.133/0.060 ms
```

The response time for a connection can depend on many different factors within the network connection. As the packets traverse the network, each network device can play a role in the total response time. The network performance tool must be able to take into account the response-time factors for each network connection.

The best use for ping response times is to establish a baseline value, or the values seen when the network is performing at normal speeds. When customers complain about slow network performance, the ping response time values taken can then be compared against response times taken during normal network performance. Any drastic deviations in these times can represent a problem with a network device.

Using traceroute for Redundant Paths

In a network that has redundant paths, it is often desirable to determine which path packets are taking at any given time. If you determine that packets are not being routed in the most efficient manner, you can often make simple configuration changes to routers to increase response times.

The Unix traceroute program allows the network administrator to determine exactly which route packets are taking to get between two points on the network. The traceroute utility uses the IP Time to Live (TTL) value to purposely force a packet to expire along the path to the destination.

The TTL value specifies how many hops an individual packet can make before expiring. When a router sees a packet with an expired TTL value, it should report the problem back to the sending network device. By starting the TTL value at 1 and incrementing it at each ping attempt, the traceroute utility forces remote routers along the network path to expire the ping packet and return an ICMP destination unreachable packet to the client. Since the router itself must return the packet, each router traversed along the network path is identified.

The format for the traceroute command is:

traceroute [-dFInrvx] [-f firstttl] [-g gateway] [-i iface] [-m maxttl] [-p port] [q nqueries] [-s srcaddr] [-t tos] [-w waittime] host [packetlength]

As can be seen from the command-line format, the ping program, like the traceroute program, has many options that can be used to fine-tune the testing.

The default values for all of the options can be used to send a simple traceroute probe to a remote host. The output from a sample traceroute across the Internet to the www.cisco.com host looks like this:

```
$ traceroute www.cisco.com
traceroute to www.cisco.com (198.133.219.25), 30 hops max, 40 byte
packets
 1 209.244.188.162 (209.244.188.162)  175 ms   170 ms   171 ms
 2 gige7-0-2.hsipacces1.Cincinnati1.Level3.net (63.212.221.2) 154 ms
150 ms  150 ms
 3 ge-6-0-0.mp1.Cincinnati1.Level3.net (64.159.0.173)  152 ms   150 ms
149 ms
 4 so-3-0-0.mp2.Chicago1.Level3.net (64.159.1.34)  150 ms   149 ms   150
ms
 5 pos9-0.core1.Chicago1.level3.net (209.247.10.170) 150 ms 150 ms 151
ms
 6 144.232.26.185 (144.232.8.185) 151 ms 152 ms 151 ms
 7 sl-bb20-chi-13-0.sprintlink.net (144.242.26.50) 151 ms   150 ms   150
ms
 8 sl-bb20-sj-6-0.sprintlink.net (144.232.8.117) 200 ms 201 ms 203 ms
 9 sl-gw11-sj-9-0.sprintlink.net (133.232.3.138) 210 ms 211 ms 210 ms
10 sl-ciscopsn2-11-0-0.sprintlink.net (144.228.44.14) 211 ms 210 ms 210
ms
11 sjce-dirty-gw1.cisco.com (128.107.239.89)  210 ms   210 ms   210 ms
12 sjck-sdf-ciod-gw2.cisco.com (128.107.239.12) 209 ms 209 ms 210 ms
13 www.cisco.com (198.133.219.25) 211 ms 210 ms 211 ms
$
```

The output from the traceroute program shows every router that responds to the expired test packet along the path to the destination host. Along with that information, the round-trip times that it took for the packet to reach each router are displayed (three separate test packets are sent with the same TTL value for each test). Remember that these values are round-trip response times, and can change with different loading on the individual routers.

Networks that use load balancing will show inconsistent route paths between two points on the network, depending on the network load at the time of the test. As with other response-time techniques, the best thing to do in these scenarios is to take baseline tests under various network loads to see how and when each network path is utilized.

Network Utilization

A major factor in network performance is the utilization of each network segment along the path between two endpoints. The *network utilization* represents the percent of time that the network is in use over a given period. By definition, individual Ethernet segments can only carry one packet at a time. For any given moment, the Ethernet segment is either at 100-percent utilization (carrying a packet), or at 0-percent utilization (idle). The network utilization percentage shows the percentage of time the network is in use over a set period.

Calculating the network utilization requires you to find out how many bytes of network traffic are being handled by the network over a set period. This value depends on the type of network interface that is being monitored.

Half-duplex devices can only carry data in one direction at a time, and therefore calculating their network utilization involves totaling the input and output byte counts for a set period, and dividing by the total capacity of the device interface for that period. To determine the total number of bits received on the interfaces, each of the packet byte rates is multiplied by 8. This value is divided by the total interface capacity multiplied by the time interval of the sample (in seconds):

```
%utilization = ((datasent + datarecv) * 8) / (intspeed * sampletime) *
100
```

For example, a 10-MB half-duplex network interface that over a 5-second period sends 700,000 bytes of data and receives 175,000 bytes would have a network utilization of:

```
%utilization = (((700,000 + 175,000) * 8) / (10,000,000 * 5) * 100 = 14%
```

The 14-percent utilization represents the network utilization only for that 5-second period. It is not uncommon to see high network utilization for a short period of time, given that Ethernet traffic is often bursty in nature. You have a problem when you take the same calculation for a longer period of time, such as a 5- or 30-minute interval, and still get high network utilization.

Although calculating network utilization on an individual network segment can be easy, determining the network utilization between two separate endpoints on the network can be complex. You must calculate the network utilization for each segment traversed along the network path, and determine how each segment's utilization affects the overall response time of the packet.

Due to the complexity of this, most network performance tools utilize different elements—the network throughput and the network bandwidth capacity—to determine network performance between two remote network endpoints.

Network Throughput

Network throughput is similar in concept to network utilization. The throughput of a network represents the amount of network bandwidth available for a network application at any given moment, across the network links. As network applications use network bandwidth, the amount of bandwidth left over for other applications is decreased. The amount of bandwidth left over is considered the network throughput.

Determining network throughput allows the network administrator to find network bottlenecks that slow down performance over a given network link between clients and servers. Often a novice network administrator places a group of clients on a high-speed network device, and the application server on another high-speed network device, to increase application performance. However, what the administrator forgets is that the two high-speed devices may be connected via a slow-speed link. Figure 1.2 demonstrates an example of this.

While the networks that contain the client and server devices are high-speed and have good network performance, it is the interconnecting network device that is causing performance problems. First off, the intermediate network link is limiting the overall speed of the end-to-end link to only 10 MB, no matter how fast the clients and server are connected to the network. Second, since the intermediate network device is a shared hub, it may contain other clients and application servers, which puts additional traffic load on the slow-speed link.

Usually, finding the network bottleneck is not this simple. On complex networks, there can be several network devices within the path of clients and servers. The hardest part of determining the network throughput is calculating the effect that each intermediate link has on the overall end-to-end network connection.

Calculating network throughput is a mathematical process that is best left to the mathematical geniuses. It involves sending periodic streams of packets, and determining the rate at which the server receives the streams. Each stream sample produces data elements used to determine the amount of bandwidth remaining on the network link. The streams are increased until the maximum bandwidth is observed, then quickly backed off so as not to affect the network performance.

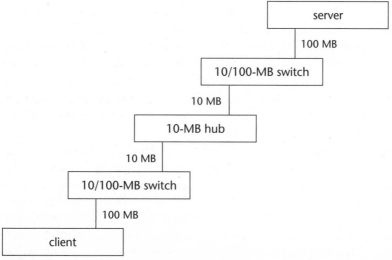

Figure 1.2   Finding the throughput bottleneck.

Of course, this calculation is extremely dependent on exiting network applications, and how they load the network at any given time. It is best to calculate network throughput at different times of the day, and on different days of the week. This enables you to gather all of the information on different applications as they are run on the network.

Many new network applications fail due to lack of available network throughput. If an application is tested in a development environment that does not include the other applications that will be running on the network, it is easy to forget about existing network throughput on the production network.

Bandwidth Capacity

Bandwidth capacity is another factor in the determination of network throughput. The total amount of bandwidth available between two network endpoints can greatly affect the performance of a network. Devices directly connected on a 100-MB network switch should have significantly better performance than devices that are remotely connected via a slower T1 circuit.

The ability to quantify this performance difference requires complex network theory to be built into the network performance tool. The network performance tool must be able to determine the possible end-to-end network bandwidth available on networks with varying link speeds. Each link that a packet must traverse must be included in the overall network performance of an application.

In an ideal network scenario, a constant data rate should be maintained between a client and a server as packets are sent back and forth. The constant data rate represents the network speed at which the two endpoints are linked together. By observing the time it takes for a packet to traverse the network, you can determine the maximum speed of the network link.

As we all know, there is no such thing as an ideal network scenario. In production networks, traffic is constantly traveling between network devices, affecting the perceived speed of a network link. In order to determine the maximum bandwidth capacity of a network link, the network performance tool must do some math tricks.

Two techniques, called *packet pairs* and *packet trains*, are used to determine the maximum network bandwidth capacity of an existing production network without affecting the normal traffic. First, a pair of packets is sent to a remote device at a known separation interval (the packet pair). As the packet pair traverses the network, the interval between the two will vary, depending on the existing traffic (the packet train). Figure 1.3 demonstrates this principle.

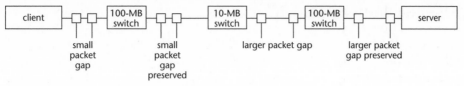

Figure 1.3   Packet separation in different speed segments.

The packets are sent from a device connected to a 100-MB network device. Along the path to the destination device, the network uses a 10-MB network link. The packets received by the switch device on the 100-MB network must be queued and wait their turn before being sent out on the 10-MB link. This affects the separation between the two packets. Again, on the other end of the network, the 10-MB link is connected to another switch, which in turn queues the packets for transmission on the 100-MB network.

When the packets arrive at the destination, the interval separating them is determined. The difference between the original interval and the calculated interval represents the loading on the network. Once the load value is calculated, a large burst of packets can be sent from the client to the server. The rate at which the packets arrive from the client represents the rate, or speed, at which the network was able to transport the data. Given the load factor and the data rate, the network performance tool can calculate the theoretical maximum speed at which the network link should be able to process data.

Methods of Collecting Performance Data

After determining which network performance elements to monitor, the network performance tool must be able to access data for the elements. Three different methods are used to obtain data from the network:

- Querying network devices for stored information
- Watching existing traffic on the network for signs of network performance issues
- Generating test traffic to send on the network to test network performance

Part of your job when evaluating a network performance tool is to determine how the tool extracts data about the network's performance, and if that method is appropriate for your particular network environment. This section describes the three different data-collecting methods, and shows how they can differ when collecting data on the network.

Querying Network Devices

One of the simplest methods used to collect network data is to go to the source of the network, the network devices. When purchasing network devices such as hubs and switches, you will find that two types of each network device are available:

- Managed network devices
- Unmanaged network devices

Managed network devices include management software that collects statistics about the network traffic traversing the device, whether it is a simple network hub or a complex network router. Unmanaged network devices do not collect any statistical information about the network traffic, and cannot be queried for information.

While managed network devices are usually more expensive than unmanaged devices, they are well worth the extra price in large networks. Many network management software packages, as well as many freely available open source network performance tools, use the network device management interface to extract network information from the managed network devices. This information is invaluable for troubleshooting network problems.

How Tools Query Devices

All managed network devices implement the Simple Network Management Protocol (SNMP). SNMP provides both a mechanism for storing network data in a hierarchical database on the network device, and a protocol for querying the database from a remote device.

All SNMP devices include a common Management Information Base (MIB) that stores basic network information about the traffic on the device. This information includes the bytes transmitted and received per interface, the number and types of errors on the interfaces, and the network utilization on each interface. This information is invaluable for determining network performance on different segments of the network.

Besides the common MIB database objects, most SNMP devices also include proprietary MIB objects that track information specific to the network device. SNMP provides an area within the hierarchical database for companies to create their own entries to track information specific to their network devices. This area of the database is called the *enterprise* MIB. Access to the enterprise MIB is usually controlled by SNMP *community names*. A community name is a password that is used to grant access to specific parts of the MIB database.

Values to Query

When using SNMP to query network devices, you must know which values are pertinent for network performance information. There are plenty of data objects that can be found in the SNMP MIB tables on network devices, and dumping all of the tables would take an extremely large amount of time and network bandwidth.

The common MIB database provides much of the basic network performance data used to track performance of a network device. The second version of the common MIB database (called *MIB-2*) has been updated to include many error statistics for network devices.

The MIB-2 database objects provide many useful fields that can be used to determine the amount of network traffic and errors on a network device. Querying these values can give you lots of information regarding network traffic on the device. Table 1.1 shows some of the more useful MIB-2 objects that should be considered.

Table 1.1   SNMP MIB Network Performance Objects

OBJECT	DESCRIPTION
IfType	The physical type of interface
IfSpeed	The data rate capacity of the interface
IfMTU	The size of the largest data packet the interface can handle
IfAdminStatus	The status of the interface (active/inactive)
IfInOctets	The total number of octets received by the interface
IfOutOctets	The total number of octets sent by the interface
IfInUcasePkts	The total number of unicast packets received by the interface
IfOutUcastPkts	The total number of unicast packets sent by the interface
IfInNUcastPkts	The total number of non-unicast packets (broadcast/multicast) received by the interface
IfOutNUcastPkts	The total number of non-unicast packets (broadcast/multicast) sent by the interface
IfInErrors	The total number of packets received that contained errors
IfOutErrors	The total number of packets that could not be sent because they contained errors
IfInDiscards	The total number of packets received that could not be processed, even though they did not contain errors

Most of the MIB-2 values are continuous counters. For example, the ifInOctets object counts the number of bytes (octets) received on the interface since it was first powered on (or the MIB-2 database was reset). This value can reach a maximum value, and then roll over to zero and start over. To determine a data rate, most network performance tools query these values over a set period of time, and subtract the difference. Care must be taken when doing this, to ensure that the value has not rolled over to zero between the measuring times, affecting the data results.

Network devices that contain multiple ports (such as switches and hubs) maintain a separate MIB-2 table for each interface on the device, as well as a system-wide MIB-2 table. The separate port tables are accessed using special indexing within the MIB value. Chapter 3, "Network Device Utilization," describes how to access this information using SNMP network tools.

Watching Existing Traffic

Another common technique used for collecting network performance data is to watch existing traffic on the network. A lot of information can be gathered from the network just by watching the packets that are traveling between network devices.

In order to capture all of the traffic traveling on the network, a device's network interface must be placed in *promiscuous mode*. By default, a network interface only accepts packets that are destined for the device, or that are sent out on a multicast or broadcast address. Promiscuous mode allows the network interface to read all packets on the network, regardless of their destination. This feature allows the network device to inspect each packet on the network, no matter where it came from, and where it is sent.

TIP When attempting to capture traffic on a network, you must be careful of devices such as switches, bridges, and routers, which segment traffic. If your network device is on one of these types of devices, it will not see all of the traffic on the network.

After the network packets have been captured, they must be decoded and analyzed to see what trends and/or problems exist on the network. A few items that can be seen by analyzing network traffic are:

- Packet retransmissions
- Frozen TCP window sizes
- Broadcast storms
- Network advertisements
- Chatty applications
- Quality of service applications

Each of these items can be a potential network performance problem, and should be watched in the network monitor.

Generating Test Traffic

Many network performance tools generate their own network traffic to determine the current performance of the network. This technique requires math skills, as well as a knowledge of network theory.

All network performance tools that analyze network performance by generating test traffic require two devices on the network. The network performance along the path between the two devices is determined by using the packet pair and packet train methods, described previously in the *Bandwidth Capacity* section. This is demonstrated in Figure 1.4.

In Figure 1.4, the network performance tool determines the performance only between devices A and B. No other paths in the network are tested. In order to test other paths on the network, the testing devices must be relocated to other points in the network. Of course the alternative is to have multiple test device pairs and locate them at different points in the network. The trick is to place the smallest number of testing points that can cover the largest area on the network.

As mentioned, calculating network performance requires you to send pairs and trains of packets across the network. The packet pairs do not take up much network bandwidth, but the packet trains can place a fair amount of data on the network. Care should be taken when using network performance tools that use packet trains, so as not to adversely affect production traffic on the network.

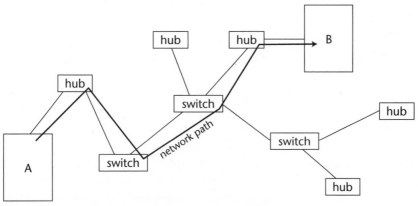

Figure 1.4 Generating test traffic on a network path.

Summary

This chapter describes what network performance is, and how a network performance tool can measure it. Network performance incorporates five separate elements: availability, response time, network utilization, network throughput, and bandwidth capacity.

The availability of the network is crucial for network applications. Testing the availability of the network is often done by using a simple ping test to determine which hosts on the network are reachable. After determining availability, you can measure the response time for various hosts on the network. Different response times can be found based on different network link types and different paths in the network.

Network utilization is measured to determine how much of the network is being used for applications, and the percentage of error transmissions. A network with high utilization will have an increased amount of errors in the network traffic. Similar to the network utilization are the network throughput and capacity. The capacity is the total amount of data that can theoretically pass between two points on the network. This can be affected by different link speeds across the network, and different types of cables used to connect the network devices. The network throughput represents the amount of network bandwidth currently available for applications.

The are three different methods of collecting network performance data from the network. The Simple Network Management Protocol (SNMP) is used to query managed network devices for network information. SNMP devices store network information in the Management Information Base (MIB) database. Information such as bytes received and sent, as well as errors received, is contained in the MIB database. A remote network management workstation can query the MIB database using SNMP to retrieve network information about the device.

Watching network traffic can also determine network performance. Telltale signs such as broadcast storms and packet retransmissions can be seen by capturing data as it flows through the network. The last method of collecting network performance data is to generate test traffic on the network. Some network performance tools generate test packets and send them across the network to determine the network capacity and performance. By using packet pairs and packet trains, network performance tools can calculate the network information based on packet separation (the spacing between packets) and throughput rates.

The next chapter describes one of the basic elements of network performance monitoring—watching network packets. By observing the actual network traffic, you can often identify the device (or devices) contributing the most to network load. There are several open source applications that are available to help you watch network traffic. Each one will be discussed and demonstrated.

Watching Network Traffic

As mentioned in Chapter 1, "Defining Network Performance," watching network traffic is one way to determine how well the network performs. This chapter shows you how to install several network-monitoring software packages for both the Unix and Windows worlds, and how to use them to watch for network traffic problems.

Watching the traffic that traverses a network can often tell you a lot about the health of your network. There are many expensive commercial monitoring tools available to help network administrators capture and decode packets on the network. These products are often standalone devices whose only function is to capture packets and monitor network activity.

However, there are also several good Open Source network monitoring tools that can perform the same functions as the expensive network monitors. Each of these tools can be loaded on an existing Unix or Windows host to monitor the network and display and decode the packets that it sees. This enables you to watch the network traffic on a specific server without having to deal with connecting any extra devices.

Catching All the Traffic

By default, network devices only capture packets that are destined for either their specific Media Access Control (MAC) address, or a broadcast or multicast address. To enable a network device to watch other traffic on the network, you must place the network card in *promiscuous mode*. Promiscuous mode enables the network card to forward all packets that it sees to higher-layer programs on the device.

Unfortunately, different network cards require different software hooks to enable promiscuous mode and pass captured packets to the higher-layer programs. To simplify things for programmers, packet-capturing libraries have been created in both the Unix and Windows worlds to provide a common application programming interface (API) for packet capturing. The two most popular packet-capturing libraries are:

- The libpcap library for Unix
- The winpcap library for Windows

Both of these libraries provide APIs for programs to easily capture packets as they travel past the network card of the host device.

The libpcap Library

The libpcap library was developed at the Lawrence Berkeley National Laboratory, and is now maintained by an organization called the Tcpdump Group. The libpcap library has been ported to every Unix distribution (including Linux and FreeBSD) to be used as a common method of capturing packets from network interface cards. Most Unix distributions include the libpcap library, and many distributions install it by default.

Downloading and Installing libpcap

If you are interested in using the latest version of libpcap, you can download the source code from the Tcpdump Group Web site and compile it yourself. At the time of this writing, the latest version of libpcap is version 0.7.1, which can be downloaded from www.tcpdump.org/release/libpcap-0.7.1.tar.gz.

After downloading the libpcap distribution file, you must unpack and compile it. The distribution file is a compressed tar file, which means that you must uncompress it using the gunzip utility, and extract the distribution files using the tar command. Many implementations of the tar command allow both steps to be performed at once using the –z option:

```
tar -zxvf libpcap-0.7.1.tar.gz
```

The distribution files will be extracted into the libpcap-0.7.1 directory. After changing to the new directory, you must run the configure script to build a Makefile file. The configure script checks the Unix distribution for specific system and compiler features to customize the libpcap library. To compile the libpcap library, your Unix distribution must have a C compiler, and the lex and bison text parsers. For Open Source Unix distributions such as Linux and FreeBSD, the gcc, flex, and bison programs provide these functions.

WARNING The current libpcap distribution requires the 2.5.4 version (or later) of flex to compile.

When you run the configure command, you must reference the local copy of it:

```
./configure
```

You should see several lines of output as the configure script checks for system and compiler features necessary to build the libpcap library. After running the configure script, you can use the make command to compile the library. The output file is called libpcap.a. To install this file on your system, you must change to the root user, and run the make program again, using the install option:

```
make install
```

This places the libpcap.a library file in the proper location on the Unix system, and registers it with the system libraries database. It is now ready to be used by any program that needs to capture network packets from the system network card.

Using libpcap

After the libpcap library is created and installed, you can use it to compile programs that require promiscuous mode access to the network. If you write programs using the libpcap library, you must include the library file in your compiles:

```
gcc program.c -lpcap
```

TIP Note that, when using the library, you do not specify the full filename on the compiler command line, just the pcap library name.

The libpcap library contains all of the API function calls that are used by applications to access packets from the network. If you are compiling the source code for the tcpdump program (described later in *The tcpdump Program* section of this chapter), you must have the libpcap library installed on your system.

The winpcap Library

The winpcap library was developed by the NetGroup at the Politecnico di Torino. It was developed as a libpcap-compatible interface for Windows platforms. As libpcap does for Unix, winpcap allows Windows programs to interface the network card with a common API to read all packets received from the network.

Downloading and Installing winpcap

The main Web site for winpcap can be found at http://winpcap.polito.it. This page contains links to several other pages, including full instructions on how to compile Windows programs with winpcap, as well as the complete winpcap downloads.

The winpcap download page (http://winpcap.polito.it/install/default.htm) provides links for several downloads:

- The latest winpcap binary package
- A developer's pack that includes library and header files for compiling applications with winpcap
- A source code pack that includes the full source code for the winpcap library

TIP Besides the most current production version of winpcap, there is often a development version of winpcap available for testing. As with all development software, you should be careful not to use this version in a production environment on a system you would not want to crash.

At the time of this writing, the most current production version of winpcap is version 2.3. If you are running Windows XP Home Edition or Professional, you must use at least the 2.3 version. Older versions of the library do not work on that platform. The binary installation file is downloaded as http://winpcap.polito.it/install.bin/WinPcap_2_3.exe.

Since the installation file is a binary executable file, after downloading the installation file, you can run it without modification. The winpcap installation program contains two separate files. The wpcap.dll file is the direct replacement for the libpcap.a library file for the Windows environment. It provides the APIs that read packets from the network interface. The packet.dll library file provides additional functionality by allowing programs to send raw packets out to the network interface as well.

WARNING If you are upgrading the version of winpcap on your system, you must completely remove it before installing the new version. This can be done from the Control Panel Add/Remove Programs program.

Developing Applications with winpcap

If you plan on creating your own network-monitoring programs using the winpcap library, you must also download the developer's pack from the winpcap Web site. At the time of this writing, the current developer's pack can be found at http://winpcap.polito.it/install.bin/Wpdpack_2_3.zip.

Unzipping the pack creates a directory, Wpdpack, with four separate subdirectories:

- **Include.** The include header files for writing C applications
- **Lib.** The library files for compiling with C applications
- **Examples.** Sample C applications showing how to write winpcap programs
- **Drivers.** The complete winpcap binary library installation file

As with libpcap, you must use the winpcap library headers and include files when creating network programs. You may want to move these files to your C language development environment.

If you want to experiment with the actual source code used to create the winpcap library, you can download it from the winpcap Web site at http://winpcap.polito.it/install/bin/WpcapSrc_2_3.zip.

Again, this is distributed as a zip file, and must be unzipped into a working directory. After you unzip the distribution file, a winpcap directory will be created containing all of the source code files. You may notice that many of the source code files used in winpcap are derived from the libpcap project.

Using winpcap

The winpcap library was written to directly support the existing libpcap library function calls in the Windows environment. Besides supporting all of the libpcap function calls, winpcap also supplies a few additional function calls specifically for Windows. If you are using the WinDump, Analyzer, or Ethereal packages described later in this chapter, you must have the winpcap libraries installed.

The tcpdump Program

The most popular network monitor program developed for the Unix environment has been the tcpdump program. Tcpdump was developed at the Lawrence Berkeley Laboratories as a way for developers to easily watch network traffic on servers. It places the host network interface in promiscuous mode, accepting all packets from the network and displaying them in different formats on the console, or storing them in a file for later analysis.

The Tcpdump Group now maintains the tcpdump application.

Most Unix distributions include the tcpdump program; however, due to security concerns, many do not install it by default. When it is installed, usually you need to have root privileges to run it.

Installing tcpdump

Depending on your Unix distribution, there are several different ways to install tcpdump. Several Linux distributions use the Resource Package Manager (RPM) method to install binary applications. This section shows you how to install tcpdump using RPM, as well as how to download the source code and install it manually on all Unix systems.

Linux RPM Installation

Many Linux distributions use the RPM package handler to install and remove applications from the system. If your Linux distribution uses RPMs (such as Red Hat, Mandrake, and Caldera) you can use the rpm installation program to easily install tcpdump.

A tcpdump rpm file should be included with your Linux distribution. On my Mandrake version 8.0 Linux system, it is included on the first installation CD as file tcpdump-3.6.1-1mdk.i586.rpm. The rpm file can be loaded using the rpm package handler:

```
#rpm -Uvh tcpdump-3.6.1-1mdk.i586.rpm
```

You must ensure that you are the root user before attempting to install the package with the rpm package manager. The three command-line options used are:

- -U to update any existing installed tcpdump application
- -v to use verbose mode when installing
- -h to use hash marks to show the progress of the install

This command installs the tcpdump application (or upgrades it, if an older version was installed), showing the progress as it goes along. When the installation is complete, the tcpdump application should be ready for use.

NOTE The binary distribution of tcpdump includes the libpcap library compiled into the application, so you do not need to download or install the libpcap files. If you download the tcpdump source code and compile it, you must have the libpcap library files installed.

Downloading the Source Code

If your Unix distribution does not include the tcpdump application, or if you want to use the latest available version, you can download the source code from the tcpdump Web site and compile it yourself.

At the time of this writing, the current version of tcpdump is version 3.7.1, which can be downloaded from www.tcpdump.org/release/tcpdump-3.7.1.tar.gz.

Like the libpcap library distribution, the tcpdump distribution comes as a compressed tar file that must be uncompressed and expanded into a working directory. If you compile the tcpdump application, you must have the libpcap library source code files as well (as discussed in the *The libpcap Library* section of this chapter). After tcpdump is compiled, you can remove the libpcap library files. It is best to keep the two distribution directories close to each other, possibly under the same directory structure, as the tcpdump compile process will look for and use the libpcap library files.

Before you can compile tcpdump, you must run the configure program to detect the system settings and create an appropriate Makefile file. The configure program detects where the libpcap library files are located on the system. You should see an output line within the configure output that references where it found the libpcap library file:

```
checking for local pcap library... ../libpcap-0.7.1/libpcap.a
```

This example shows that the libpcap library directory was found one directory level up from where the tcpdump working directory was located. If no libpcap library files are found on the system, you will see an error message in the configure output:

```
checking for local pcap library... not found
checking for main in -lpcap... no
configure: error: see the INSTALL doc for more info
```

After the configure program has run successfully, you can run make to create the tcpdump executable file, and makeinstall (as root) to install it on your system. Once the executable file is created, you can remove the libpcap and tcpdump source code files.

Using tcpdump

The first part of using tcpdump is to determine which interface you want to monitor. Many Unix systems have multiple network interfaces, and possibly PPP connections as well. You must know which interface you are monitoring on the system. The interfaces can be displayed with the Unix ifconfig program.

To display all of the active network interfaces on a system, you must use the –a option. The following code shows what a sample ifconfig output for a Linux system looks like:

```
# ifconfig -a
eth0      Link encap:Ethernet  HWaddr 00:E0:29:51:06:D2
          inet addr:192.168.1.6  Bcast:192.168.1.25 Mask:255.255.255.0
          UP BROADCAST RUNNING MULTICAST  MTU:1500  Metric:1
          RX packets:1043006 errors:0 dropped:0 overruns:0 frame:0
          TX packets:79946 errors:0 dropped:0 overruns:0 carrier:0
          collisions:0 txqueuelen:100
          RX bytes:334058983 (318.5 Mb)  TX bytes:66614501 (63.5 Mb)
          Interrupt:10 Base address:0x8000
lo        Link encap:Local Loopback
          inet addr:127.0.0.1   Mask:255.0.0.0
          UP LOOPBACK RUNNING  MTU:16436  Metric:1
          RX packets:1552 errors:0 dropped:0 overruns:0 frame:0
          TX packets:1552 errors:0 dropped:0 overruns:0 carrier:0
          collisions:0 txqueuelen:0
          RX bytes:151972 (148.4 Kb)  TX bytes:151972 (148.4 Kb)
#
```

This system contains two network interfaces, a network interface card, called eth0, and the network loopback interface, lo. The loopback interface is often used for testing network programs without using the actual network. The ifconfig output also shows the basic information for the network card, such as the MAC and IP addresses, along with network statistics. On a FreeBSD system, the output looks like the following:

```
# ifconfig -a
vx0: flags=8943<UP,BROADCAST,RUNNING,PROMISC,SIMPLEX,MULTICAST> mtu 1500
inet 192.168.1.6 netmask 0xffffff00 broadcast 192.168.1.255
ether 00:a0:24:9c:69:02 lp0: flags=8810<POINTOPOINT,SIMPLEX,MULTICAST>
mtu 1500
ppp0: flags=8010<POINTOPOINT,MULTICAST> mtu 1500
lo0: flags=8049<UP,LOOPBACK,RUNNING,MULTICAST> mtu 16384
inet 127.0.0.1 netmask 0xff000000
#
```

The default network interface on this device is called vx0. There is also a PPP connection on this system, called ppp0, as well as the standard loopback interface, called lo0.

By default, tcpdump monitors the lowest-numbered active interface, which is listed first in the ifconfig output. To choose a different interface, the –i option must be used. This command monitors packets sent and received on the PPP interface of the FreeBSD device shown:

```
$tcpdump -i ppp0
```

There are many command-line options that can be used to modify the behavior of the tcpdump program. Table 2.1 shows the command-line options that can be used.

Table 2.1   The tcpdump Command-Line Options

OPTION	DESCRIPTION
-a	Attempt to convert network and broadcast addresses to names.
-c	Exit after receiving count packets.
-C filesize	If the file is larger than *filesize*, close the current savefile and open a new one.
-dd	Dump packet-matching code as a C program fragment.
-ddd	Dump packet-matching code as decimal numbers (preceded with a count).
-e	Print the link-level header on each dump line.
-E algo:secret	Use *algo:secret* for decrypting IPsec ESP packets.
-f	Print foreign Internet addresses numerically.
-F file	Use *file* as input for the filter expression.
-i interface	Listen on *interface*.
-l	Make stdout line buffered.
-m module	Load SMI MIB module definitions from file *module*.
-N	Don't print domain name qualification of hostnames.
-O	Don't run the packet-matching code optimizer.
-p	Don't put the interface into promiscuous mode.
-q	Quick output. Fewer lines per packet are displayed.
-R	Assume ESP/AH packets to be based on old specification.
-r file	Read packets from *file*.
-S	Print absolute, rather than relative, TCP sequence numbers.
-s snaplen	Get *snaplen* bytes of data from each packet. The default is 68 bytes.

(continued)

Table 2.1   *(continued)*

OPTION	DESCRIPTION
-T type	This option specifies the type of packet (rtp, snmp, rtcp, vat, or wb).
-t	Don't print a timestamp on each dump line.
-tt	Print an unformatted timestamp on each dump line.
-ttt	Print the delta time between packets.
-tttt	Print a timestamp in default format proceeded by date on each dump line.
-u	Print undecoded NFS handles.
-v	Show verbose output.
-vv	Show more verbose output.
-vvv	Show even more verbose output.
-w file	Write the raw packets to *file* rather than printing them out.
-x	Print each packet in hex.
-X	When printing hex, print ASCII text as well.

Most of the command-line options can be mixed and matched together. tcpdump allows you to specify as many command-line options as you desire, separating each with a space:

```
$tcpdump -i eth0 -s 200 -x
```

This example instructs tcpdump to monitor the eth0 network interface, capture and display the first 200 bytes of each packet, and display the results in hexadecimal format. If no options are specified, only the packet header information is displayed. The following code shows a sample output from the default command:

```
# tcpdump
tcpdump: listening on eth0
18:07:12.648173 192.168.1.6.1043 > shadrach.blum.lan.telnet: . ack
760172632 win
 17264 (DF)
18:07:12.648348 shadrach.blum.lan.telnet > 192.168.1.6.1043: P 1:29(28)
ack 0 wi
n 32120 (DF)
18:07:12.848468 192.168.1.6.1043 > shadrach.blum.lan.telnet: . ack 29
win 17236
(DF)
```

```
3 packets received by filter
0 packets dropped by kernel
#
```

The first line of each displayed packet shows the timestamp indicating when the packet was received. Next, the vital information for the packet is displayed—the source and destination addresses of the connection (the hostname is used by default if it is known), and any protocol-specific information, such as TCP flags, as seen in this example.

The WinDump Program

While the tcpdump program is popular in the Unix environment, the WinDump program is used in the Windows environment to capture and display network packets from a command prompt. This section describes how to install and use the WinDump network monitor program.

Downloading and Installing WinDump

The WinDump program is available on the Politecnico de Torino Web site. At the time of this writing the most current version of WinDump is version 3.6.2. The WinDump program is distributed as a single executable file. The file is not compressed, so it can be run exactly as downloaded.

The download URL for the WinDump executable is http://windump .polito.it/install.bin/alpha.WinDump.exe.

There is no installation procedure to do; this is the complete WinDump executable file. As long as the winpcap libraries are loaded, you can begin using WinDump immediately.

Using WinDump

The WinDump program behaves similarly to the tcpdump program, but there are a few command-line option differences. The WinDump program provides a command-line option that displays the available network interfaces on the device:

```
C:\monitor>windump -D
1.\Device\Packet_{E0D13BFC-D26F-45D6-BC12-534854E3AD71} (Novell 2000
Adapter.)
2.\Device\Packet_NdisWanIp (NdisWan Adapter)
3.\Device\Packet_NdisWanBh (NdisWan Adapter)

C:\monitor>
```

The configuration on this sample workstation contains one network card (emulating a Novell 2000 network adapter), and a modem that has two separate PPP connections configured. By default, WinDump will monitor traffic on the number 1 interface. If you want to monitor traffic on a different interface, you must specify it on the command line, using the -i option:

```
C:\monitor>windump -i 2

windump: listening on\Device\Packet_NdisWanIp
```

Note that the -i option for WinDump can specify either the interface number, as specified by the -D option, or the full interface text name. If the full text name is used, it must be specified exactly as shown in the -D option output.

Table 2.2 shows the command line options that are available for the WinDump program.

Table 2.2   The WinDump Command-Line Options

OPTION	DESCRIPTION
-a	Attempt to convert network and broadcast addresses to names.
-B size	Set the receive buffer size to *size*.
-c count	Capture *count* packets and stops.
-D	Display all available network interfaces on the system.
-e	Print the link-level information on each line of the output.
-F file	Read the filter expression from the filename *file*.
-I interface	Monitor the network interface. *interface* can be either the interface name or a number shown from the -D command.
-n	Don't convert addresses to names.
-N	Don't print fully qualified domain names.
-q	Print quick (less) packet information.
-r file	Read the packets from dumpfile *file*.
-S	Print absolute TCP sequence numbers.
-s snaplen	Capture *snaplen* bytes from the packets. The default value is 68.
-t	Don't print a timestamp on each line.
-w file	Write the output to *file*.
-X	Print each packet in hex and ASCII.
-x	Print each packet in hex.

As with tcpdump, multiple options can be combined on the command line to create the network-monitoring environment you need. For example, to capture the first 200 bytes of each packet, print them in hex, and write the output to a file, you would type:

```
C:\>windump -s 200 -x -w testcap
```

By default, WinDump attempts to capture all packets it sees on the network interface. Depending on your network (and the placement of your analyzer workstation on the network), this may be a large amount of traffic. Often it is difficult trying to track a single IP session within a bunch of extraneous network packets. With WinDump, you can specify a filter to limit the amount of traffic captured to just the information you are interested in monitoring. The next section describes how to set monitor filters in WinDump.

Filtering Packets with tcpdump and WinDump

Trying to watch a specific network session while capturing all the packets on the network can be a difficult thing to do. To make this job easier, both the tcpdump and WinDump programs allow you to specify filters on the command line. A filter can be configured to filter out all background network traffic except the specific session you are trying to analyze.

The filter uses a specific syntax to define the types of packets to accept. The filter consists of an *expression* that each captured packet is compared against. The expression defines one or more *primitives* that consist of an ID and one or more *qualifiers*. The primitive ID defines the type of packet to capture, such as TCP or UDP. The qualifiers define values to match against the primitives.

There are lots of primitives that can be used in the filter. Table 2.3 shows some of the primitive types that can be used.

Table 2.3   The tcpdump and WinDump Primitives

PRIMITIVE	DESCRIPTION
dst host *host*	Specifies a hostname or IP address of the destination host
src host *host*	Specifies a hostname or IP address of the source host
host *host*	Specifies a hostname or IP address of either the source or destination host
ether dst *host*	Specifies the Ethernet address of the destination host
ether src *host*	Specifies the Ethernet address of the source host

(continued)

Table 2.3 *(continued)*

PRIMITIVE	DESCRIPTION
ether host *host*	Specifies the Ethernet address of either the source or destination host
gateway *host*	Specifies the hostname or IP address of a gateway used by the packet
dst net *net*	Specifies the network name or IP network address of the destination network
src net *net*	Specifies the network name or IP network address of the source network
net *net*	Specifies the network name or IP network address of the source or destination network
net *net* mask *mask*	Specifies the network name or IP address of *net* and the subnet mask of *mask*
net *net/len*	Specifies the network IP address of *net* with the subnet mask of *len* bits wide
dst port *port*	Specifies the TCP or UDP destination port of *port*
src port *port*	Specifies the TCP or UDP source port of *port*
less *length*	Indicates that the packet size is less than *length*
greater *length*	Indicates that the packet size is greater than *length*
ip proto *protocol*	Indicates the next-layer IP protocol in the packet
ether multicast	Indicates that the packet is an Ethernet multicast packet
ip multicast	Indicates that the packet is an IP multicast packet
ether proto *protocol*	Indicates the next-layer Ethernet protocol in the packet

Some primitives can be used without qualifiers, while some qualifiers can be used without primitives. For example, the primitive ip proto tcp can be shortened to just the qualifier, tcp. This restricts captured packets to just TCP packets. Some examples of using expressions in the command line are:

```
tcpdump ip host meshach.isptest.net
```

The primitive in this example is ip. The qualifier, host meshach.isptest.net, specifies that only packets sent and received by the host meshach.isptest.net will be captured.

```
tcpdump ip host 192.168.1.6 and port not 23
```

This example demonstrates a more complicated expression. The first part is normal; it specifies all packets sent and received by host 192.168.1.6. The second part further limits the capture by specifying that the packets should not be to or from port 23.

The Analyzer Program

The Analyzer program is a Windows application that provides a graphical environment for capturing and analyzing network packets. It uses the winpcap library to capture packets from the network interface on the Windows system. It has the same functionality as the WinDump program, but with a more convenient user interface.

To start the Analyzer program, double-click on the analyzer.exe file, or click on the Analyzer desktop icon if you elected to create it during the installation. There are four basic functions the analyzer program can perform:

- Capture and display network packets
- Display packets stored in a file
- Capture network statistics
- Perform real-time network monitoring

Since the point of this section is to discuss capturing network packets, I will not describe the network statistics and real-time monitoring functions of the analyzer program. These are, however, useful for doing network troubleshooting, and you should investigate them on your own.

To capture network packets, you must click the packet capture icon, which is the first icon on the third row of toolbars. When you click the icon, a Filter Selection window appears, as shown in Figure 2.1.

The Filter Selection window allows you to select the network interface to capture packets from, and to define a filter for the packet capturing. By clicking the Select Adapter button, you can select which network adapter to use. The list that appears should be the same as from the WinDump -D command-line option. Again, any PPP connections that you have defined will show up here as well.

If you want to capture all network packets, you must check the Promiscuous Mode check box; otherwise, all you will see are packets destined for your local device. After you select the network adapter to use, you may define a specific filter to use. In the right-hand window, the analyzer program shows a tree of several common filters. By expanding a particular network layer, you can select a specific packet type to capture.

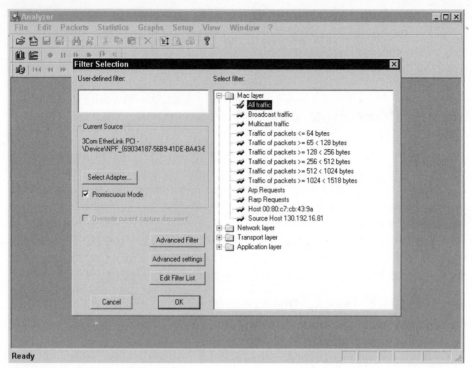

Figure 2.1   Filter Selection window.

After you select the desired filter options and click the OK button, the Analyzer program begins capturing packets. The Capture in Progress window appears, showing the elapsed time the capture has been running, how many packets have been accepted by the filter, how many packets have been analyzed by the analyzer, and how many packets have been lost (dropped). To end the capture session, press the Stop button.

When you stop the capture, a Capture document window appears, as shown in Figure 2.2.

This window contains three sections:

- A packet index showing all of the packets captured in order
- A hex and ASCII printout of the current packet
- A tree view of the packet type information

The tree view contains all of the detailed information about the packet, divided by the different protocols present in the packet data. For example, for a typical TELNET session packet, the following protocols would be present:

- The Ethernet layer transport information
- The IP network layer information

- The TCP transport layer information
- The TELNET application data

To successfully trace and debug a network application, you should know how to decode and understand each of the different layers of information contained in the network packet. The next section shows the different layers present in the IP network packet, and describes how to decode the information contained in them.

The Ethereal Program

The Ethereal program is a graphical network-monitoring application that runs in both the Unix and Windows environments. It uses either the libpcap or winpcap library to capture packets from the network interface on the host machine. It also uses the GTK+ graphical library to produce its windows and dialog boxes. This enables it to have the same graphical interface in either operating system.

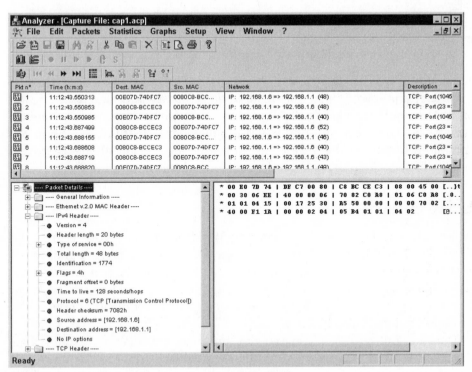

Figure 2.2 The Analyzer Capture document window.

Downloading and Installing Ethereal

The Ethereal Web site is located at www.ethereal.com. It includes a download area that contains both binary and source code distributions for all environments. The main download URL is www.ethereal.com/distribution/.

If you are using the Windows environment, you can download the binary distribution file from the Win32 distribution area. At the time of this writing, the current Windows version of Ethereal is 0.9.7, and it is distributed in the download file ethereal-setup-0.9.7.exe. You can run this executable file to install the Ethereal package.

If you are using a Unix environment, you can either download the binary distribution file for your Unix distribution, or download the source code and compile the Ethereal package yourself. Either way, you need the following additional software to install Ethereal in the Unix environment:

The GTK+ libraries, which provide the graphical libraries for the Windows system

The GLIB libraries, which provide additional graphic libraries for GTK

The libpcap libraries, which provide the packet capture libraries

The ucd-snmp libraries (also called net-snmp), which provide SNMP decoding capabilities

The zlib libraries, which provide compression utilities for compressing saved capture files

On my Mandrake Linux system, all of these library packages are available as RPM installation packages. All of these contain two separate installation files: a basic library distribution, and a developer's distribution. If you are compiling the Ethereal source code, you must also install the development version of each of these packages, as well as the basic library files.

Using Ethereal

After installing Ethereal on the Unix or Windows system, you can run the Ethereal executable file to start the program (on Unix systems, you must have root privileges to capture packets). When the application starts, it produces the main Ethereal capture screen. The program options are contained in the menu bar items. If you click the Capture menu item, and select the Start option, the Capture Options dialog box appears.

The Filter button allows you to define and select packet capture filters, similar to the tcpdump and WinDump filter expressions. You can configure and save several different capture filters, and use them by selecting them at this point.

To start the capture, click the OK button in the Capture Options dialog box. When the capture starts, the Capture dialog box appears, showing how many packets are being captured by the application. To stop the capture, click the Stop button.

After the capture session is stopped, Ethereal decodes the packets (which may take some time for large captures), and displays the results in the main program window (as shown in Figure 2.3).

The display window is divided into three separate sections:

- The top section shows the header information of the captured packets.

- The middle section shows the decoded information from the packets.

- The bottom section shows the raw hex and ASCII display of the packet data.

Like the Analyzer program the Ethereal program allows you to step through each captured packet, showing the details of both the packet header fields and the data portion of the packet. One nice feature of Ethereal is that it decodes a lot more packet types for you, allowing you to see what is happening on the network without having to manually decode packets.

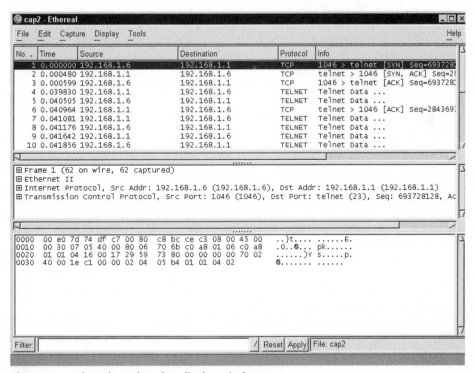

Figure 2.3 The Ethereal packet display window.

Summary

This chapter shows how you can use standard Unix and Windows hosts to monitor network traffic, without having to purchase expensive network-monitoring equipment or software. The libpcap (for Unix) and winpcap (for Windows) libraries enable applications to access device network interfaces in promiscuous mode, capturing all packets that traverse the network. After capturing the network packets, you will want to decode their meaning to determine network performance issues.

There are several Open Source network-monitoring packages that use the libpcap and winpcap libraries to capture, decode, and display network traffic. The tcpdump package is the most popular Unix network-monitoring package. It uses filter options to specify which type of packets to capture. The WinDump program performs the same function in the Windows environment.

If you prefer graphical interfaces, the Analyzer program is a Windows graphical network-monitoring application that can monitor network interfaces and be configured with capture filters. The Ethereal package is unique in that it can be used in both the Unix and Windows environments. Both the Analyzer and Ethereal packages show both decoded and raw packet data, enabling you to easily analyze network packets.

The next chapter discusses how to determine network device utilization using SNMP. The snmpwalk and snmpget applications allow you to query network devices using SNMP, to determine how they are handling network traffic.

## CHAPTER 3

Network Device Utilization

Directly monitoring network devices is an easy way to gather information about network performance. This chapter describes how to use the Simple Network Management Protocol (SNMP) to query managed network devices for performance data. The net-snmp family of SNMP tools for Unix platforms is used to directly query network devices for performance data.

As described in Chapter 1, "Defining Network Performance," managed network devices use SNMP to query network devices for information about the traffic that they are handling. You can use SNMP to obtain baseline information about the network data and error rates before doing any external performance testing.

The net-snmp Package

To query remote SNMP devices for network information, you must have an SNMP package running on your system. The most popular SNMP package available for the Unix platform is the net-snmp package. The net-snmp package was developed at the University of California, Davis, and is now maintained by the net-snmp group. It provides complete SNMP functions for Unix hosts.

NOTE The net-snmp package is a new name for the original ucd-snmp package, starting at version 5.0. The last version of ucd-snmp was version 4.9.2. All new versions will use the new name, net-snmp. Many Linux distributions still include the older ucd-snmp package. Most of the functionality between the two packages is the same, although the net-snmp package started using slightly different syntax for command-line options.

The net-snmp package contains several utilities that are useful in communicating with remote network devices via SNMP. The net-snmp package can be easily loaded on any Unix platform, including Linux and FreeBSD, providing a framework for network management tools.

The SNMP functions that the net-snmp package provides are:

- Send SNMP queries to remote devices
- An SNMP agent to respond to SNMP queries from other devices
- Send and receive SNMP trap messages
- Provide an SNMP API library for other applications
- Query remote hosts for netstat command output

The net-snmp package consists of a set of library and executable files, and a set of configuration files for defining the SNMP agent information. This section describes the net-snmp package and explains how to use it to obtain network information from network devices.

Downloading and Installing net-snmp

The main net-snmp Web site, http://www.net-snmp.org, contains information about the latest version of net-snmp, along with other miscellaneous SNMP information. There are several binary versions that can be downloaded, as well as the source code distribution. The main download site is located at:

```
http://sourceforge.net/project/showfiles.php?group_id=12694
```

The current source code version at the time of this writing is net-snmp-5.0.6. This package includes all of the net-snmp utilities, along with libraries and man pages. After downloading the source code file, you must compile it on your Unix system.

Before compiling the software, you must run the configure program to allow net-snmp to detect what software is installed on the system, and to specify which features to compile information on for the final executable programs. The configure program uses several command-line options to modify how to compile and install the application. To see a list of all the possible options, you can use the —help option:

```
$ ./configure —help
```

You can use the standard configure —enable and —disable parameters to enable or disable features within the net-snmp package. To create a standard installation with all of the features, just run the configure program with no options. As the configure program runs, it checks installed software necessary to support features within the net-snmp package. One of these features is encryption.

NOTE If you want to implement SNMP version 2 and 3 encryption, you must have the OpenSSL package libraries installed on your system.

When the configuration runs, it asks some questions to create the configuration files. Most of these questions pertain to the SNMP agent feature of the net-snmp package, providing the system information details to remote SNMP devices.

The first question asked is important even if you do not use the SNMP agent feature. It pertains to the version of SNMP you want to use by default in the net-snmp utilities:

```
Default version of SNMP to use (3):
```

If you are planning on using mostly SNMP version 1 queries, you can enter a 1 to set it as the default query type. This will enable you to enter SNMP version 1 queries on the command lines without having to specify the version. As you will see later, you can always specify which version of query to use on the SNMP utility command line.

After the configure program is finished, you must run the make program to build and install the SNMP utilities:

```
make
```

```
make install
```

The make install command installs all of the library and executable files, as well as the manual pages for the software package. Remember that you need to be logged in as the root user to run the install option. After you run the make commands, the net-snmp package should be ready to use.

Using net-snmp Utilities

The net-snmp package contains many SNMP utilities that can be used to query remote network devices for SNMP information. The command line of each utility uses essentially the same format:

```
command [options] agent OID
```

The agent value is the IP address or hostname of the remote SNMP device to query. The OID value is the MIB structure to send in the query. The MIB structure can be specified in several different ways:

- Using the complete numeric MIB value: 1.3.6.1.2.1.1.3.0

- Using the complete text MIB values: iso.org.dod.internet.mgmt.mib-2.system.sysUpTime.0

- Using a shorthand text MIB value, starting from the MIB management object: system.sysUpTime.0

- Using a combination of numeric and text MIB values: 1.3.6.1.2.1.1.sysUpTime.0

WARNING Earlier versions of ucd-snmp required that the numeric MIB values be preceded by a period. Version 5.0 of net-snmp does not have this requirement. If you are using older versions of ucd-snmp, remember to use the period at the start of the full numeric MIB value.

The options section of the utility command line allows you to specify one or more options to modify the behavior of the utility. There are lots of options that can be used with all of the net-snmp utilities. To see a complete list of the available options, you can refer to the man page for the generic snmpcmd command. Although this is not an actual net-snmp command, it is used as a man page to list all of the common options that can be used on all of the net-snmp utilities. Table 3.1 lists some of the more common and useful options that you will run into.

Table 3.1 Some Standard net-snmp Utility Options

OPTION	DESCRIPTION
-a prot	Sets the authentication protocol to *prot*
-A passwd	Sets the authentication password to *passwd*
-c comm	Sets the community string to *comm*
-d	Dumps the sent and received SNMP packets in hexadecimal

Table 3.1   *(continued)*

OPTION	DESCRIPTION
-D [TOKEN]	Turns on debugging for the given *TOKEN*s
-e engine	Sets the authoritative engine for SNMP version 3 requests to *engine*
-I	Specifies input parsing options
-l seclevel	Sets the security level used in SNMP version 3 requests to *seclevel*
-M dir	Sets a colon-separated list of directories to search for MIBs
-O	Specifies output parsing options
-P	Specifies MIB parsing options
-r retries	Specifies the number of retries to be used in requests, with a default of 5
-t timeout	Specifies the timeout in seconds between retries, with a default of 1
-u secname	Sets the security name used in SNMP version 3 requests to *secname*
-v	Specifies the SNMP version to use (overrides the default set in the configure process)
-x privprot	Sets the privacy protocol used for SNMP version 3 messages
-X privpasswd	Sets the privacy pass phrase used in SNMP version 3 messages

The –I and –O options allow you to specify options used to parse the inputs and outputs for the net-snmp commands. These options allow you to specify how MIBs are searched and displayed in the commands.

The following sections describe some of the more popular SNMP query utilities that can be used to query remote SNMP devices for network traffic information.

snmpget

The snmpget command queries a remote SNMP device for a single value in the MIB database, using the SNMP GET command. The command line for snmpget is:

```
snmpget [options] agent OID
```

If you are querying an SNMP version 1 device, you must specify the community name used with the –c option:

```
snmpget -c public 192.168.1.100 system.sysUpTime.0
```

Remember when using the snmpget command that you need to specify the trailing .0 on the MIB value, to ensure that you are querying a single value in the database; otherwise, you will get an error.

Some examples of using the snmpget command are:

```
$ snmpget -c public 192.168.1.100 system.sysUpTime.0
SNMPv2-MIB::sysUpTime.0 = Timeticks: (17134241) 1 day, 23:35:42.41
$
```

This example queries the 192.168.1.100 host for the sysUpTime MIB-II value. The returned output contains four different items:

- The original MIB value queried: SNMPv2-MIB::sysUpTime.0
- The data type of the returned data: Timeticks
- The raw value of the returned data: 17134241
- The formatted value of the returned data: 1 day, 23:35:42.41

Note that since this was an SNMP version 1 query, a value read community name for the remote device was specified using the –c option.

An example of the snmpget command that uses the numeric MIB object is:

```
$ snmpget -c public 192.168.1.100 1.3.6.1.2.1.1.1.0
SNMPv2-MIB::sysDescr.0 = STRING: Bay Networks, Inc., 3000 Chassis,
Ethernet NMM 331XA, Agent V5.3.1
Compiled Date: Jun 22 1995, Time: 14:58:05
$
```

In this example, the MIB object (sysDescr) was specified on the command line, using the full numeric MIB version. The returned data for this MIB object is a string value, with the full text value of the string returned.

snmpgetnext

The snmpgetnext command uses the SNMP GetNext request packet to retrieve the next value in the MIB table. This is often used when querying a table of values, such as interface values on a hub or switch. The returned value will specify the next MIB that should be used to continue walking the table, as well as the value of the MIB queried.

An example of the use of snmpgetnext is:

```
$ snmpgetnext -c public 192.168.1.100 1.3.6.1.2.1.2.2.1
IF-MIB::ifIndex.1 = INTEGER: 1
$ snmpgetnext -c public 192.168.1.100 IF-MIB::ifIndex.1
IF-MIB::ifDescr.1 = STRING: Ethernet
$ snmpgetnext -c public 192.168.1.100 IF-MIB::ifDescr.1
IF-MIB::ifType.1 = INTEGER: ethernetCsmacd(6)
$ snmpgetnext -c public 192.168.1.100 IF-MIB::ifType.1
IF-MIB::ifMtu.1 = INTEGER: 1500
$ snmpgetnext -c public 192.168.1.100 IF-MIB::ifMtu.1
IF-MIB::ifSpeed.1 = Gauge32: 10000000
$ snmpgetnext -c public 192.168.1.100 IF-MIB::ifSpeed.1
IF-MIB::ifPhysAddress.1 = STRING: 0:0:81:24:30:86
$ snmpgetnext -c public 192.168.1.100 IF-MIB::ifPhysAddress.1
IF-MIB::ifAdminStatus.1 = INTEGER: up(1)
$ snmpgetnext -c public 192.168.1.100 IF-MIB::ifAdminStatus.1
IF-MIB::ifOperStatus.1 = INTEGER: up(1)
$ snmpgetnext -c public 192.168.1.100 IF-MIB::ifOperStatus.1
IF-MIB::ifLastChange.1 = Timeticks: (0) 0:00:00.00
$ snmpgetnext -c public 192.168.1.100 IF-MIB::ifLastChange.1
IF-MIB::ifInOctets.1 = Counter32: 481651898
$ snmpgetnext -c public 192.168.1.100 IF-MIB::ifInOctets.1
IF-MIB::ifInUcastPkts.1 = Counter32: 166060
$ snmpgetnext -c public 192.168.1.100 IF-MIB::ifInUcastPkts.1
IF-MIB::ifInNUcastPkts.1 = Counter32: 1935111
$
```

This example uses the MIB-II interfaces object, which maintains information and statistics for each physical interface on a network device. Note how each query produces the next MIB object in the table, along with the MIB value response. You can continue using the next MIB object to manually walk your way down the MIB table, viewing all of the values. Or, you can use the snmp-walk function, discussed next, to do this automatically.

snmpwalk

The snmpwalk command is similar to the snmpgetnext command, in that it uses the SNMP GetNext request packet to retrieve the next value in the MIB table—but with a twist. The snmpwalk command automatically queries the remote device with the MIB that is returned as the next MIB value. This allows you to retrieve information from an entire table from a single function call.

An example of the use of snmpwalk is:

```
$ snmpwalk -c public 192.168.1.100 1.3.6.1.2.1.2.2.1
IF-MIB::ifIndex.1 = INTEGER: 1
IF-MIB::ifDescr.1 = STRING: Ethernet
```

```
IF-MIB::ifType.1 = INTEGER: ethernetCsmacd(6)
IF-MIB::ifMtu.1 = INTEGER: 1500
IF-MIB::ifSpeed.1 = Gauge32: 10000000
IF-MIB::ifPhysAddress.1 = STRING: 0:0:81:24:30:86
IF-MIB::ifAdminStatus.1 = INTEGER: up(1)
IF-MIB::ifOperStatus.1 = INTEGER: up(1)
IF-MIB::ifLastChange.1 = Timeticks: (0) 0:00:00.00
IF-MIB::ifInOctets.1 = Counter32: 486732814
IF-MIB::ifInUcastPkts.1 = Counter32: 167851
IF-MIB::ifInNUcastPkts.1 = Counter32: 1955195
IF-MIB::ifInDiscards.1 = Counter32: 501
IF-MIB::ifInErrors.1 = Counter32: 0
IF-MIB::ifInUnknownProtos.1 = Counter32: 0
IF-MIB::ifOutOctets.1 = Counter32: 8204530
IF-MIB::ifOutUcastPkts.1 = Counter32: 167436
IF-MIB::ifOutNUcastPkts.1 = Counter32: 34763
IF-MIB::ifOutDiscards.1 = Counter32: 0
IF-MIB::ifOutErrors.1 = Counter32: 0
IF-MIB::ifOutQLen.1 = Gauge32: 0
IF-MIB::ifSpecific.1 = OID: SNMPv2-SMI::mib-2.22
$
```

As expected, the snmpwalk command walked through all of the objects under the specified node object, showing the object name and value for each object.

snmpdelta

Many network statistics rely on obtaining MIB values at regular intervals. The snmpdelta command allows you to monitor a MIB value at a regular interval, providing you with information for network calculations. The snmpdelta command uses the –Cp option to specify how often (in seconds) the new value should be retrieved. The default is every 1 second.

An example of this command is:

```
$ snmpdelta -c public -Cp 5 192.168.1.100 1.3.6.1.2.1.2.2.1.10.
1
IF-MIB::ifInOctets.1 /5 sec: 3866
IF-MIB::ifInOctets.1 /5 sec: 2172
IF-MIB::ifInOctets.1 /5 sec: 2314
IF-MIB::ifInOctets.1 /5 sec: 8871
IF-MIB::ifInOctets.1 /5 sec: 2775
IF-MIB::ifInOctets.1 /5 sec: 3744
IF-MIB::ifInOctets.1 /5 sec: 2304
IF-MIB::ifInOctets.1 /5 sec: 12510
IF-MIB::ifInOctets.1 /5 sec: 25124
IF-MIB::ifInOctets.1 /5 sec: 45604

$
```

This example uses the MIB-II interfaces object to show the input octets read by the interface. The output from the snmpdelta command does not display the actual value of the ifInOctets MIB object. Instead, it displays the change in the value every 5 seconds.

Standard Network Performance MIBs

Now that you have the net-snmp utilities at your disposal, you can start querying network devices for performance data. The next step is to decide what data you should mine from the network devices to give you the information you need. This section describes some of the values that you should look for in network devices to help your study of network performance.

Data Rates

One of the most important items to monitor on network devices is the amount of traffic they are handling. The data rate of a device can give you important information about how busy the network segment is, and how overloaded the network devices may be.

The MIB-II database contains the interfaces MIB object, which tracks information about each network interface on the device. You can query the interface MIB to obtain packet statistics used to analyze network performance.

The interfaces MIB object (1.3.6.1.2..1.2) contains two objects:

- **ifNumber.** The number of network interfaces on the device
- **ifTable.** A table containing one entry for each interface on the device

The ifTable object contains an ifEntry object, which holds the statistical information for one interface on the device. There is one ifEntry object for each interface. The ifEntry object contains the objects that hold the statistical information about the interface. Table 3.2 shows the important ifEntry objects that you will want to use to monitor network performance.

Table 3.2 The ifEntry Information Objects

ENTRY	DESCRIPTION
ifIndex	A unique index value for each interface
ifDescr	A description of the interface
ifType	The type of interface
ifSpeed	The network speed of the interface

(continued)

Table 3.2   *(continued)*

ENTRY	DESCRIPTION
ifAdminStatus	The administration status of the interface
ifOperStatus	The operational status of the interface
ifInOctets	The number of bytes received by the interface
ifInUcastPkts	The number of unicast packets received by the interface
ifInNUcastPkts	The number of non-unicast packets received by the interface
ifInErrors	The number of errors found on received packets
ifOutOctets	The number of bytes sent by the interface
ifOutUcastPkts	The number of unicast packets sent by the interface
ifOutNUcastPkts	The number of non-unicast packets sent by the interface

Each of these objects can be referenced in net-snmp by the IF-MIB object name. For example, to display the number of interfaces on a device, you would use the command:

```
$ snmpget -c public@100 192.168.1.100 IF-MIB::ifNumber.0
IF-MIB::ifNumber.0 = INTEGER: 155
$
```

This shows that there are 155 interfaces on this device (a Cisco switch). Next, you can use the snmpwalk command to obtain the ifInOctets for each of the device interfaces:

```
$ snmpwalk -c public@100 192.168.1.100 IF-MIB::ifInOctets
IF-MIB::ifInOctets.1 = Counter32: 3263693885
IF-MIB::ifInOctets.2 = Counter32: 0
IF-MIB::ifInOctets.3 = Counter32: 680005263
IF-MIB::ifInOctets.4 = Counter32: 1535913171
IF-MIB::ifInOctets.5 = Counter32: 0
IF-MIB::ifInOctets.9 = Counter32: 0
IF-MIB::ifInOctets.10 = Counter32: 72
     .

     .
     .
IF-MIB::ifInOctets.150 = Counter32: 606586528
IF-MIB::ifInOctets.151 = Counter32: 768458000
IF-MIB::ifInOctets.152 = Counter32: 85185680
IF-MIB::ifInOctets.153 = Counter32: 206787112
IF-MIB::ifInOctets.159 = Counter32: 0
IF-MIB::ifInOctets.192 = Counter32: 2215972217
$
```

Note that although there are 155 interfaces, they do not necessarily have to be indexed numerically in order (as seen by the last two index numbers). You can use the same technique with snmpwalk to obtain the ifOutOctet values for each interface.

The octet counts are cumulative since the last time the interface was reset. To obtain the network utilization for an interface, you must take samples over a set time period, and subtract the values to determine the counts. This is a perfect example of the purpose of the snmpdelta utility:

```
$ snmpdelta -c public@100 -Cp 5 -CT 192.168.1.100 IF-MIB::ifInOc tets.23
IF-MIB::ifOutOctets.23
IF-MIB::ifInOctets.23     IF-MIB::ifOutOctets.23          8080.00   8080.00
42382.00          12810.00          12810.00      174024.00
22527.00          22527.00          141483.00     17827.00
17827.00          170875.00         11703.00      11703.00
90228.00          7804.00  7804.00  65305.00      2913.00   2913.00
48177.00          3916.00  3916.00  40330.00      6367.00   6367.00
50510.00          4257.00  4257.00  20633.00      2934.00   2934.00
53747.00          7157.00  7157.00  274228.00
```

By using the –CT option, you can format the output to be in tables. You can also use the –Cs option to timestamp each table entry, and redirect the output to a file, to analyze at a later time. Once you know the input and output octets for an interface for a given time period, you can determine the utilization with the equation:

```
% Utilization = (((inOctets + outOctets) * 8) / (ifSpeed * time) * 100
```

In this example, the first entry shows 8080 input octets, and 42382 output octets. Using the equation, and assuming a 10-Mbps half-duplex line, the % utilization would be about 0.81 percent.

NOTE Be careful when calculating network utilization using the interface speed. Remember that full-duplex connections allow twice the amount of traffic at the same speed, so a 100-Mbps connection would have a real capacity of 200 Mpbs.

Error Rates

You can also use the same net-snmp technique to calculate error rates on network interfaces. The equation that is commonly used to determine the error rate of a network interface is:

```
Error rate = (ifInErrors * 100) / (ifInUcastPkts + ifInNUcastPkts)
```

Like the percent utilization, the error rate is calculated over a specific time period. Since all of the values represent changes (deltas), no time value is required in the equation.

Again, the snmpdelta utility is ideal for obtaining the data necessary for these calculations:

```
$ snmpdelta -c public@100 -Cp 60 -Cs 192.168.1.100 IF-MIB::ifInEr
rors.23 IF-MIB::ifInUcastPkts.23 IF-MIB::ifInNUcastPkts.23
[07:51:10 10/7] IF-MIB::ifInErrors.23 /5 sec: 0
[07:51:10 10/7] IF-MIB::ifInUcastPkts.23 /5 sec: 220
[07:51:10 10/7] IF-MIB::ifInNUcastPkts.23 /5 sec: 0
[07:51:15 10/7] IF-MIB::ifInErrors.23 /5 sec: 0
[07:51:15 10/7] IF-MIB::ifInUcastPkts.23 /5 sec: 121
[07:51:15 10/7] IF-MIB::ifInNUcastPkts.23 /5 sec: 1
[07:51:20 10/7] IF-MIB::ifInErrors.23 /5 sec: 0
[07:51:20 10/7] IF-MIB::ifInUcastPkts.23 /5 sec: 0
[07:51:20 10/7] IF-MIB::ifInNUcastPkts.23 /5 sec: 0
[07:51:25 10/7] IF-MIB::ifInErrors.23 /5 sec: 1
[07:51:25 10/7] IF-MIB::ifInUcastPkts.23 /5 sec: 835
[07:51:25 10/7] IF-MIB::ifInNUcastPkts.23 /5 sec: 0
$
```

Often, to notice errors, you must use the –Cp option to increase the sample period to a fairly large value, such as 1 minute or more. As can be seen from the output data, most of the time this interface did not have any input errors to report. In the one time sample that showed errors, there was 1 error in 835 packets, resulting in a 0.12-percent error rate for that time period.

NOTE You may have noticed the odd community name format used when accessing the Cisco switch device in the examples. Cisco switches use an SNMP v2 feature called community string indexing, which references a specific VLAN number in the community name. This makes it possible to use the same community name to obtain information from multiple VLANs.

Using Vendor MIBs

Most network device vendors utilize the enterprise MIB object (1.3.6.1.4.1) to add their own device configurations and statistics, to augment the standard MIB-II statistics. The IAB assigns child-node values to vendors under this object. When writing real-world SNMP network applications, you often have to use enterprise database objects to control network devices and extract useful information.

This section describes how to interpret vendor MIB data, and how to create an SNMP shell script to query information from a network device, using objects from the vendor MIB. This is an SNMP application that has come in handy for me as a network administrator.

With several Cisco-brand routers on the network, it is nice to see how each one is working throughout the day without having to manually TELNET to each router and read the statistics. One useful statistic to monitor on Cisco routers is the CPU utilization. By watching the CPU utilization of a router, you can often tell when network segments are being overloaded, or when strange things are happening on the network. The sample script presented in this section sends an SNMP packet to a Cisco router, using a Cisco vendor MIB to query the 5-minute CPU utilization average on the router.

The CISCO CPU MIB

The first step to writing the SNMP script is to obtain the vendor's MIB data for the device you want to monitor.

Fortunately, Cisco provides a large variety of MIB files for all its network devices, freely available to download at ftp://ftp.cisco.com/pub/mibs/v1/. Different MIB categories and devices are defined in different MIB files. Usually a quick search on the Cisco Web page (http://www.cisco.com) produces the MIB filename that contains the data you are looking for. The MIB information for router CPU utilization is contained in the OLD-CISCO-CPU-MIB.my file, which defines the MIBs used for monitoring CPU statistics on Cisco devices.

NOTE There is a newer MIB file available for obtaining CPU statistics, but this MIB is not guaranteed to be compatible with all of the Cisco router models. The OLD-CISCO-CPU-MIB.my file is usable with all models of Cisco routers.

The MIB file uses ASN.1 syntax to define each of the separate MIB objects and object identifiers. The top of the MIB file lists each of the high-level objects that these MIBs are based on. Depending on how often you want to monitor CPU utilization on your router, you can use one of three different MIB objects, shown in Table 3.3.

Table 3.3 The Cisco CPU Utilization MIBs

MIB OBJECT	DESCRIPTION
busyPer	The 5-second CPU utilization average
avgbusy1	The 1-minute CPU utilization average
avgbusy5	The 5-minute CPU utilization average.

Each MIB object has its own unique object identifier to use to obtain the values stored in the device database. The ASN.1 definitions of the objects show the node value for the object, but not the whole object identifier to use. Here are the three MIB values that can be used:

```
busyPer OBJECT-TYPE
    SYNTAX  INTEGER
    ACCESS  read-only
    STATUS  mandatory
    DESCRIPTION
            "CPU busy percentage in the last 5-second
             period. Not the last 5 real-time seconds, but
             the last 5-second period in the scheduler."
    ::= { lcpu 56 }

avgBusy1 OBJECT-TYPE
    SYNTAX  INTEGER
    ACCESS  read-only
    STATUS  mandatory
    DESCRIPTION
            "1-minute exponentially-decayed moving
             average of the CPU busy percentage."
    ::= { lcpu 57 }

avgBusy5 OBJECT-TYPE
    SYNTAX  INTEGER
    ACCESS  read-only
    STATUS  mandatory
    DESCRIPTION
            "5-minute exponentially-decayed moving
             average of the CPU busy percentage."
    ::= { lcpu 58 }
```

The ASN.1 notation defines five separate values:

- The datatype (called SYNTAX)
- The access mode
- Whether the object is optional or mandatory in each device
- A text description of the object
- The ASN.1 definition of the object identifier

The MIB indicates that the avgBusy5 object has a node value of 58, and is a child node of the lcpu object. This in itself does not give you enough information to define the object identifier for the object. You must do some legwork to determine the complete object identifier.

To find the complete object identifier for the object, you must backtrack through the MIBs to find each object's identifier in the chain.

The lcpu object is defined in the same MIB file. It is defined as:

```
lcpu     OBJECT IDENTIFIER ::= { local 1 }
```

The lcpu object is defined as node 1 under the local object. So now you at least know that the avgBusy5 object identifier ends with 1.58.

Unfortunately, the local object is not defined in this MIB file. Fortunately, in the comments of the MIB file, the local object is referenced as coming from the CISCO-SMI MIB file.

To find the rest of the MIB object identifier, you must also download the CISCO-SMI-V1SMI.my MIB file from the Cisco ftp site. In that MIB file, the local object is defined as:

```
local OBJECT IDENTIFIER ::= { cisco 2 }
```

The local object is child node 2 under the cisco object. The cisco object is also defined in the same MIB file as:

```
cisco OBJECT IDENTIFIER ::= { enterprises 9 }
```

OK, now we're getting somewhere. The cisco object is child node 9 under the enterprises object. The enterprises object is one of the standard MIB objects, with an object identifier of 1.3.6.1.4.1.

Putting all of the pieces together, the whole object identifier for the avg-Busy5 object instance is 1.3.6.1.4.1.9.2.1.58.0. Now that you know what MIB object to query, you can write an SNMP script to query the router for the avg-Busy5 MIB object, and run it at 5-minute intervals.

Using the Cisco CPU MIB

If you have done any shell script programming in Unix, this task should be simple for you. If not, then follow along with this example, and you will quickly pick up on it.

Obviously, the first thing is to get the command down that will get the avg-Busy5 MIB object value. This is done using the snmpget command, with the appropriate command-line parameters. An example of this would be:

```
snmpget 192.168.1.100 -c public .1.3.6.1.4.1.9.2.1.58.0
```

The output from this command is the full MIB, the data type of the returned object, and the value of the returned object:

```
iso.3.6.1.4.1.9.2.1.58.0 = INTEGER: 31
```

This output shows that currently, the 5-minute CPU utilization average is 31 percent. While the output from the snmpget provides the information we are looking for, it is not in a very friendly format. The next step is to spruce things up a bit.

You can use the awk utility to filter out the unwanted information from the snmpget output. The awk utility parses lines, and allows you to specify filters and commands to operate on the data. Describing the whole awk program is well beyond the scope of this book, but for this utility, we will use the print function.

The awk process separates each data line into fields based on a separation token. By default, it uses spaces and tabs to separate fields. Using this approach, the snmpget output is divided into four fields:

- Field1 consists of: iso.3.6.1.4.1.9.2.1.58.0
- Field2 consists of: =
- Field3 consists of: INTEGER:
- Field4 consists of: 31

The information that we need is in field 4 of the data line. By feeding the snmpget output into an awk command, and telling it to print only field 4, we can single out the utilization value. In a script, this would look like this:

```
snmpget 192.168.1.100 -c public .1.3.6.1.4.1.9.2.1.58.0 | awk '{print $4}'
```

The output of this script is just the utilization value, exactly what we wanted. Now, you can assign the utilization value to a script variable, and do whatever you want with it.

Besides the utilization value, you will want to get the time (and possibly the date) when the script ran, to be able to associate the utilization average with the time when it happened. This can be done using the date command. By default, the date command displays the full text of the date and time on the system:

```
$ date
Fri Oct  4 13:02:26 EST 2002
$
```

You can use this, as is, in your output file, or you can use the special date formatting options:

```
$ date +"%x %T"
10/04/2002 14:05:36
$
```

This format will work perfectly for creating the log file. Now, you can put all the pieces together in a simple shell script program:

```
#!/bin/sh
datenow=`date +"%x,%T"`
util=`snmpget 192.168.1.100 -c public .1.3.6.1.4.1.9.2.1.58.0 | awk
'{print $4}'`
echo $datenow,$util >> utilization.txt
```

The shell script assigns the output from the date command to the $datenow variable, and the output from the snmpget (fed through awk) command to the $util variable (this is done using the backtick characters placed around the commands). After the variables are created, they can either be displayed on the console or sent to a text file for later retrieval. In this example, commas are used to separate the data fields, so that the file can be easily read into a spreadsheet application, such as Microsoft Excel, and examined.

NOTE Remember to change the mode of the script file so that it can be executed on the system. This is done using the chmod **command:**

chmod 700 cisco

The next step is to get the shell script to run every 5 minutes. This is done with some help from the cron program. The cron program is used to schedule jobs to perform at predetermined times. The crontab file controls the times the scheduled job is run. It can be edited using the crontab –e command.

Each line in the crontab file contains information for a single job. A sample crontab file entry to run the shell script created would look like:

```
0,5,10,15,20,25,30,35,40,45,50,55 0-23, * * 1-5 /home/rich/cisco
```

After the crontab file entry is created, the system will automatically run the script every 5 minutes from Monday to Friday. You may want to change this schedule, depending on when your network operating times are heaviest.

Summary

The Simple Network Management Protocol (SNMP) allows you to query remote network devices to easily watch performance on your network. You can utilize SNMP tools, such as the net-snmp package for Unix hosts, to contact and query network devices.

SNMP utilizes the Management Information Base (MIB) database, which provides a method for network devices to track basic network statistics for the segment(s) they are connected to. Basic information—such as the total input and output bytes, as well as errors received on the network—is stored in the SNMP database for easy retrieval.

Besides the common MIB database items, most vendors implement their own database objects to monitor device-specific features, such as CPU utilization of the device. You can download the MIB file from the vendor to determine the appropriate MIB objects to query.

The next chapter begins the *Network Performance Tools* section by describing the netperf application. Netperf allows you to monitor network performance by sending different types of test data between two endpoints, and measuring the response of the test data.

PART

Two

Network Performance Tools

netperf

Part II of this book covers common Open Source tools that can be used to help analyze the performance of your networks. This chapter introduces the net-perf program, which can determine TCP and UDP end-to-end performance across most types of networks.

The netperf program was developed at the Information Network Division of the Hewlett-Packard Company to help customers benchmark their network performance using HP Unix hosts. It has been released to the public, and can be compiled and run on most Unix platforms, including the Linux and FreeBSD platforms. There are many valuable tests that can be performed using netperf, allowing you to benchmark different data transfer types across the network.

This chapter describes the basics of the netperf program, and explains how to use it to extract useful performance information about your networks and hosts.

What Is netperf?

The netperf program can be used to measure several different types of performance parameters on your network. The netperf program works as a client/server application, consisting of *netserver*, a server program that listens for connections from remote hosts, and *netperf*, a client program that is used to initiate the network tests with the server. The client and server programs pass specified traffic patterns back and forth, measuring performance as the traffic is passed through the network. The following sections describe the TCP and UDP traffic tests that netperf can perform.

TCP Network Performance

Many applications use TCP to transfer streams of data between network endpoints. TCP is known for its reliability, but also for its overhead in establishing network connections and tracking packet sequences (see Chapter 2, "Watching Network Traffic"). Netperf can be used to simulate three different types of TCP traffic:

- A single TCP connection used to bulk transfer a large quantity of data
- A single TCP connection used to transfer client requests and server responses
- Multiple request/response pairs, each one a separate TCP connection

The default test mode in netperf sends blocks of data from the client to the server, measuring how fast the data is sent and received by the hosts. Parameters can be set to alter some of the variables that affect the performance of the data transfer, such as the size of the sockets and the size of the buffers used to send and receive the data.

UDP Network Performance

Applications that do not require a dedicated stream to send data to a remote host often use UDP. UDP is faster, in that it does not require the overhead of establishing a connection between the two hosts, but it does not guarantee delivery of all data packets. The application must perform the task of tracking packets and retransmitting lost packets. Netperf can perform two types of UDP packet tests:

- A unidirectional bulk data transfer from the client to the server
- A request/response session using UDP

Both of the simulated UDP traffic patterns produced by netperf can be used to determine UDP characteristics of the network. Often, network devices handle UDP packets differently than TCP packets, resulting in drastically different performance. As with the TCP tests, the netperf parameters that affect the UDP data transfer, such as buffer sizes, can be altered at the command line.

NOTE When performing UDP tests with netperf, you must be careful not to set the sending buffer size larger than the receiving buffer size, as data will be lost, and netperf will produce an error.

It is important to remember that, since UDP does not guarantee packet delivery, the data statistics for received packets may be incorrect. When reporting UDP traffic statistics from netperf, you should take care to include both the sending and receiving statistics.

Downloading and Installing netperf

The home Web page for the netperf program can be found at http://www. netperf.org. It contains information about the netperf program, sample network performance statistics uploaded by users, and, of course, a download area where you can obtain the program.

Downloading netperf

The main download area for netperf is on an FTP server sponsored by Hewlett-Packard on the server ftp.cup.hp.com. The netperf distributions can be found at the URL:
ftp://ftp.cup.hp.com/dist/networking/benchmarks/netperf/
At the time of this writing, the most current production version of netperf available on the Web site is netperf version 2.2, patch level 2. This is located in the file netperf-2.2pl2.tar.gz.

After downloading the distribution file, you must uncompress and expand it into a working directory. Depending on your Unix system, this can be done either in one step, by using the –z option of the tar command, or in two steps, by using the gunzip command to uncompress the distribution file, then using the standard tar expanding command:

```
tar -zxvf netperf-2.2pl2.tar.gz
```

The tar expansion creates the directory netperf-2.2pl2, containing all of the files necessary to compile the netperf application, along with some script files that make using netperf easier.

Installing the netperf Package

The netperf installation files contain a makefile that must be modified to fit your Unix environment before the application can be compiled. There are several compiler options that must be set, depending on which functions you want to include in the installed netperf application. Table 4.1 shows a list of the features that can be compiled into the application.

Table 4.1   The netperf Compiler Features

COMPILER OPTION	DESCRIPTION
-Ae	Enable ANSI C compiler options for HP-UX systems.
-DDIRTY	Include code to dirty data buffers before sending them. This helps defeat any data compression being done in the network.
-DHISTOGRAM	Include code to keep a histogram of request/response times in tests. This is used to see detailed information in verbose mode.
-DINTERVALS	Include code to allow pacing of packets in TCP and UDP tests. This is used to help prevent lost packets on busy nerworks.
-DDO_DLPI	Include code to test DLPI implementations.
-DDO_UNIX	Include code to test Unix domain sockets.
-D$(LOG_FILE)	This option specifies where the netserver program will put debug output when debug is enabled.
-DUSE_LOOPER	Use looper or soaker processes to measure CPU performance.
-DUSE_PSTAT	For HP-UX 10.0 or later systems, use the pstat() function to compute CPU performance.
-DUSE_KSTAT	For Solaris 2.x systems, use the kstat interface to compute CPU performance.
-DUSE_PROC_STAT	For Linux systems, use the /proc/stat file to determine CPU utilization.
-DDO_IPV6	Include code to test Ipv6 socket interfaces.
-U__hpux	This is used when compiling netperf on an HP-UX system for running on an HP-RT system.
-DDO_DNS	Include code to test performance of the DNS server. Experimental in the 2.2 version.
-DHAVE_SENDFILE	Include code to test sending data using the sendfile() function as well as send().
-D_POSIX_SOURCE	This is used only for installation on an MPE/ix system.
-D_SOCKET_SOURCE	This is used only for installation on an MPE/ix system.
-DMPE	This is used only for installation on an MPE/ix system.

After deciding which features you want (or need) to include in the netperf program, you must edit the makefile file to add them to (or remove them from) the appropriate makefile lines:

```
NETPERF_HOME = /opt/netperf
LOG_FILE=DEBUG_LOG_FILE="\"/tmp/netperf.debug\""
CFLAGS = -Ae -O -D$(LOG_FILE) -DUSE_PSTAT -DHAVE_SENDFILE -
DDO_FIRST_BURST
```

The LOG_FILE entry defines where the debug log file should be located on the host. By default it is placed in the /tmp directory, which will be erased if the system is rebooted.

The default CFLAGS line is set for compiling netperf on an HP Unix system. You must modify this value for it to compile on any other type of Unix system. An example that I used for my Linux system is:

```
CFLAGS = -O -D$(LOG_FILE) -DDIRTY -DHISTOGRAM -DUSE_PROC_STAT
```

After modifying the makefile, you must compile the source code using the make command, and install it using the make command with the install option:

```
make
make install
```

NOTE You must be logged in as root to run the make install option.

After the netperf package is compiled and installed, you must configure your system to run the netserver program to accept connections from the netperf clients.

Running netserver

The netserver program is the application that receives requests from remote netperf clients, and performs the requested tests, transferring data as necessary. There are two ways to install netserver on a Unix system:

- As a standalone application on the server
- Automatically running from the inetd or xinetd program

This section describes both of these methods of running netserver. The method you choose is entirely dependent on your Unix environment.

Using netserver in Standalone Mode

If you do not plan on using netperf on a regular basis, you can start and stop the netserver application program as necessary on your Unix system. In the installation process, the netserver application should have been installed in the directory specified as the NETPERF_HOME in the makefile (/opt/netperf by default).

To start netserver, just run the executable file:

```
$ /opt/netperf/netserver
Starting netserver at port 12865
```

When netserver starts, it indicates which port it is using to listen for incoming client connections, and it will automatically run in background mode. You can check to make sure it is running by using the ps command, with the appropriate option for your Unix system:

```
$ ps ax | grep netserver
15128 ?        S      0:00 /opt/netperf/netserver
$
```

As can be seen from this example, the netserver program is running as process ID (PID) 15128 on the system. To make sure that netserver is indeed listening for incoming connections, you can use the netstat command to display all network processes on the system:

```
$ netstat -a
Active Internet connections (servers and established)
Proto Recv-Q Send-Q Local Address          Foreign Address
State
tcp        0      0 *:1024                  *:*
LISTEN
tcp        0      0 *:12865                 *:*
LISTEN
tcp        0      0 *:mysql                 *:*
LISTEN
tcp        0      0 *:6000                  *:*
LISTEN      tcp       0      0 *:ssh                   *:*
LISTEN
tcp        0      0 *:telnet                *:*
LISTEN      udp       0      0 *:xdmcp                 *:*
```

This is just a partial listing of all the processes listening on the Unix host. The output from the netstat command shows that the system is listening on TCP port 12865 for new connections.

If you start netserver in standalone mode, it will continue to run in the background until you either reboot the server or manually stop it. To manually stop netserver, you must use the Unix kill command, along with the PID number of the running instance of netserver:

```
$ ps ax | grep netserver
15148 ?         S       0:00 /usr/local/netperf/netserver
$ kill -9 15148
$ ps ax | grep netserver
15175 pts/1     S       0:00 grep netserver
$
```

The –9 option on the kill command stops the netserver program. After stopping the program, you should not see it when performing the ps command.

Autostarting netserver

The Unix system offers two methods for automatically starting network programs as connection attempts are received. The inetd program is an older program that listens for connections on designated ports, and passes the received connection attempts to the appropriate program as configured in a configuration file. The xinetd program is a newer version that accomplishes the same task with a slightly different configuration file format.

For the inetd method, you must create an entry in the inetd.conf file for netserver to be started automatically when a connection attempt is detected. The line can be placed anywhere in the file, and should look like:

```
netserver   stream  tcp  nowait  root   /opt/netperf/netserver   netserver
```

The inetd.conf entry specifies the location of the netserver executable file, which may be different on your system, depending on how you installed netperf. Also, this example uses the root user to start the netserver application.

> **NOTE** Since netserver does not use a protected TCP port number, it can be started by any user on the system. You may prefer to create a separate user ID with few or no permissions to start the netserver application.

The xinetd process is similar in function to the original inetd process, but uses a different format for the configuration file to define the network services that it supports. Because the xinetd program is not limited to listening to services defined in the /etc/services file, it can be used for services other than network applications. However, it is still a good idea to configure the netserver entry in the /etc/services file so that you are aware that the application is on the system. The process for doing this is the same as that for the inetd program, with the addition of the netserver entry in the list of available ports.

A sample xinetd configuration file for netserver would look like:

```
service netserver
{
        socket_type = stream
        wait        = no
        user        = root
        server      = /opt/netperf/netserver
}
```

netperf Command-Line Options

After the netserver program is running on a server, you can run the netperf client program from any Unix host on the network (including the local host), to communicate with the server and test network performance. There are many different command-line options used in netperf to control what kind of test is performed, and to modify the parameters used in a specific test. The netperf command-line options are divided into two general categories:

- Global command-line options
- Test-specific command-line options

Options within the same category are grouped together on the command line, with the two categories separated with a double dash:

```
netperf [global options] -- [test-specific options]
```

Global command-line options specify settings that define what netperf test is performed, and how it is executed. These options are used to control the basics of the netperf test, and are valid for all of the netperf test types. Table 4.2 lists the available global commands in netperf version 2.2.

Table 4.2   The netperf Global Command-Line Options

OPTION	DESCRIPTION
-a *sizespec*	Defines the send and receive buffer alignments on the local system, which allows you to match page boundaries on a specific system
-A *sizespec*	The same as –a, except that it defines the buffer alignments on the remote system
-b *size*	Sets the size of the burst packets in bulk data transfer tests

Table 4.2 *(continued)*

OPTION	DESCRIPTION
-c [*rate*]	Specifies that CPU utilization calculations be done on the local system
-C [*rate*]	Specifies that CPU utilization calculations be done on the remote system
-d	Increases the debugging level on the local system
-f *meas*	Used to change the unit of measure displayed in stream tests
-F *file*	Prefills the data buffer with data read from *file*, which helps avoid data compression techniques
-h	Displays the help information
-H *host*	Specifies the hostname or IP address of the remote netperf netserver program
-i *min,max*	Sets the minimum and maximum number of iterations for trying to reach specific confidence levels
-I *lvl,[int]*	Specifies the confidence level and the width of the confidence interval as a percentage
-l *testlen*	Specifies the length of the test (in seconds)
-n *numcpu*	Specifies the number of CPUs on the host system
-o *sizespec*	Sets an offset from the alignment specified with the −a option for the local system
-O *sizespec*	The same as −o, but for the remote system
-p *port*	Specifies the port number of the remote netserver to connect to
-P [*0/1*]	Specifies to either show (1) or suppress (0) the test banner
-t *testname*	Specifies the netperf test to perform
-v *verbose*	Sets the verbose level to *verbose*
-V	Enables the copy-avoidance features on HP-UX 9.0 and later systems

The global command-line options can be specified in any order, as long as they are in the global option section (listed before the double dash). The –t option is used to specify the netperf test that is performed. The next section describes the possible tests that can be performed.

Measuring Bulk Network Traffic

This section describes the netperf tests that are used to determine the performance of bulk data transfers. This type of network traffic is present in many network transactions, from FTPs to accessing data on shared network drives. Any application that moves entire files of data will be affected by the bulk data transfer characteristics of the network.

TCP_STREAM

The default test type used in netperf is the TCP_STREAM test. This test sends bulk TCP data packets to the netserver host, and determines the throughput that occurs in the data transfer:

```
$ netperf -H 192.168.1.100 -l 60
TCP STREAM TEST to 192.168.1.100 : histogram : dirty data
Recv   Send    Send
Socket Socket  Message  Elapsed
Size   Size    Size     Time      Throughput
bytes  bytes   bytes    secs.     10^6bits/sec

 16384  16384  16384    60.03       7.74
$
```

This example uses two global command-line options, the –H option to specify the address of the remote netserver host, and the –l option to set the test duration to 60 seconds (the default is 10 seconds). The output from the netperf TCP_STREAM test shows five pieces of information:

- The size of the socket receive buffer on the remote system: 16384 bytes
- The size of the socket send buffer on the local system: 16384 bytes
- The size of the message sent to the remote system: 16384 bytes
- The elapsed time of the test: 10.02 seconds
- The calculated throughput for the test: 7.74Mbps

The basic netperf test shows that the throughput through this network connection is 7.74 Mbps. By default, netperf will set the message size to the size of the socket send buffer on the local system. This minimizes the effect of the local socket transport on the throughput calculation, indicating that the network bottleneck between these two devices appears to be a 10-Mbps link, with a throughput of almost 8 Mpbs—not too bad.

Many factors can affect this number, and you can modify the netperf test to test the factors. Table 4.3 shows the test-specific options that can be used in the TCP_STREAM test.

Table 4.3 TCP_STREAM Test Options

OPTION	DESCRIPTION
-s *size*	Sets the local socket send and receive buffers to *size* bytes
-S *size*	Sets the remote socket send and receive buffers to *size* bytes
-m *size*	Sets the local send message size to *size*
-M *size*	Sets the remote receive message size to *size*
-D	Sets the TCP_NODELAY socket option on both the local and remote systems

Remember to separate any test-specific options from the global options using a double dash (--). By modifying the size of the socket buffers or the message size used in the tests, you can determine which factors are affecting the throughput on the connections.

For example, if you think that an internal router is having problems forwarding larger packets due to insufficient buffer space, you can increase the size of the test packets and see if there is a throughput difference:

```
$ netperf -H 192.168.1.100 -- -m 2048
TCP STREAM TEST to 192.168.1.100 : histogram : dirty data
Recv    Send     Send
Socket  Socket   Message  Elapsed
Size    Size     Size     Time       Throughput
bytes   bytes    bytes    secs.      10^6bits/sec

 16384   16384    2048     60.02       7.75
$
```

In this example, the message size was decreased to 2 KB, and the throughput remained pretty much the same as with the default larger-sized message (16 KB). A significant increase in throughput for the smaller message size could indicate a buffer space problem with an intermediate network device.

UDP_STREAM

Similar to the TCP_STREAM test, the UDP_STREAM test determines the throughput of UDP bulk packet transfers on the network. UDP differs from TCP in that the message size used cannot be larger than the socket receive or send buffer size. If netperf tries to run with a larger message size, an error is produced:

```
$ netperf -t UDP_STREAM -H 192.168.1.100
UDP UNIDIRECTIONAL SEND TEST to 192.168.1.100 : histogram : dirty data
udp_send: data send error: Message too long
$
```

To avoid this, you must either set the message size to a smaller value, or increase the send and receive socket buffer sizes. The UDP_STREAM test uses the same test-specific options as the TCP_STREAM test, so the –m option can be used to alter the message size used in the test. A sample successful UDP_STREAM test is:

```
$ netperf -t UDP_STREAM -H 192.168.1.100 -- -m 102
4
UDP UNIDIRECTIONAL SEND TEST to 192.168.1.100 : histogram : dirty data
Socket  Message  Elapsed      Messages
Size    Size     Time         Okay Errors   Throughput
bytes   bytes    secs            #      #   10^6bits/sec

65535   1024     9.99       114839      0      94.15
41600            9.99        11618              9.52

$
```

The output from the UDP_STREAM test is similar to that of the TCP_STREAM test, except that there are two lines of output data. The first line shows the statistics for the sending (local) system. The throughput represents the throughput of sending UDP packets to the socket. For this local system, all of the packets sent to the socket were accepted and sent out on the network. Unfortunately, since UDP is an unreliable protocol, there were more packets sent than were received by the remote system.

The second line shows the statistics for the receiving host. Notice that the socket buffer size is different on the receiving host than on the sending host, indicating that 41,600 bytes is the largest UDP packet that can be used with the remote host. The throughput to the receiving host was 9.52 Mbps, which is reasonable for the network being tested.

Measuring Request/Response Times

One the most common types of network traffic used in the client/server environment is the request/response model. The request/response model specifies individual transactions that occur between the client and the server. Figure 4.1 demonstrates this type of traffic.

The client network device usually sends small packets that query information from the server network device. The server receives the request, processes it, and returns the resulting data. Often the returned data is a large data message.

The netperf package can be used to test request/response rates both on the network, where they relate to network performance, and on the client and server hosts, where rates are affected by system loading.

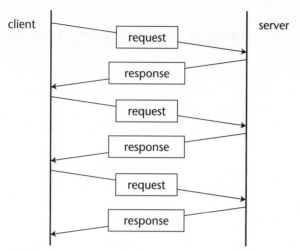

Figure 4.1 Request/response network traffic diagram.

TCP_RR

The TCP_RR test tests the performance of multiple TCP request and response packets within a single TCP connection. This simulates the procedure that many database programs use, establishing a single TCP connection and transferring database transactions across the network on the connection. An example of a simple TCP_RR test is:

```
$ netperf -t TCP_RR -H 192.168.1.100 -l 60
TCP REQUEST/RESPONSE TEST to 192.168.1.100 : histogram : dirty data
Local /Remote
Socket Size   Request  Resp.   Elapsed  Trans.
Send   Recv   Size     Size    Time     Rate
bytes  Bytes  bytes    bytes   secs.    per sec

16384  87380  1        1       59.99    1994.22
16384  16384
$
```

The output from the TCP_RR test again shows two lines of information. The first line shows the results for the local system, and the second line shows the information for the remote system buffer sizes. The average transaction rate shows that 1,994.22 transactions were processed per second. Note that the message size for both the request and response packets was set to 1 byte in the default test. This is not a very realistic scenario. You can change the size of the request and response messages using test-specific options. Table 4.4 shows the test-specific options available for the TCP_RR test.

Table 4.4   The TCP_RR Test Options

OPTION	DESCRIPTION
-r *req,resp*	Sets the size of the request or response message, or both
-s *size*	Sets the size of the local socket send and receive buffers to *size* bytes
-S *size*	Sets the size of the remote socket send and receive buffers to *size* bytes
-D	Sets the TCP_NODELAY socket option on both the local and remote system

Using the –r option, you can alter the size of the request and response packets. There are several different formats you can use to do this:

- -r 32, sets the size of the request message to 32 bytes, and leaves the response message size at 1 byte.

- -r 1, 024 sets the size of the response message to 1,024 bytes, and leaves the request message size at 1 byte.

- -r 32,1024 sets the size of the request message to 32 bytes, and the response message size to 1,024 bytes.

Using the –r option, you can now set meaningful message sizes for the test:

```
$ netperf -t TCP_RR -H 192.168.1.100 -l 60 -- -r 32,1034
TCP REQUEST/RESPONSE TEST to 192.168.1.100 : histogram : dirty data
Local /Remote
Socket Size   Request  Resp.   Elapsed  Trans.
Send    Recv   Size     Size    Time     Rate
bytes   Bytes  bytes    bytes   secs.    per sec

16384   87380  32       1034    59.99    551.71
16384   16384
$
```

With the larger message sizes, the transaction rate dramatically drops to 551.71 transactions per second, significantly lower than the rate obtained with the single-byte messages. This is more representative of the actual transaction rate experienced by production applications.

NOTE This transaction rate represents only the network performance and minimal system handling. An actual network application would incorporate application-handling delays that would also affect the transaction rate.

TCP_CRR

Some TCP transactions require a new TCP connection for each request/response pair. The most popular protocol that uses this technique is HTTP. Each HTTP transaction is performed in a separate TCP connection. Since a new connection must be established for each transaction, the transaction rate is significantly different than the one you would get from the TCP_RR test.

The TCP_CRR test is designed to mimic HTTP transactions, in that a new TCP connection is established for each transaction in the test. A sample TCP_CRR test is:

```
$ netperf -t TCP_CRR -H 192.168.1.100 -l 60
TCP Connect/Request/Response TEST to 192.168.1.100 : histogram : dirty
dataLocal /Remote
Socket Size    Request  Resp.   Elapsed  Trans.
Send    Recv   Size     Size    Time     Rate
bytes   Bytes  bytes    bytes   secs.    per sec

131070 131070 1         1       60.00       17.25
16384   16384
$
```

The transaction rate for even the default message size of 1 byte has significantly dropped to only 17.25 transactions per second. Again, this difference is due to the additional overhead of having to create and destroy the TCP connection for each transaction. The TCP_CRR test can also use the same test-specific options as the TCP_RR test, so the request and response message sizes can be altered using the –r option.

UDP_RR

The UDP_RR test performs request/response tests using UDP packets instead of TCP packets. UDP does not use connections, so there is no connection overhead associated with the UDP_RR transaction rates. A sample UDP_RR test is:

```
$ netperf -t UDP_RR -H 192.168.1.100 -l 60
UDP REQUEST/RESPONSE TEST to 192.168.1.100 : histogram : dirty data
Local /Remote
Socket Size    Request  Resp.   Elapsed  Trans.
Send    Recv   Size     Size    Time     Rate
bytes   Bytes  bytes    bytes   secs.    per sec

65535  65535  1         1       60.00    2151.32
9216    41600
$
```

The transaction rate for the UDP request/response test was faster than the TCP request/response transaction rate. Again, if you see a significant drop in UDP transaction rate from the TCP rate, you should look for network devices such as routers that use separate buffer spaces or handling techniques for UDP packets.

Using netperf Scripts

With the vast variety of test-specific options that are available for use, it can be confusing trying to determine not only which tests to run in your network environment, but how to configure the individual tests to produce meaningful results. Fortunately, the netperf designers have helped out, by providing some specific testing scripts that can be used to test specific network situations.

The snapshot_script provides a general overview of all the TCP and UDP tests. Seven separate tests are performed by the snapshot_script test:

- TCP_STREAM test, using 56-KB socket buffers and 4-KB message sizes
- TCP_STREAM test, using 32-KB socket buffers and 4-KB message sizes
- TCP_RR test, using 1-byte request packets and 1-byte response packets
- UDP_RR test, using 1-byte request packets and 1-byte response packets
- UDP_RR test, using 516-byte request packets and 4-byte response packets
- UDP_STREAM test, using 32-KB socket buffers and 4-KB message sizes
- UDP_STREAM test, using 32-KB socket buffers and 1-KB message sizes

The snapshot_script also uses the –I global option, which specifies a confidence level for each test. The confidence level ensures that the tests are repeated a sufficient number of times to establish the consistency of the results. To limit the number of times the tests are performed, the –i option is used to specify a minimum number of 3 times, and a maximum number of 10 times. Since each test is also configured to run for 60 seconds, the seven tests run at a minimum of 3 times would take 21 minutes to complete.

Before running the script, you must check to see if the netperf executable is defined properly for your installation environment. The script uses the default location of /opt/netperf/netperf. If this is not where netperf is installed on your system, you can either modify the location in the script, or assign the NETPERF_CMD environment variable before running the script.

To change the script, modify the location on the line:

```
NETPERF_CMD=${NETPERF_CMD:=/opt/netperf/netperf}
```

The /opt/netperf/netperf text defines where netperf should be located on the system. If you prefer to set an environment variable instead of modifying the script file, you must set the NERPERF_CMD variable to the location of the netperf executable. For a bourne or bash shell, the script would look like this:

```
NETPERF_CMD=/usr/local/netperf/netperf ; export NETPERF_CMD
```

When the snapshot_script is run, it first silently performs three tests without displaying the results, as a warmup. After the three tests have been completed, each test is run again, in succession, with banner text describing which test is being performed. The output from each test is displayed, showing the standard information generated from the test. A sample section of the output looks like:

```
$ snapshot_script 192.168.1.100
Netperf snapshot script started at Thu Oct 10 14:45:46 EST 2002
Starting 56x4 TCP_STREAM tests at Thu Oct 10 14:46:21 EST 2002
------------------------------------
Testing with the following command line:
/usr/local/netperf/netperf -t TCP_STREAM -l 60 -H 192.168.1.156 -i 10,3
-I
99,5 -- -s 57344 -S 57344 -m 4096

TCP STREAM TEST to 192.168.1.100 : +/-2.5% @ 99% conf. : histogram :
interval : dirty data
Recv    Send    Send
Socket  Socket  Message  Elapsed
Size    Size    Size     Time      Throughput
bytes   bytes   bytes    secs.     10^6bits/sec

 57344 131070   4096     60.06       6.89


Starting 32x4 TCP_STREAM tests at Thu Oct 10 14:49:21 EST 2002

------------------------------------
```

A line of dashes separates the output for each test run from the other two. The exact netperf command line used to produce the test is also displayed.

Summary

The netperf program is used to measure network performance for different types of networks. Netperf's specialty is measuring end-to-end throughput and response times between hosts on the network, using both TCP and UDP data packets.

The netperf program can be configured to support several types of network tests from the command-line options. The default netperf test performs a bulk data transfer using TCP, and determines the throughput speed of the transfer. Other tests include UDP bulk data transfers, and TCP and UDP request/response data transfers. Each test can be configured to support different socket buffer sizes, as well as different message sizes within the test packets.

The next chapter discusses the dbs performance-testing tool. You will see that it has some similarities to netperf, but there are also some significant differences in the ways they are used.

dbs

This chapter looks at another network performance tool that can be used to determine how TCP and UDP traffic is handled on your network. The Distributed Benchmark System (dbs) allows you to set up simultaneous traffic tests between multiple hosts on your network, and control the tests from any of the test hosts, or from a completely different host on the network.

The dbs performance tool was developed at the Nara Institute of Science and Technology in Japan, by Yukio Murayama, as a method of testing TCP and UDP functions on a network. The Distributed Benchmark System has the ability to perform simultaneous network tests, placing a load on the network and observing how the network handles traffic under the load condition. This chapter describes the dbs performance tool, along with two separate tools that are required to use dbs—the ntp network time package and the gnuplot plotting package. A detailed example is presented, showing how you can use dbs to perform a three-way simultaneous network test, testing network performance among three separate hosts at the same time.

dbs Features

The philosophy behind dbs is different from that of other network performance tools. While dbs allows you to perform the standard test of sending a single flow of traffic between two hosts on the network, it also allows you to perform more complicated tests involving multiple hosts.

Often, network problems aren't apparent unless the network is operating under a load condition. Usually, it is not appropriate to test network applications under a load condition, as it would adversely affect the normal production network traffic. To compensate for this, dbs allows you to simulate actual production traffic flows by generating your own network load for observing network behavior. As a result, you can test during nonproduction hours, which won't affect existing network operations.

The following sections describe the individual features of dbs, and explain how they relate to testing performance on the network.

The Components of dbs

The dbs application consists of three components that are used to perform the network tests and display the test results. These programs are:

- **dbsc** A program used to control all the network tests from a single location
- **dbsd** A program that runs on the test hosts to perform the tests
- **dbs_view** A Perl script that is used to display the results of the tests in a graphical form

The dbsc program communicates with each of the test hosts, using TCP port 10710. Each test host uses the dbsd program to listen for test commands and perform tests as instructed. After the tests are performed, the dbs_view program is used to view the results.

The dbs Output

The dbs program produces tables of test data that show the output from the tests performed. Each test produces a separate table, showing the time and traffic information generated during the test. This information looks like this:

send_sequence	send_size	send_time	recv_sequence	recv_size	recv_time
0	2048	0.007544	0	2048	0.017666
2048	2048	0.007559	2048	2048	0.018018
4096	2048	0.007570	4096	2048	0.018164
6144	2048	0.007583	6144	2048	0.018338
8192	2048	0.007595	8192	2048	0.018472
10240	2048	0.007609	10240	2048	0.018629
12288	2048	0.007621	12288	2048	0.018744
14336	2048	0.007633	14336	2048	0.018889
16384	2048	0.007646	16384	2048	0.018991
18432	2048	0.007674	18432	2048	0.019329
20480	2048	0.007688	20480	2048	0.019442
22528	2048	0.007700	22528	2048	0.019580
24576	2048	0.007722	24576	2048	0.019688

Each line of data in the output file shows the results of the traffic as it was sent by one test host and received by another test host. The timing information received from the test hosts must be synchronized using the ntp application to ensure that the data is correct.

After the dbs output file is generated, the dbs_view script can be used to generate additional tables for different network statistics. From those tables, dbs_view can produce graphs to show the data's relation to the communication session. TCP sessions can be analyzed for communications problems, such as repeated sequence and acknowledgment information, indicating a retransmission problem. By observing the data displayed in the graph, you can see how the sequence numbers were incremented in the test sessions.

Before Installing dbs

As mentioned, the dbs program utilizes both the ntp and gnuplot applications to perform its functions. Both of these applications are freely available for any Unix system, and must be installed before installing dbs. This section describes how to do this.

The ntp Program

Many network applications rely on the time setting on remote hosts to be the same as their own. The Network Time Protocol (NTP) was developed to allow systems to synchronize their system clocks with a common time source. There are several applications available on the Unix platform to synchronize the system clock on the host with an NTP server. The ntp application was developed as a free NTP server and client package, allowing a Unix host to both receive NTP transactions to synchronize its own clock, and also send NTP transactions to allow other hosts on the network to synchronize their clocks.

The ntp program can be downloaded from a link on the main ntp Web site at http://www.ntp.org. At the time of this writing, the current production version of ntp available for download is 4.1.1a, which can be downloaded at URL:

```
http://www.eecis.udel.edu/~ntp/ntp_spool/ntp4/ntp-4.1.1a.tar.gz
```

WARNING Older versions of ntp suffered from a buffer overflow security bug. If your Unix distribution comes with a version of ntp older than 4.0, please do not use it. Instead, download the latest version and install it.

The gnuplot Program

The dbs application generates lots of data from the tests it performs. An easy way to analyze the data is to put it in graphical form. The dbs_view script uses the gnuplot program to do that. This program is a freeware application that runs on Unix systems running the X-Windows graphical display system.

WARNING Although gnuplot has the term gnu in it, the application is not produced or distributed by the GNU project. You should carefully read the license agreement distributed with gnuplot before using it. While it is freeware, you are only free to use it, not modify and redistribute it.

The gnuplot program can plot two- and three-dimensional graphs from either data tables or equations. The results are displayed as a graphical window with proper axis labeling and legends.

The main Web site for gnuplot is http://www.gnuplot.info. From that site, you can download the FAQ describing gnuplot, and link to one of several download sites that contain distributions of gnuplot. At the time of this writing, the latest version of gnuplot is version 3.7.1. It can be downloaded from the following URL:

```
ftp://ftp.gnuplot.info/pub/gnuplot/gnuplot-3.7.1.tar.gz
```

Downloading and Installing dbs

The dbs application can be downloaded from the dbs Web site at http://ns1.ai3.net/products/dbs/. This site contains links to the download area, along with lots of information about how dbs works. At the time of this writing, the current production version of dbs is version 1.1.5, which can be downloaded using the URL:

```
http://www.kusa.ac.jp/~yukio-m/dbs/software1.1.5/dbs-1.1.5.tar.gz
```

WARNING Even though the filename uses the .gz suffix to indicate it is a compressed file, it isn't. You do not need to uncompress the distribution file.

The distribution file must be expanded into a working directory using the tar command before it can be compiled:

```
tar -xvf dbs-1.1.5.tar.gz
```

This creates the working directory dbs-1.1.5, which contains the source code package. Several subdirectories are created within the working directory:

- **doc** contains the installation file and the dbs manual pages.
- **sample** contains sample command files and test outputs.
- **script** contains the dbs-view Perl script.
- **src** contains the dbsc and dbsd program source code.

You must perform several steps to compile and install the dbs package properly. First, you need to create an obj directory within the working directory, to use as a temporary working directory to hold the object files created by the compile. This is done using the Unix mkdir command:

```
[rich@test dbs-1.1.5]$ mkdir obj
```

After creating the obj directory, you must change to the src directory, and use the make command to create a working directory specific to your Unix distribution:

```
[rich@test dbs-1.1.5]$ cd src
[rich@test src]$ make dir
(cd  ../obj/`uname|tr -d '/'``uname -r|tr -d '/'`; ln -sf
../../src/*.[hc]
.)
cp Makefile ../obj/`uname|tr -d '/'``uname -r|tr -d '/'`/makefile
[rich@test2 src]$
```

The make command creates a new subdirectory under the obj directory that contains links to the source code. This produces a clean work area for you, in which to perform the source code compile. The new directory is named using the Unix uname command results for your system. On my test Mandrake system, it created the directory Linux2.4.3-20mdk.

Change to the new directory, and examine the generated makefile file to ensure that it will compile dbs in your Unix environment:

```
[rich@test src]$ cd ../obj/Linux2.4.3-20mdk
[rich@test Linux2.4.3-20mdk]$ vi makefile
```

NOTE By default, the makefile is set to install the dbs application programs in the /usr/local/etc directory (the BIN variable). You may want to change this for your Unix environment.

If you are installing dbs in a Linux environment, there is one more change you will need to make. The tcp.trace.c program uses the nlist.h header file, which is not present in Linux systems. You must comment this line out from the source code. The complete line looks like this:

```
#include <nlist.h>
```

To comment it out, surround it with the standard C comment symbols, so it looks like this:

```
/* #include <nlist.h> */
```

Then save the file, using the original filename. After this is completed, you can run the make command to build the executable files. Depending on your Unix distribution, you may see several warning messages as the compiles are performed. You should be able to ignore these warning messages. The end results should produce the two executable files, dbsc and dbsd.

After the executable files are produced, you can install them in the installation directory specified in the makefile, using the 'make install'.

WARNING In the 1.1.5 version of dbs, the install section of the makefile has an error. You must change the reference to the dbs_view file from ../script/ dbs_view to ../../script/dbs_view, or it will not be installed in the installation directory.

When this is complete, the dbsc, dbsd, and dbs_view programs should be copied to the installation directory. You can add the installation directory location (/usr/local/etc by default) to your PATH environment variable to easily run the dbs application from any directory on your system.

Running the dbsd Program

Each host that will participate in dbs testing must be running the dbsd program. The format of the dbsd command is:

```
dbsd [-p port] [-d] [-D] [-v] [-h host]
```

The dbs program does not use a configuration file. Instead, it uses command-line parameters to define its behavior. Table 5.1 describes the parameters that can be used with the dbsd program.

Table 5.1 The dbsd Program Parameters

PARAMETER	DESCRIPTION
-p *port*	Listen for incoming command connections on port *port*.
-d	Use debug mode, producing verbose output.
-D	Use the inetd process to accept incoming connections.
-v	Display version number and parameter options.
-h *host*	Only accept command connections from *host*.

For simple dbs tests, the dbsd program can be run directly from the command prompt in standalone mode. All debug messages will be sent to the standard output of the console terminal. For environments that need to perform frequent tests, you most likely will want to configure inetd or xinetd to run the dbsd program automatically for each incoming command connection. As with the netserver application in Chapter 4, an entry must be made in the /etc/services file defining the TCP port used for dbsd. By default, it should be 10710:

```
dbsd    10710/tcp    dbsd
```

If your Unix system uses the inetd application to launch network programs, the /etc/inetd.conf entry that would be used for dbsd is:

```
dbsd  stream  tcp  nowait  root  /usr/local/etc/dbsd  dbsd -D
```

NOTE This example shows the root user being used to start the dbsd program. For security purposes, you may choose to run it under a different user.

For Unix systems that use the xinetd application to launch network programs, the dbsd configuration file should contain information similar to that of the inetd.conf configuration line:

```
service dbsd
{
        socket_type     = stream
        wait            = no
        user            = root
        server          = /usr/local/etc/dbsd
        server_args     = -D
}
```

NOTE When using the inetd or xinetd programs to launch dbsd, remember to include the -D parameter to make it a daemon process.

After you have made the appropriate configuration changes to either the inetd or xinetd system, you must restart the process for it to recognize dbsd connections.

Configuring Command Files

After the dbsd program is running on each of the hosts that will participate in the tests, it's time to create a command file to control the testing from the dbsc control program. The dbsc command file is used to:

- Define the hosts participating in the test
- Define the socket parameters used in the test connections
- Define the start, end, and duration of the test
- Define the output files used to store data from the test

The command file can define multiple tests that are to be performed. Each test definition has three sections: the sender parameters, the receiver parameters, and the test parameters. Each of these sections is surrounded with braces, within the command file. Each individual test itself is also contained within braces. The basic command file structure looks like this:

```
# Test 1
{
    sender {
        .. sender commands ..
    }
    receiver {
        .. receiver commands ..
    }
    .. test commands ..
}
# Test 2
{
    sender {
        .. sender commands ..
    }
    receiver {
        .. receiver commands ..
    }
    .. test commands ..
}
```

This section defines two separate tests within a single command file. Each test has its own section, which defines the parameters used for the test. When multiple tests are configured, they can be set to perform on different hosts, and at either the same or at different times. The following sections of the chapter describe these command file sections.

Sender and Receiver Commands

The sender and receiver commands define the host configurations that are used in the test. Both the sending and receiving host addresses are defined, along with the socket settings and data pattern used for the test. Table 5.2 shows the commands that can be used in the sender and receiver sections.

Table 5.2   The Sender and Receiver Section Commands

COMMAND	DESCRIPTION
hostname	The host name or IP address of the host performing the function
hostname_cmd	The host name or IP address of the command connection for the host (usually the same as the hostname, and can be omitted)
port	The port number used for the test. If the host is a sender, the port can be specified as 0, so the system can choose any port
So_debug	If set to ON, the socket debug option is enabled for the host
Tcp_trace	If set to ON, the TCP_DEBUG option is enabled on the kernel (if the OS supports it)
No_delay	If set to ON, the socket no_delay option is set
recv_buff	Sets the size of the socket receive buffer. If omitted, the default system value is used
send_buff	Sets the size of the socket send buffer. If omitted, the default system value is used
mem_align	Arranges the size of both send and receive buffers in a page boundary
pattern	Defines a data pattern used for the test data

The Pattern Command

Most of these commands are self-explanatory. The pattern command is less so. The pattern command defines the data that is used for the performance test. Its format depends on whether it is in the sender or receiver section.

The Sender Pattern

The sender pattern command has the following syntax:

```
pattern {data size, message size, interval, wait time}
```

The *data size* parameter defines the amount of data that is sent in one iteration of the test. The *message size* parameter defines how much of the data is contained within a single packet. If the data size is specified as 2,048 bytes, and the message size is specified at 1,024 bytes, the test will send two 1,024-byte packets to complete the test. Conversely, if the data size is set to 1,024 and the message size is set to 2,048, the entire test data will be sent in a single packet.

When multiple packets are sent in the test, the *interval* parameter defines the length of time from the start of one packet to the start of the next packet. This can be used as a throttle mechanism, controlling how fast the packets are sent to the remote hosts. If this value is zero, the system will send the packets as fast as possible.

Finally, the *wait time* parameter defines the amount of time between packets. This value differs from the interval in that it is measured from the end of one packet to the start of the next packet. If this value is zero, the system will send the packets as fast as possible.

A sample sender data pattern command would look like:

```
pattern {2048, 1024, 0.0, 0.0}
```

This pattern defines a test using two packets, each containing 1,024 bytes of data, sent at normal system packet separation.

To complicate things even more, you can specify multiple data patterns within the same pattern command. A semicolon is used to separate the groups of parameters:

```
pattern {2048, 2048, 0.0, 0.0;
         2048, 1024, 0.0, 0.0;
         10000, 1024, 0.0, 0.0;
         1024, 1024, 0.0, 0.0 }
```

This pattern defines four separate data patterns. Each pattern is used once in the test, in sequence from the first listed pattern to the last. This test pattern would produce 14 separate data packets (1 for the first pattern, 2 for the second, 10 for the third, and 1 for the fourth). You could alternately specify an interval or wait time value to separate the data packet streams.

The Receiver Pattern

The receiver pattern command has the following syntax:

```
pattern {buffer, message size, interval, wait time}
```

The *buffer* parameter defines the total size of the buffer used for receiving the test data. The *message size* parameter defines the socket buffer size, representing the largest packet size that can be received. The *interval* parameter defines the time interval for receiving the next message from the sender. Finally, the *wait time* parameter defines a system overhead value that can be used to simulate a busy host.

WARNING Be careful when performing UDP tests. If the message size parameter is less than the sender's message size, data will be lost and the test statistics will be flawed.

A sample receiver pattern command would look like:

```
pattern {2048, 1024, 0.0, 0.0}
```

This pattern defines a 2,048-byte buffer to hold the data, and socket buffers set to 1,024 bytes. No interval or wait time value is set.

Sample Sender and Receiver Sections

A sample sender and receiver command file section would look like:

```
sender{
      hostname = 192.168.1.2;
      port = 0;
      recv_buff = 32678;
      send_buff = 32768;
      pattern {2048, 1024, 0.0, 0.0}
}
receiver{
      hostname = 192.168.1.100;
      port = 2102;
      mem_align = 2048;
      pattern {1024, 1024, 0.0, 0.0}
}
```

This sample test defines the two test hosts, and sets the socket information for the sender, allowing it to use large socket buffers. The receiving host is set to receive the data using port 2102 (the protocol used will be specified in the test command section).

Test Commands

The remaining commands used in the command file define the characteristics of the test. Table 5.3 describes these commands.

A sample test command section would look like:

```
file = data/test1;
protocol = TCP;
connection_mode = AFTER;
start_time = 0.0;
end_time = 30;
send_times = 1024;
```

These commands define that the test data output should be stored in the file test1, located under the data subdirectory in the current directory. TCP is used to transfer the data, and the data pattern is repeated 1,024 times, or for 30 seconds, whichever occurs first.

Performing Tests

This section shows the steps necessary to perform a sample dbs test session from start to finish.

Table 5.3   Test Section Commands

COMMAND	DESCRIPTION
File	Defines the location of the output data file (as a Unix pathname)
protocol	Defines the protocol used to transmit the data (TCP or UDP)
connection_mode	Defines when the session connection is established, either BEFORE the data trace is started, or AFTER the data trace starts
server	Defines which host acts as the server device, either the SENDER or the RECEIVER
end_time	Defines when the test will stop (in seconds)
start_time	Defines a delay value (in seconds) when the test should begin
send_times	Defines the number of times the test data pattern should be sent

Define the Test Environment

This test performs two separate tests between three separate hosts on different parts of the network simultaneously. This demonstrates the power of the dbs network performance tool. Testing all three hosts at the same time allows network traffic loads on the internal network devices to be tested.

The test host configurations used in this test are shown in Figure 5.1.

The details of the test are:

- Host1 sends a TCP data pattern to Host3

- Host2 sends a TCP data pattern to Host1

- Host3 sends a TCP data pattern to Host2

Each host sends the same data pattern, which defines a 2K data buffer to send in 1K messages, with no interval or wait time. This pattern is repeated 1,000 times, or for 60 seconds.

Create the Command File

Since all of the tests are to be performed simultaneously, they must all be configured in the same command file. Figure 5.2 shows the command file used for the test.

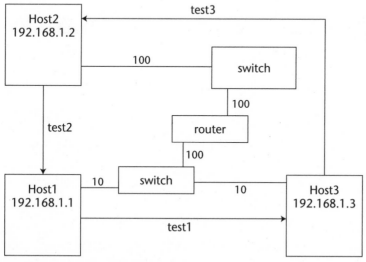

Figure 5.1   Host setup for dbs test.

```
# Test 1
{
    sender {
        hostname = 192.168.1.1;
        port = 0;
        send_buffer = 65535;
        recv_buffer = 65535;
        pattern {2048, 1024, 0.0, 0.0}
    }
    receiver {
        hostname = 192.168.1.3;
        port = 21001;
        pattern {2048, 1024, 0.0, 0.0}
    }
    file = data/test1;
    protocol = TCP;
    start_time = 0.0;
    end_time = 60;
    send_times = 1000;
}

# Test 2
{
    sender {
sender {
        hostname = 192.168.1.2;
        port = 0;
        send_buffer = 65535;
        recv_buffer = 65535;
        pattern {2048, 1024, 0.0, 0.0}
    }
    receiver {
        hostname = 192.168.1.1;
        port = 21001;
        pattern {2048, 1024, 0.0, 0.0}
    }
    file = data/test2;
    protocol = TCP;
    start_time = 0.0;
    end_time = 60;
    send_times = 1000;
}

# Test 3
{
    sender {
sender {
        hostname = 192.168.1.3;
```

Figure 5.2   The test.cmd command file.

```
        port = 0;
        send_buffer = 65535;
        recv_buffer = 65535;
        pattern {2048, 1024, 0.0, 0.0}
    }
    receiver {
        hostname = 192.168.1.2;
        port = 21001;
        pattern {2048, 1024, 0.0, 0.0}
    }
    file = data/test3;
    protocol = TCP;
    start_time = 0.0;
    end_time = 60;
    send_times = 1000;
}
```

Figure 5.2   *(continued)*

Each test is defined in its own section of the command file. Since the tests will be performed simultaneously, each of the start_time commands is set to 0.0. If, instead, you want to run the tests separately, you can specify different start times for each test.

Run the Test

After the test.cmd command file is created, you can use the dbsc controller program from any host on the network (including one of the test participants) to start the test:

```
$ dbsc test.cmd
Command File: OK
Setup:(192.168.1.1.0, 192.168.1.3.21001, TCP):End
Setup:(192.168.1.2.0, 192.168.1.1.21001, TCP):End
Setup:(192.168.1.3.0, 192.168.1.2.21001, TCP):End
Test Start. Test time=80s
Test End.
Results:(192.168.1.1,192.168.1.3,0,21001,TCP):Received
Results:(192.168.1.2,192.168.1.1,0,21001,TCP):Received
Results:(192.168.1.3,192.168.1.2,0,21001,TCP):Received
DBSC: Normal END.
$
```

The first thing dbsc does is read and parse the command file. If any errors are found in the command file, an error message is produced, pointing out the location of the faulty statement. As shown in this example, the command file was parsed with no errors.

The next step is for dbsc to send the test information to each of the test participants. This is called the Setup section. As seen in the output, each of the setup commands was successfully sent to the appropriate test host. If any of the setup commands failed, dbsc would halt the test.

After configuring each of the test participants, dbsc coordinates the start and end of the test. Since all of the tests in this example ran simultaneously, there is only one start and end test time. This requires that each of the systems be synchronized with the clock on the system running dbsc. A small amount of variance is permitted. If this variance is detected, a warning message will be produced, but the test will continue. If the clock variance is too great, dbsc will stop the test and produce an error message.

After the test is completed, the test results are transferred from the test host back to the host running dbsc. The appropriate data files are created containing the results from the test.

Analyze the Data

When the test results have been created, it is time to run the dbs_view script to view and analyze the data. The dbs_view script is unusual in that you do not directly specify the test data created by the dbsc program. Instead, you must specify the original command file used to perform the test. The dbs_view script interprets the command file, and accesses the appropriate data file.

The dbs_view script uses command-line parameters to define which test results to graph. Table 5.4 shows the possible parameters that can be used.

Table 5.4   The dbs_view Command-Line Parameters

PARAMETER	DESCRIPTION
-a *area*	Defines the area of the graph to draw
-color	Displays the graph in color when writing to a postscript or eps output file
-delay	Displays delay time at the application level
-dth	Displays the throughput relative to the data sent (bps/bytes)
-eps	Outputs the graph as an eps file
-f *file*	Specifies the command file to read
-jitter	Displays the application-level jitter
-p	Processes data for display
-ps	Outputs the graph as a postscript file
-sq	Displays the connection sequence numbers

Table 5.4 *(continued)*

PARAMETER	DESCRIPTION
-sd	Displays the connection sequence numbers relative to data sent
-t *time*	Defines the time interval
-tdelay	Displays delay time at the kernel level
-th	Displays throughput of the connection
-title	Displays the selected title on the graph
-tjitter	Displays the kernel-level jitter
-tlost	Calculates lost data segments
-trtt	Displays round-trip time at the kernel level
-tsq	Displays the packet sequence numbers at the kernel level
-tth	Displays the throughput at the kernel level
-twin	Displays TCP packet window sizes
-ulost	Calculates the lost UDP packets

The parameters that display packet statistics must also specify whether the send (s) or receive (r) data is used. For example, to display the sequence numbers of the sending data (as shown back in Figure 5.2), you would use the command:

```
$ dbs_view -p -f test.cmd -sq s
```

If you wanted to see the receive sequence numbers, you would use the r option.

WARNING It is important to remember to use the -p option the first time you display a statistic. dbs_view must create the data file for the statistic from the raw data before it can be graphed.

The dbs_view graphs are an excellent way to visualize the data extracted from the tests. A good example of this is to watch the throughput graphs produced from the sample test:

```
$ dbs_view -p -f test.cmd -th s
data/test1 Send: Mean Throughput    3.6780 Mbps
data/test2 Send: Mean Throughput    4.9521 Mbps
data/test3 Send: Mean Throughput    6.8266 Mbps
Hit Return Key

$
```

The dbs_view program displays the mean throughput of the tests on the console screen. Going by this information, it appears that the test1 hosts had a difficult time sending the test data across the network, more so than the other test hosts. The throughput graph produced by this command is shown in Figure 5.3.

The throughput graph displays the results of all three tests on a single graph. This enables you to analyze and compare what was happening during the tests. As can be seen from this graph, test1 had a terrible throughput rate while test2 and test3 were running. However, as soon as the other two tests stopped, the throughput rate for test1 jumped back to a normal range. Obviously, there was some network congestion involved in the slow throughput rate (or a poorly performing host).

This kind of information is crucial to identifying network performance problems. With the information provided by the dbs graph in hand, you can now configure additional test scenarios to attempt to isolate the performance problem on the network.

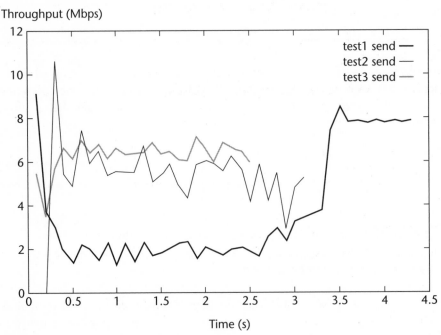

Figure 5.3   The test.cmd throughput graph.

Summary

The Distributed Benchmark System (dbs) can be used to perform multiple performance tests on the network, and control the tests from a single point. This allows you to test multiple hosts and network segments under a load condition without affecting production network traffic.

The dbs application uses three separate programs to function. The dbsd program is the core of the test. It must run on each test host to accept test instructions from the controller, and perform the desired tests with remote test hosts. The dbsc program controls the test environment, sending commands to the individual test hosts on how and when to perform the tests. The dbs_view program is used to graph the test results in a user-friendly form.

The next chapter describes the Iperf network performance tool. It can be used to determine the total network bandwidth available between two points on the network.

Iperf

The next network performance tool to discuss is the Iperf application. Iperf provides several different types of TCP and UDP communication tests between two hosts on the network, and can be used in both the Unix and Windows environments. This chapter describes the benefits of Iperf, and explains how to install and use it in your network environment.

The Iperf application was developed at the National Laboratory for Applied Network Research (NLANR), and is currently maintained at the University of Illinois. Its primary purpose is to help system administrators fine-tune TCP parameters on network applications and servers. Iperf can be used to determine the standard performance statistics of the network, as well as the TCP window performance of network test streams between both Unix and Windows hosts. By fine-tuning network hosts and applications, you can improve the performance of applications within your network environment.

Iperf Features

The Iperf application was designed to work as a simple, interactive application that allows network and system administrators to see how TCP socket parameters used in applications and in host configurations can affect network performance. This section describes some of the basic features of Iperf, along with the concepts behind the features.

The Components of Iperf

The Iperf application consists of an executable file, used as a single application for both the client and server functions; a Java application that provides a graphical front end to the Iperf application; and a set of library files used to provide additional functions for socket programs. This section describes these pieces of the Iperf application package.

The Iperf Program

Unlike the previous performance tools discussed, the Iperf application uses a single program that contains both the client and server functions of the application. Only a single file (iperf) needs to be loaded on the test devices on the network, and any device can be used as both a client and a server. The Iperf application also contains a distribution for the Windows environment, allowing you to use Windows-based workstations or servers as test devices on the network. This can greatly expand the number of testing devices on the network.

As with the previous performance tools discussed, when Iperf is run in server mode, it can be run in either foreground or background mode (both in the Unix and Windows environments). In the Windows environment, Iperf can be run as a service, allowing it to operate in the background without interfering with other applications on the workstation or server. In the Unix environment, it can be run as a daemon process in the background, without the help of the inetd or xinetd program. For short-term tests in either environment, you can run the Iperf program in standalone server mode, providing a quick and easy way to perform tests.

The jperf Front End

If you download the source code distribution package for Iperf, you get an additional package (at no additional charge). The jperf package is included as a graphical front end to Iperf.

Jperf provides a fancy graphical interface to Iperf, allowing you to perform the same performance tests, and produce the same output results. Each of the command-line options available in Iperf is provided in various radio buttons and text boxes in the jperf Java application. All of the Iperf command-line options available can be set using the jperf front end.

NOTE To run jperf, you must have a Java runtime or SDK package installed on the host. Jperf will operate in either a Java 1.1 or 1.2 environment. When you run jperf, the Iperf executable file for your host environment must also be available in the PATH environment variable. Jperf is just a front-end program; it still needs access to the Iperf executable file to perform the network tests.

The Iperf library

One additional feature of the Iperf application is a set of C and C++ library files that can be used to add functionality to socket-based applications, or to make normal socket programming functions easier. It is often difficult to create network programs using C++ as there are no standard classes available. The Iperf library provides several classes to help network programmers. Table 6.1 shows the C++ library classes that are included with Iperf.

Besides these C++ library classes, Iperf also contains several C functions that can be used to make creating and using socket applications easier. These functions are shown in Table 6.2.

If you do network programming in the Unix environment, these C++ classes and C functions can save you time by providing commonly used network functions.

Iperf Tests

The Iperf application provides several network performance tests for both the TCP and UDP network environments. It can be used to measure the following TCP network characteristics:

- Total bandwidth of the test connection
- Stream bandwidth assigned to multiple test connections
- Default TCP window size value used by the test host
- Default Path MTU Discovery value used by the test host
- Router handling of IP Type-of-Service (TOS) packets

Table 6.1   Iperf C++ Library Classes

CLASS	DESCRIPTION
Socket	Provides simplified socket functions to applications
Queue	Provides simplified queue functions to applications
Thread	Provides simplified thread functions to applications
Timestamp	Provides simplified timestamp functions to applications

Table 6.2   Iperf C Functions

FUNCTION	DESCRIPTION
getsock_tcp_windowsize(*sock*)	Retrieves the socket send buffer size
setsocket_tcp_windowsize(*sock*, *size*)	Sets the socket send and receive buffer sizes
getsock_tcp_mss(*sock*)	Retrieves the socket maximum segment size value
setsock_tcp_mss(*sock*, *size*)	Sets the socket maximum segment size value
readn(*sock*, **buff*, *len*)	Reads a full buffer of data from the socket
writen(*sock*, **buff*, *len*)	Writes a full buffer of data to the socket

Besides detecting the default in addition to these standard tests, Iperf also has modes that automatically determine the optimal TCP widow size and MTU size used for socket connections. This feature alone can greatly improve network performance when configuring network applications for your network environment.

Besides the TCP tests, Iperf can also be used to measure some UDP network characteristics:

- UDP performance at a specified bandwidth
- UDP packet loss in a stream of packets
- UDP delay jitter in a stream of packets
- UDP multicast packet performance

The UDP multicast test feature of Iperf is unique in that it allows you to set the Iperf client to send packets to a specific multicast address, and set one or more Iperf servers to listen to the same multicast address. This allows you to easily test multicast network performance on separate network segments. This can often be tricky, as network routers must be configured to provide multicast support to individual network segments.

Iperf Output

The Iperf application uses the standard console display to output all of the results from network tests. The format of the test results can be altered by defining what units of measurement (such as kilobytes, megabytes, or gigabytes) to use in the values presented.

Both the client and server devices used in the test output results from the test, allowing you to quickly see the results from either host in the test. A default Iperf test looks something like this:

```
host1>iperf -s
------------------------------------------------------------
Server listening on TCP port 5001
TCP window size:  8.0 KByte (default)
------------------------------------------------------------
[188] local 192.168.1.100 port 5001 connected with 192.168.1.6 port 1332
[ ID] Interval        Transfer      Bandwidth
[188]  0.0-10.0 sec    110 MBytes  92.3 Mbits/sec

host2$ iperf -c 192.168.1.100
------------------------------------------------------------
Client connecting to 192.168.1.100, TCP port 5001
TCP window size: 16.0 KByte (default)
------------------------------------------------------------
[   3] local 192.168.1.6 port 1332 connected with 192.168.1.100 port
5001
[ ID] Interval        Transfer      Bandwidth
[   3]  0.0-10.0 sec    110 MBytes  92.3 Mbits/sec
$
```

The host1 device is used as the Iperf server. Its output shows that the server is listening for connections on the standard Iperf TCP port (5001), along with the current value of the TCP window size. When a new connection is accepted, the remote client IP address and port number are displayed. At the end of the test (which by default is 10 seconds long), the raw test data is displayed: the number of bytes transferred between the devices, and the bandwidth calculated for the transfer.

The client Iperf host (host2) uses the -c option to indicate the address of the Iperf server to connect to. Similar to the server output, the client output indicates the IP address and TCP port number of the remote server, along with the current value of the TCP window size of the client machine. When a connection is established, the information is displayed on a separate line, indicating both the client and server connection information. When the test is complete, the test information is displayed, again similar to the server output.

Downloading and Installing Iperf

The Iperf application Web site (http://dast.nlanr.net/Projects/Iperf/) contains information about the latest release of Iperf (version 1.6.3 at the time of this writing), as well as links to the download area. The download area contains links for downloading several different binary packages for various platforms (including MacOS X and Microsoft Windows), as well as the source code package. If your particular Unix distribution does not have a binary package, you must download the source code and compile it yourself.

Downloading the Source Code

At the time of this writing, the most current source code distribution URL is:

```
http://dast.nlanr.net/Projects/Iperf/iperf-1.6.3.tar.gz
```

Similar to the other package distributions used in this book, the Iperf source code is distributed as a compressed tar file. To compile the package on a Unix system, you must first extract it into a working directory:

```
tar -zxvf iperf-1.6.3.tar.gz
```

This command creates the subdirectory iperf-1.6.3 under the current directory, and extracts the Iperf source code package into the directory.

Compiling the Source Code

Once the source code package has been downloaded and extracted into a working directory, you can compile and install it on your system. The Iperf application package does not use the configure command, as other packages do. It uses the make command to both determine system configuration settings and generate the executable files on the system.

> **WARNING** The Iperf programs are written in C++. You must have a C++ compiler on your system to compile the Iperf package. The most popular package for Linux and FreeBSD systems is the GNU C++ compiler, gc++.

When the make program is running, you will see lots of messages indicating which files are being compiled. When it is done, the iperf executable will appear in the working directory, along with the jperf script to start the jperf application, and the jperf.jar Java file that contains the jperf classes.

Installing Iperf

Even though the Iperf executable file will work perfectly fine at this point, it's best to place it in a common location so it can be easily accessed. To do this, you must run the make command again, this time using the install option. The install option first asks a question about where to install the binary files, then proceeds with the installation:

```
# make install

Where should the iperf binary be installed? [/usr/local/bin]


make[1]: Entering directory `/home/rich/iperf-1.6.3/src'
../install-sh -c -d /usr/local/bin
../install-sh -c ../iperf /usr/local/bin
make[1]: Leaving directory `/home/rich/iperf-1.6.3/src'

make[1]: Entering directory `/home/rich/iperf-1.6.3/jsrc'
../install-sh -c -d /usr/local/bin
../install-sh -c ../jperf /usr/local/bin
../install-sh -c -m 0644 ../jperf.jar /usr/local/bin
make[1]: Leaving directory `/home/rich/iperf-1.6.3/jsrc'
#
```

If you want to use the default installation directory, you can just hit the Enter key when asked for the path (the path will default to /usr/local/bin). Next the install process installs both the Iperf and jperf pieces into the selected installation directory.

Using Iperf

This section shows you how to run various performance tests using the Iperf application. Except where noted, the Iperf application performs exactly the same, no matter which platform it is running on.

Starting the Iperf Server

The -s option is used to place the Iperf program in server mode. While in server mode, Iperf will listen to port 5001 for incoming test connections. As mentioned earlier in the *Iperf Features* section, Iperf can be run in server mode as either a standalone server or a background daemon.

Standalone Mode

When just using the -s option, Iperf operates in standalone mode. All messages generated by Iperf are displayed on the standard output for the terminal:

```
$ iperf -s
------------------------------------------------------------
Server listening on TCP port 5001
TCP window size:  8.0 KByte (default)
------------------------------------------------------------
```

By default, Iperf will use the default TCP window size assigned by the host system. If you want to use an alternate window size, you can use the -w option:

```
$ iperf -s -w 130k
------------------------------------------------------------
Server listening on TCP port 5001
TCP window size:  8.0 KByte (WARNING: requested  130 KByte)
------------------------------------------------------------
```

If the system allows the send and receive socket buffers to be altered, the new window size will be displayed. If not, a warning message is shown.

Daemon Mode

The -s option can also be used with the -D option, which places the Iperf program in background mode (or runs it as a service in Windows platforms):

```
$ iperf -s -D
------------------------------------------------------------
Server listening on TCP port 5001
TCP window size: 16.0 KByte (default)
------------------------------------------------------------
Running Iperf Server as a daemon
The Iperf daemon process ID : 18074
$
```

The output from the -s -D options shows that the Iperf program is running as a daemon, and indicates the PID of the running process.

The output from the Iperf program will still be displayed on the standard output, at least while the standard output exists. If you prefer, you can redirect the output to a file, which will then contain all of the output from any tests performed with the Iperf program:

```
$ iperf -s -D > /home/rich/iperf.log
```

WARNING When redirecting the output to a log file, make sure that you have proper permissions to create and write to the file, or Iperf will not run.

Performing Simple Tests

After a copy of Iperf is running in server mode, you can run Iperf in client mode from any other device on the network to connect to the server, using the -c option, and specifying the hostname or IP address of the Iperf server:

```
$ iperf -c 192.168.1.100
------------------------------------------------------------
Client connecting to 12, TCP port 5001
TCP window size: 16.0 KByte (default)
------------------------------------------------------------
[  3] local 192.168.1.6 port 1337 connected with 192.168.1.100 port 5001
[ ID] Interval        Transfer     Bandwidth
[  3]  0.0-10.0 sec   111 MBytes  93.2 Mbits/sec
$
```

By default, the client sends 8-KB data packets for 10 seconds to the remote server. The total amount of data transferred, along with the calculated network bandwidth, is displayed. You can alter some of the test features using command-line parameters. Table 6.3 lists the parameters that can be used.

If you want to extend the test to 60 seconds, showing an update every 5 seconds, you use the following command:

```
$ iperf -c 192.168.1.100 -t 60 -i 5
------------------------------------------------------------
Client connecting to 192.168.1.100, TCP port 5001
TCP window size: 16.0 KByte (default)
------------------------------------------------------------
[  3] local 192.168.1.6 port 1340 connected with 192.168.1.100 port 5001
[ ID] Interval        Transfer     Bandwidth
[  3]  0.0- 5.0 sec   55.5 MBytes  93.1 Mbits/sec
[  3]  5.0-10.0 sec   55.4 MBytes  92.9 Mbits/sec
[  3] 10.0-15.0 sec   55.4 MBytes  93.0 Mbits/sec
[  3] 15.0-20.0 sec   53.5 MBytes  89.6 Mbits/sec
[  3] 20.0-25.0 sec   53.4 MBytes  89.6 Mbits/sec
[  3] 25.0-30.0 sec   54.8 MBytes  91.9 Mbits/sec
[  3] 30.0-35.0 sec   54.8 MBytes  91.9 Mbits/sec
[  3] 35.0-40.0 sec   55.0 MBytes  92.3 Mbits/sec
[  3] 40.0-45.0 sec   55.5 MBytes  93.2 Mbits/sec
[  3] 45.0-50.0 sec   55.5 MBytes  93.0 Mbits/sec
[  3] 50.0-55.0 sec   55.6 MBytes  93.2 Mbits/sec
[  3] 55.0-60.0 sec   55.5 MBytes  93.2 Mbits/sec
[  3]  0.0-60.0 sec   660 MBytes  92.2 Mbits/sec
$
```

A report is displayed every 5 seconds of the test. A final report is also displayed, showing the results for the overall, 60-second test.

The -P option can be used to run simultaneous tests between the two test hosts. Each test stream will contain the same data pattern, and the same data and time limits as defined on the command-line parameters:

```
$ iperf -c 192.168.1.100 -P 2
------------------------------------------------------------
Client connecting to 192.168.1.100, TCP port 5001
TCP window size: 16.0 KByte (default)
```

```
---------------------------------------------------------------
[  3] local 192.168.1.6 port 1346 connected with 192.168.1.100 port 5001
[  6] local 192.168.1.6 port 1347 connected with 192.168.1.100 port 5001
[ ID] Interval       Transfer      Bandwidth
[  6]  0.0-10.0 sec  55.4 MBytes   46.4 Mbits/sec
[  3]  0.0-10.0 sec  55.4 MBytes   46.4 Mbits/sec
$
```

Both tests are assigned a unique ID value, which allows you to track the test statistics (especially if you are obtaining interval reports). Note that the total bandwidth for the individual tests should be similar to the total bandwidth used for a single test.

Testing TOS Traffic

With the increased use of special-purpose video and audio connections across networks, it is important to determine if network equipment is handling this traffic properly. Video and audio traffic must maintain a set bandwidth, or the result will be choppy and possibly useless display frames and unintelligible voice.

Most video and audio traffic uses the IP Type-of-Service (TOS) feature to tag IP packets containing the data as higher priority than regular data packets on the network. This lets routers identify these packets as higher priority, and handle them with a higher preference than other packets being routed.

The IP TOS field can identify several different classes of data, shown in Table 6.4.

Table 6.3   Iperf Client Command-Line Parameters

PARAMETER	DESCRIPTION
-f format	Sets the units of the output data (b = bits/s, B = bytes/s, k = Kbits/s, K = Kbytes/s, etc)
-I interval	Sets the interval (in seconds) at which Iperf will display a status report (default = 0, only one report at the end of the test)
-l length	Sets the length of the test data packets (in bytes)
-n num	Sets the number of test data packets to send (overrides the time restriction)
-p port	Sets the port to use to contact the server
-t time	Sets the time (in seconds) to transmit data packets
-P clients	Sets the number of concurrent client connections to clients

Table 6.4 IP TOS Types

TOS	VALUE	DESCRIPTION
Minimize cost	0x02	Chooses the routes with the least monetary cost to send the packet
Maximize reliability	0x04	Chooses the most reliable routes to send the packet
Maximize throughput	0x08	Chooses the paths with the highest throughput to send the packet
Minimize delay	0x10	Chooses the paths with the least delay to send the packet

The -S option can be used on the Iperf client command-line options to specify the TOS value to use for the test. The value can be entered in hexadecimal notation (0x02), octal notation (002), or decimal notation (2). A sample test would look like the following:

```
$ iperf -c 192.168.1.100 -S 16
------------------------------------------------------------
Client connecting to 192.168.1.100, TCP port 5001
TCP window size: 16.0 KByte (default)
------------------------------------------------------------
[  3] local 192.168.1.6 port 1353 connected with 192.168.1.100 port 5001
[ ID] Interval       Transfer     Bandwidth
[  3] 0.0-10.0 sec   107 MBytes   89.9 Mbits/sec
$
```

With TOS traffic, the thing to watch for is whether the bandwidth increases for different TOS values, indicating that intermediary routers are actually passing the packets at a higher priority than normal network traffic.

NOTE To utilize the TOS feature of Iperf, you must perform the test across one or more routers that are configured to handle TOS traffic at a different priority than normal network traffic.

Testing UDP Traffic

The Iperf application also allows you to test the performance of UDP traffic on your network. To test UDP traffic, you must use the -u command-line option on both the server and client programs:

```
C:\>iperf -s -u
------------------------------------------------------------
Server listening on UDP port 5001
```

```
Receiving 1470 byte datagrams
UDP buffer size:  8.0 KByte (default)
------------------------------------------------------------
[136] local 192.168.1.100 port 5001 connected with 192.168.1.6 port 1024
[ ID] Interval    Transfer   Bandwidth    Jitter   Lost/Total
Datagrams
[136] 0.0-10.0 sec 1.3 MBytes 1.0 Mbits/sec 2.084 ms   0/  893 (0%)

$ iperf -c 192.168.1.100 -u
------------------------------------------------------------
Client connecting to 1192.168.1.100, UDP port 5001
Sending 1470 byte datagrams
UDP buffer size: 64.0 KByte (default)
------------------------------------------------------------
[  3] local 192.168.1.6 port 1024 connected with 192.168.1.100 port 5001
[ ID] Interval        Transfer     Bandwidth
[  3]  0.0-10.0 sec   1.3 MBytes   1.0 Mbits/sec
[  3] Sent 893 datagrams
$
```

You may notice one thing that's different with the UDP test—the detailed test result is shown on the server host, and not the client host. This is due to the way UDP operates. Since it is not a connection-oriented protocol, the client has no idea how many packets actually make it to the server. Instead, it can tell the server how many packets are sent, and the server can determine how many actually make it.

The other feature of the UDP test is the *jitter value*. The jitter of a connection shows the amount of change in the delay between sent packets. If two hosts are on the same subnet, the jitter value should be extremely small (as shown in the preceding example). However, if the UDP packets must traverse a large network that includes switches and routers, the delay between packets may increase, depending on the load of the network devices.

For packets that contain time-sensitive data (such as voice and video data), changes in the delay between packets can be devastating. As the delay between packets increases, the flow of the video or voice data is altered, severely affecting the end-result of the data.

The UDP option allows only a set bandwidth of data to be sent on the network during the test. By default, this is 1 Mbps of bandwidth. You can alter the desired bandwidth by using the -b command-line option:

```
>iperf -s -u
------------------------------------------------------------
Server listening on UDP port 5001
Receiving 1470 byte datagrams
UDP buffer size:  8.0 KByte (default)
------------------------------------------------------------
[136] local 192.168.1.100 port 5001 connected with 192.168.1.6 port 1024
```

```
[ ID] Interval     Transfer   Bandwidth    Jitter   Lost/Total
Datagrams
[136]0.0-10.0 sec   113 MBytes 94.9 Mbits/sec 0.488 ms  582/81518 (0.71%)
[136]   0.0-10.0 sec  1 datagrams received out-of-order


$ iperf -c 192.168.1.100 -u -b 100M
------------------------------------------------------------
Client connecting to 192.168.1.100, UDP port 5001
Sending 1470 byte datagrams
UDP buffer size: 64.0 KByte (default)
------------------------------------------------------------
[  3] local 192.168.1.6 port 1024 connected with 192.168.1.100 port 5001
[ ID] Interval      Transfer    Bandwidth
[  3]  0.0-10.0 sec   114 MBytes  95.9 Mbits/sec
[  3] Sent 81518 datagrams
$
```

The test with the larger UDP bandwidth (set to 100 Mbps) resulted in a few dropped packets (0.71 percent), and one packet received out of order. However, the overall bandwidth for the UDP session was still close to the test goal (about 95 Mbps).

NOTE Unfortunately, you cannot use the same Iperf server when testing UDP and TCP applications. If you need to perform both TCP and UDP simultaneously, you can run two separate servers, one using the default port number of 5001 and a second with an alternate port number.

Testing Multicast Traffic

As mentioned earlier, one nice feature of Iperf is the ability to test the performance of multicast packets on the network. This is done using the -B command-line option, which allows you to bind the test program to an IP address different from the one configured on the host:

```
>iperf -s -u -B 224.100.0.1
------------------------------------------------------------
Server listening on UDP port 5001
Binding to local address 192.168.1.100
Receiving 1470 byte datagrams
UDP buffer size: 8.0 KByte (default)
------------------------------------------------------------
[136] local 192.168.1.100 port 5001 connected with 192.168.1.6 port 1024
[ ID] Interval     Transfer   Bandwidth    Jitter   Lost/Total
Datagrams
```

```
[136] 0.0-10.0 sec 113 MBytes 94.9 Mbits/sec 0.293 ms 678/81518 (0.83%)


$ iperf -c 224.100.0.1 -u -b 100M
-----------------------------------------------------------
Client connecting to 224.100.0.1, UDP port 5001
Sending 1470 byte datagrams
Setting multicast TTL to 1
UDP buffer size: 64.0 KByte (default)
-----------------------------------------------------------
[  3] local 192.168.1.6 port 1024 connected with 224.100.0.1 port 5001
[ ID] Interval        Transfer      Bandwidth
[  3]  0.0-10.0 sec   114 MBytes   95.9 Mbits/sec
[  3] Sent 81518 datagrams
$
```

Remember to include the -u option, since the multicast test must use UDP packets. This example also used the -b option to specify the bandwidth to attempt to send to the remote server. For multicast tests you can also use multiple servers, as each server should receive the same multicast packets as the others.

By default, the Iperf multicast test uses an IP Time to Live (TTL) value of 1. The TTL value is used to define the number of router hops the packet is allowed to take. Setting the value to 1 restricts it to the local network, with no router hops.

If you need to perform the multicast test using devices on other subnets, you must increase the TTL value, using the -T option on the client side:

```
$ iperf -c 224.100.0.1 -u -b 100M -T 10
```

This test allows the multicast packets to traverse up to 9 router hops from the local subnet when the client is located.

WARNING Be careful when running multicast tests. First, ensure that any routers involved in the test are capable of forwarding packets for the specific multicast group used in the test. Second, do not use arbitrary large values for the TTL, as your test streams could possibly work their way through your network routers out onto the Internet (assuming your Internet routers enable multicast traffic to pass for the group used).

Testing a File Transfer

Besides sending meaningless streams of data to test network performance, Iperf allows you to test an actual file transfer performance using real-world files. This is a nice feature, in that you can use it to predict what type of performance actual client file transfers would realize, without actually moving the data.

Often, just sending arbitrary data generated in memory on the machine does not provide an accurate picture of a real data transfer on the network. When you transfer a file from one host to another, there are also the read and write speeds on the host disks, along with the CPU load on both systems.

The -F command-line option can be used at the Iperf client side to define a file that you would like to simulate transferring to the remote server host. The file can be any type or size, as long as its path relative to the current directory is defined in the command line:

```
$ iperf -c 192.168.1.100 -F testfile
------------------------------------------------------------
Client connecting to 192.168.1.100, TCP port 5001
TCP window size: 16.0 KByte (default)
------------------------------------------------------------
[  4] local 192.168.1.6 port 1368 connected with 192.168.1.100 port 5001
[ ID] Interval       Transfer     Bandwidth
[  4]  0.0- 0.2 sec   2.3 MBytes   88.9 Mbits/sec
$
```

If the test file is not found, Iperf will revert to performing a default test:

```
$ iperf -c 192.168.1.100 -F badfile
Unable to open the file stream
Will use the default data stream
```

Testing TCP Window Sizes

Besides showing the TCP window sizes used by default in the test hosts, Iperf can calculate the preferred TCP window size for a network connection. This feature is used to determine the optimal TCP window size to use when transferring data across the network, given the current network conditions.

The -W command-line option is used with the Iperf client program to allow Iperf to determine the optimal TCP window size for the test:

```
>iperf -c 192.168.1.100 -W
------------------------------------------------------------
Client connecting to 192.168.1.100, TCP port 5001
TCP window size:  8.0 KByte (default)
------------------------------------------------------------
[136] local 192.168.1.6 port 1623 connected with 192.168.1.100 port 5001
------------------------------------------------------------
TCP window size:  8.0 KByte (default)
```

```
[ ID] Interval        Transfer     Bandwidth
[136]  0.0- 1.0 sec  11.1 MBytes  93.3 Mbits/sec
------------------------------------------------------------
TCP window size: 16.0 KByte (default)
[136]  1.0- 2.0 sec  11.1 MBytes  93.1 Mbits/sec
------------------------------------------------------------
TCP window size: 16.0 KByte (default)
[136]  2.0- 3.0 sec  11.1 MBytes  93.2 Mbits/sec
------------------------------------------------------------
TCP window size: 16.0 KByte (default)
[136]  3.0- 4.0 sec  11.1 MBytes  93.2 Mbits/sec
------------------------------------------------------------
TCP window size: 12.0 KByte (default)
[136]  4.0- 5.0 sec  11.1 MBytes  93.1 Mbits/sec
------------------------------------------------------------
TCP window size: 16.0 KByte (default)
[136]  5.0- 6.0 sec  11.1 MBytes  93.3 Mbits/sec
------------------------------------------------------------
TCP window size: 12.0 KByte (default)
[136]  6.0- 7.0 sec  11.0 MBytes  93.1 Mbits/sec
------------------------------------------------------------
TCP window size: 16.0 KByte (default)
[136]  7.0- 8.0 sec  11.1 MBytes  92.8 Mbits/sec
------------------------------------------------------------
TCP window size: 16.0 KByte (default)
[136]  8.0- 9.0 sec  11.1 MBytes  92.9 Mbits/sec
------------------------------------------------------------
TCP window size: 16.0 KByte (default)
[136]  9.0-10.0 sec  11.1 MBytes  92.8 Mbits/sec
------------------------------------------------------------
Optimal Estimate
TCP window size:  8.0 KByte (default)
------------------------------------------------------------
[136]  0.0-10.0 sec   111 MBytes  93.1 Mbits/sec

>
```

When performing the TCP window-size test, instead of sending a single 10-second stream of data, Iperf sends 10 1-second streams, altering the TCP window size of the client during each stream test. It will attempt to match the stream to the best client TCP window size, given the network utilization at the time of the test, and the TCP window settings on the server.

Using jperf

If you have the Java runtime or SDK package installed on your system (either Unix, Mac, or Windows), you can use the jperf program to provide a simple, graphical interface to the Iperf command line. Figure 6.1 shows the jperf window.

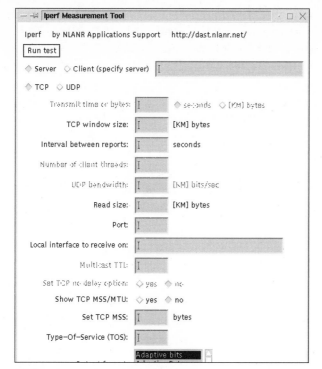

Figure 6.1   The jperf window.

You can select which mode you want Iperf to run in (server or client), along with the address of the remote server if it is running in client mode. There are text boxes to enter information for each of the different command-line options that are available. Fields that only apply to the client program are shadowed-out when the server option is selected.

Summary

The Iperf application is a versatile network performance tool that can be used in both the Unix and Windows environments. Its specialty is determining optimal TCP window sizes for TCP connections, allowing the system administrator to configure network hosts for optimal performance.

The main feature of Iperf is the ability to determine the TCP window size that will produce the best throughput for the network conditions. This feature can be used to determine optimal default network settings for network hosts, as well as assist network programmers in determining optimal socket buffer sizes when creating programs to operate in the network environment.

The TCP windows size regulates how much data is on the network for a connection. The receiving host can inform the sending host to either slow down or speed up the amount of data sent before an acknowledgment packet is sent. By regulating the data transfer, the receiving host can control how fast the data is sent on the network.

Iperf also provides a way for you to test how multicast packets are handled by the network devices. Multicast packets are used to send the same data to multiple network devices at the same time, with the same packet stream. Routers must be specifically configured to forward multicast packets, and often can add delays in processing multicast packets.

The next chapter presents the Pathrate and Pathload tools, which can be invaluable in determining both the total bandwidth and the available bandwidth between two network points.

Pathrate

One of the crucial elements of network performance is bandwidth capacity. The Pathrate application provides a method for you to determine the total possible bandwidth capacity for a network link between two endpoints, even when the link in under load. The Pathrate application has a companion application, Pathload, which can be used to determine the actual load on a network link between two endpoints. This chapter describes how network bottlenecks can affect your network performance, and how these applications can be used to find them.

The Pathrate and Pathload applications were developed, and are maintained, by Constantinos Dovrolis, who is currently working at Georgia Tech. Both applications rely on advanced network statistical calculations, involving the delays present in transferring packets across network devices along the path between the two endpoints.

The Pathrate application can be used to determine the maximum theoretical throughput (often called the bottleneck speed) of a network path between two points, even when parts of the network are under loading conditions (such as during normal production operations). This value represents the fastest possible speed at which a packet can be transferred between the two hosts, given ideal conditions. The Pathload application can be used to determine the throughput of the link, given the current traffic levels. By using both of these applications, the network administrator can obtain a clearer picture of the network, and how well traffic is funneling through it.

Using Statistics to Measure Bandwidth

The unique feature of Pathrate and Pathload is the way they use statistical analysis to determine the maximum capacity of an operating network, and determine the available bandwidth of the network using the statistical data. This section describes the processes that Pathrate and Pathload use to perform the calculations and estimate the bandwidth capacity and available bandwidth.

How Pathrate Works

There are several different statistical tests that are performed throughout the test period. The tests are grouped into phases that are used to obtain different information about the connection. This section describes each phase of the Pathrate test.

Initial Phase

In the initial phase of operation, Pathrate sends a limited number of packet trains to the remote host to "test the waters" of the network link. The packet trains used vary in size and interpacket gap, allowing for varying network conditions.

During this phase, Pathrate can use the packet train data to determine if any special network devices are present within the network link. Two special types of network devices that Pathrate tests for are:

- Load-balancing devices
- Traffic-shaping devices

Load-balancing devices allow multiple network lines to be trunked together to provide a single, larger bandwidth pipe.

In traffic shaping, routers can limit the bandwidth allocated to bursts of packets, while allowing normal traffic to consume a set (higher) bandwidth. This helps prevent a single-burst application from dominating the network bandwidth.

If the network link is not heavily loaded with other traffic, the results from the initial Pathrate tests may result in a consistent bandwidth calculation value (or within a small deviation). If this is the case, Pathrate will produce an estimation of the network capacity without performing any other tests.

Phase I

If the initial results vary greatly, Pathrate determines that the link was heavily loaded, and the application enters the first phase of statistical calculations.

During this phase Pathrate generates 1,000 variable-length packet pairs to test the network link.

The Phase I tests perform measurements using groups of 27 packet trains. Each group maintains a consistent packet size. The first group uses 600-byte packet sizes, and each successive group increases the packet size by 25 bytes until the maximum MTU size is reached (1,500 bytes for Ethernet connections).

The results produced by this phase are used to determine trends within the packet-pairs data, and to determine minimum and maximum values.

Phase II

In Phase II, Pathrate uses 500 large packet trains to attempt a statistical calculation to determine which of the Phase I results were closest to the true bandwidth capacity. Pathrate measures the dispersion of the large packet trains to estimate the ADR of the connection.

When its statistical analysis has determined which of the results from Phase I are the most likely candidates for the correct bandwidth, Pathrate reports this as the capacity estimation.

WARNING Since Pathrate uses statistical calculations to determine the final bandwidth estimate, it is possible that it can determine the wrong value. It is always best to perform more than one test on the network link to see what values Pathrate can generate.

How Pathload Works

The Pathload application uses similar statistical calculations to estimate the current network load between two devices on the network. Pathload sends packet streams between two points on the network (the test hosts), using increasing rates (less delay time between packets). The rate at which the packets are sent is saved as a state variable (R) in the program.

When the rate at which the packets are sent exceeds the available bandwidth on the network, a delay occurs between the packets, as shown in Figure 7.1.

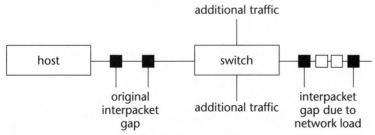

Figure 7.1 Packet delay introduced by loaded network.

The rate at which the packets are sent is represented by the interpacket (between sent packets) gap. When the network is loaded, additional packets from other traffic flows must be interspersed between the original packets, increasing the interpacket gap. Pathload detects this additional delay, and determines that the test stream was sent at a rate larger than the available bandwidth. The rate state variable (R) is then decreased, and another test is performed. This process is continued until the rate state variable maintains a value within a predetermined resolution.

NOTE Unlike other network bandwidth calculation programs, Pathload presents the available bandwidth estimation as a range of possible values. Since Pathload determines the available bandwidth using statistics, there is a range of possibilities that could include the actual available bandwidth, not a set available bandwidth value.

Using Pathrate

This section describes the Pathrate application programs, and how to download and install them on a Unix host on the network.

The Pathrate Programs

The Pathrate application consists of two programs:

- pathrate_snd waits for new test connections.
- pathrate_rcv establishes connection with the server and begins the capacity test.

The pathrate_snd program must be running either in background mode or as a standalone application on a host on the network. The hostname or IP address of the host running the pathrate_snd program must be specified on the pathrate_rcv program to identify the remote endpoint. The pathrate_rcv program establishes a TCP connection using port 48699 to the pathrate_snd server. The TCP connection is used to send control information between the two test hosts. After the control connection is established, the test data is sent from the server program to the receiver, using UDP port 48698.

NOTE Since Pathrate uses nonreserved TCP and UDP ports, you do not have to be logged in as the root user to use it.

Downloading Pathrate

The Pathrate application source code can be downloaded from the Pathrate Web site, www.pathrate.org. At the time of this writing, the current version of Pathrate is 2.2.1, and can be downloaded using the URL:

```
http://www.cc.gatech.edu/fac/Constantinos.Dovrolis/pathrate-2.2.1..tar
```

As usual, you must expand the distribution file into a working directory, using the tar command:

```
tar -xvf pathrate-2.2.1.tar
```

This command creates a working directory pathrate-2.2.1, and places the source code files in the directory.

Compiling Pathrate

Before building the executable files for Pathrate, there is one decision you need to make. By default, the pathrate_rcv program produces a fair amount of text output to the standard output file. If you are connecting remotely to the host to perform the tests, this traffic could affect the results of the bandwidth tests. You can prevent pathrate_rcv from displaying the text output by modifying the makefile file in the source code before compiling. The section of the makefile to modify looks like:

```
pathrate_rcv.o: pathrate_rcv.c pathrate.h

        $(CC) -c -DVERBOSE_RCV  $(CPPFLAGS) $(DEFS) $(CFLAGS) $<
```

The -D compile option is used to define the VERBOSE_RCV flag. You can remove this from the line in the makefile to prevent pathrate_rcv from displaying the text output during the tests.

To build the Pathrate executable files, you must use the configure and make commands:

```
$ ./configure
```

```
$ make
```

The configure command performs the usual checks of the system to determine which libraries are present to compile the programs, and the make command creates the programs. The result is the pathrate_rcv and pathrate_snd executable files.

There is no installation procedure for the make command, so you can either run the Pathrate programs from the working directory, or manually move them to a common directory, such as /usr/local/bin.

WARNING You do not need to be the root user to use the pathrate_snd and pathrate_rcv programs. If you are using Pathrate on a system that has other users on it, be careful where you place these executable programs. Any user on the system could run Pathrate, which may or may not be what you have in mind.

Starting the Pathrate Server

One test host must run the pathrate_snd program, either as a standalone application at the command prompt, or as a background process.

WARNING The pathrate_snd program cannot be set up as a process in inetd or xinetd. It must be run from the command prompt. If you want to run pathrate_snd in background mode, use the ampersand sign.

To run the pathrate_snd program as a standalone process, you simply run it from the command prompt. When it is started, Pathrate displays a message indicating that it is waiting for a connection from a remote client:

```
$ pathrate_snd

Waiting for receiver to establish control stream =>
```

At this point the pathrate_rcv program can be run from the second test host.

NOTE The pathrate_snd program will only accept one test connection at a time. You cannot run multiple simultaneous Pathrate tests.

Starting the Pathrate Client

The pathrate_rcv program is used on the client host to initiate the test with the Pathrate server. The command line uses a single parameter, the hostname or IP address of the remote Pathrate host:

```
$ pathrate_rcv 192.168.1.100
```

The pathrate_rcv program will attempt a TCP control connection to the remote pathrate_snd program at the specified address. If the VERBOSE_RCV flag was left in the makefile when you built the executable files, the pathrate_rcv program will display the information for the connection, and start the test:

```
$ pathrate_rcv 192.168.1.100
pathrate run from 192.168.1.6 to 192.168.1.100 on Wed Oct 30 19:24:15
2002


--> Minimum acceptable packet pair dispersion: 42 usec
```

When the client program connects to the server program, it determines the minimum acceptable dispersion value for the connection, and displays the results. This value is used to determine the acceptable values used in the statistical calculations for the bandwidth.

Pathrate Test Output

The Pathrate application produces lots of output from the various tests that are performed to determine the network bandwidth. This section describes the test outputs, and how to interpret the data produced.

Quick Termination Mode

When the Pathrate connection is established, the initial test phase is started, using increasing length of packet trains to estimate the bandwidth. The output should look like this:

```
-- Maximum train length discovery --
        Train length: 2 ->          9.7 Mbps
        Train length: 3 ->          9.8 Mbps
        Train length: 4 ->          9.8 Mbps
        Train length: 5 ->          9.7 Mbps
        Train length: 6 ->          9.7 Mbps
        Train length: 8 ->          9.7 Mbps
        Train length: 10 ->         9.7 Mbps
        Train length: 12 ->         9.7 Mbps
        Train length: 16 ->         9.7 Mbps
        Train length: 20 ->         9.7 Mbps
        Train length: 24 ->         9.7 Mbps
        Train length: 28 ->         9.7 Mbps
        Train length: 32 ->         9.7 Mbps
        Train length: 36 ->         9.7 Mbps
        Train length: 40 ->         9.7 Mbps
        Train length: 44 ->         9.7 Mbps
        Train length: 48 ->         9.7 Mbps
        --> Maximum train length: 48 packets
```

On a lightly loaded network, the estimated bandwidth for each packet train should be similar. If the network is more heavily loaded, the estimations will have a wider variance. Next, the output shows the preliminary measurements that were made during the packet-train tests (lines slightly modified so they fit on the page):

```
-- Preliminary measurements with increasing packet train lengths --
2  -> 9.7 Mbps    9.8 Mbps    9.7 Mbps    9.8 Mbps    9.8 Mbps    9.7 Mbps   9.7 Mbps
3  -> 9.7 Mbps    9.3 Mbps    9.7 Mbps    9.8 Mbps    9.8 Mbps    9.8 Mbps   9.7 Mbps
4  -> 9.8 Mbps    9.7 Mbps    9.7 Mbps    9.7 Mbps    9.7 Mbps    9.7 Mbps   9.7 Mbps
5  -> 9.7 Mbps    9.7 Mbps    9.7 Mbps    9.7 Mbps    9.8 Mbps    9.7 Mbps   9.8 Mbps
6  -> 9.7 Mbps    9.7 Mbps    9.6 Mbps    9.7 Mbps    9.7 Mbps    9.7 Mbps   9.7 Mbps
7  -> 9.7 Mbps    9.7 Mbps    9.7 Mbps    9.7 Mbps    9.5 Mbps    9.7 Mbps   9.7 Mbps
8  -> 9.7 Mbps    9.7 Mbps    9.7 Mbps    9.7 Mbps    9.7 Mbps    9.7 Mbps   9.7 Mbps
9  -> 9.7 Mbps    9.7 Mbps    9.7 Mbps    9.7 Mbps    9.7 Mbps    9.3 Mbps   9.7 Mbps
10 -> 9.7 Mbps 9.7 Mbps    9.7 Mbps    9.7 Mbps    9.7 Mbps    9.5 Mbps   9.7 Mbps
          --> Resolution:    5 kbps
```

The resulting resolution shows that the results from the initial phase tests were within 5 kbps of each other. This qualified for the quick termination mode, and a final bandwidth capacity estimation is displayed:

```
--> Coefficient of variation: 0.001
    Sufficiently low measurement noise - `Quick-termination'


------------------------------------------------
Final capacity estimate :   9.7 Mbps   to   9.7 Mbps
------------------------------------------------


$
```

The final estimation of the bandwidth capacity of this link was 9.7 Mbps. The actual limiting link in this path was a 10-Mbps hub connection. In this test, Pathrate correctly determined the bandwidth of the network link tested. However, during this test there was minimal load on the network. In the next test, Pathrate will have to deal with a much more heavily loaded network.

Full Testing Mode

If the network link that is being tested has traffic on it (as will be the case in most instances), and the load on the network is more than light, it is more difficult for Pathrate to determine the limiting bandwidth capacity. In these scenarios, Pathrate cannot perform a quick termination mode test, and must perform all of the tests, as outlined in the *How Pathrate Works* section.

Initial Phase Results

Pathrate determines when it must perform a full test by analyzing the results of the initial phase tests. If the deviation between the test samples is large, Pathrate automatically starts the Phase I tests:

```
-- Preliminary measurements with increasing packet train lengths --
2 -> 7.5 Mbps 8.7 Mbps  7.5 Mbps  8.2 Mbps  8.0 Mbps  8.1 Mbps  8.5 Mbps
3 -> 8.4 Mbps 8.3 Mbps  9.6 Mbps  8.4 Mbps  9.7 Mbps  8.4 Mbps  8.9 Mbps
4 -> 796 kbps 805 kbps  8.7 Mbps  837 kbps  9.6 Mbps  9.4 Mbps  8.8 Mbps
5 -> 7.2 Mbps 9.1 Mbps  6.0 Mbps  9.0 Mbps  9.2 Mbps  8.6 Mbps  6.1 Mbps
6 -> 9.6 Mbps 9.3 Mbps  9.2 Mbps  9.4 Mbps  8.8 Mbps  9.5 Mbps  6.6 Mbps
7 -> 9.4 Mbps 9.0 Mbps  9.3 Mbps  9.1 Mbps  7.8 Mbps  9.3 Mbps  6.9 Mbps
8 -> 1.9 Mbps 9.3 Mbps  7.2 Mbps  8.8 Mbps  9.3 Mbps  9.4 Mbps  9.8 Mbps
9 -> 7.4 Mbps 2.4 Mbps  9.6 Mbps  9.4 Mbps  9.4 Mbps  9.5 Mbps  2.0 Mbps
10-> 2.7 Mbps 9.4 Mbps  9.1 Mbps  9.4 Mbps  9.2 Mbps  9.4 Mbps  9.1 Mbps
          --> Resolution:  425 kbps
```

The results from the preliminary measurements show a wide range of test results from the initial tests. This wide range of results is due to the loading of the network path by additional traffic. The resolution of the test results is much larger than that produced in the quiet network environment (425 kbps versus 5 kbps from the quick termination test). With the large variance of data, Pathrate cannot make a determination of the bandwidth capacity, and must continue with the other phases of the test.

Phase I Results

Pathrate automatically starts the Phase I test, initiating the packet-train tests with the remote server, and displaying the results to the standard output. The Phase I test consists of multiple groups of 27 packet trains. Each packet within the group test is set to a specific packet size. The packet size is increased by 25 bytes for each successive group until the maximum MTU size has been reached. For an Ethernet connection, this value is 1,500 bytes.

The results from each packet-train group are displayed on the standard output, along with the Phase I results:

```
-- Local modes --
   * Mode: 9.5 Mbps to 9.8 Mbps  - 534 measurements
      Modal bell: 736 measurements - low : 7.4 Mbps - high : 10.3 Mbps
   * Mode: 6.7 Mbps to 7.1 Mbps  - 60 measurements
      Modal bell: 198 measurements - low : 5.9 Mbps - high : 8.2 Mbps
```

After the last packet-train group is processed, the statistical information is presented, showing the estimates of the bandwidth capacity based on the information presented in the Phase I test results. Automatically, the Phase II tests are started.

Phase II Results

The Phase II test attempts to estimate the ADR using 500 separate packet trains. Each packet train is 48 packets, and the packet sizes are set for each train at the maximum MTU size for the interface. At the end, the Phase II results are displayed:

```
-- Local modes --
     * Mode: 9.4 Mbps to 9.8 Mbps  - 499 measurements
        Modal bell: 499 measurements - low : 9.4 Mbps - high : 9.8 Mbps
```

After obtaining all of the data from the Phase I and Phase II tests, Pathrate is prepared to estimate the bandwidth of the network link:

```
     The capacity estimate will be based on the ADR mode.

--> Asymptotic Dispersion Rate (ADR) estimate: 9.6 Mbps

--> Possible capacity values:
        9.5 Mbps to 9.8 Mbps  - Figure of merit: 38.82

--> There are no Phase I modes larger than the ADR

--> The capacity estimate will be based on figure of merit of Phase II
measurements
        9.4 Mbps to 9.8 Mbps  - Figure of merit: 99.80


-------------------------------------------------
Final capacity estimate :  9.4 Mbps  to  9.8 Mbps
-------------------------------------------------
$
```

Due to the extra traffic found on the network link, Pathrate was not able to return as narrow an estimate for the final capacity value as the quick termination mode test, but again, the final result is accurate for the network link used.

WARNING The results of the Pathrate tests are dependent on the CPU load of the test systems. It is recommended to use Pathrate on systems that are not heavily (or at all) loaded.

After the test is over, the pathrate_snd program will reset and be ready to accept a new connection for another test.

Using Pathload

This section describes the Pathload application programs, and how to download and install them on a Unix host on the network for testing the available network bandwidth.

Pathload

Similarly, the Pathload application consists of two programs:

- pathload_snd waits for new test connections.
- pathload_rcv establishes connection with the server and begins the capacity test.

The pathload_snd program must be running to accept connection requests from remote hosts. It can be run as either a background mode daemon or a standalone application from the command prompt. The pathload_rcv program uses the remote hostname or IP address on the command line to specify the location of the Pathload server.

Downloading and Configuring Pathload

The Pathload application can also be found at the Pathrate Web site, www .pathrate.org. At the time of this writing, the current version of Pathload is 1.0.2, and can be found at the URL:

```
http://www.cc.gatech.edu/fac/Constantinos.Dovrolis/pathload_1.0.2.tar.gz
```

Since this file is a compressed tar file, you must either uncompress it using the gunzip program, or use the -z option with the tar command:

```
tar -zxvf pathload_1.0.2.tar.gz
```

This command creates the working directory pathload_1.0.2, and places the source code files into the directory. To build the Pathload executable files, you must use the configure and make commands:

```
$ ./configure
$ make
```

As usual, the configure program is used to determine the appropriate files required to build the executable programs, pathload_snd and pathload_rcv.

The Pathload application works similarly to the Pathrate application, in that you must start a server program on one test host before the client program can be started on another test host.

Starting the Pathload Server

The pathload_snd program can be started either in background mode (using the ampersand sign after the command) or as a normal application on the command prompt:

```
$ pathload_snd
```

Like the Pathrate application, Pathload displays a message indicating that it is waiting for a connection attempt from a client:

```
Waiting for receiver to establish control stream =>
```

The server program is now ready to accept connections from remote clients.

NOTE The pathload_snd program will only accept one test connection at a time. You cannot perform simultaneous tests using Pathload.

Starting the Pathload Client

The pathload_rcv program must be started on a remote host, specifying two command-line parameters:

```
pathload_rcv hostname resolution
```

The hostname parameter defines the hostname or IP address of the host that is running the Pathload server program. The *resolution* parameter defines the precision (in Mbps) with which Pathload should estimate the available bandwidth on the network link. Pathload will stop when the different bandwidth estimates fall within the defined resolution value.

Once pathload_rcv starts, it attempts to establish the TCP control connection with the Pathload server specified on the command-line parameter:

```
$ pathload_rcv 192.168.1.100 1

Receiver 192.168.1.6 starts measurements on sender 192.168.1.100 at
Wed Oct 30 19:37:51 2002
Requested bandwidth resolution :: 1.00
Minimum packet spacing :: 225 usec
Max rate 53.33mbps :  Min rate 1.17mbps
Estimate Asymptotic Dispersion Rate (ADR) --  9.59 (mbps)
```

Once the control connection is established, the Pathload fleet tests will automatically begin. The results of each fleet test, along with the final results, will be displayed on the standard output of the device from which pathload_rcv was run. The next section discusses the pathload_rcv output.

Pathload Output

The pathload_rcv output displays the values used for a particular fleet test, along with the results from the fleet test for each test performed. The fleet test information output looks like:

```
Receiving Fleet 0
 Fleet Parameter(req):: R=9.57Mbps, L=713B, K=100packets, T=620usec
 Lossrate per stream :: :0.0:0.0:0.0:0.0:0.0:0.0:0.0:0.0:0.0:0.0:0.0:0.0
 Fleet Parameter(act):: R=9.57Mbps, L=713B, K=100packets, T=627usec
 CS @ sender         :: [0][0][0][4][2][0][2][2][1][0][0][1]
 Discard[ 0]         :: [0][0][0][0][0][0][0][0][0][0][0][0]
 Trend per stream[12]:: UNNNNUNNNNNN
 Aggregate trend     :: NO TREND
 Rmin                :: 9.57Mbps
```

Each set of fleet test results is displayed separately. The fleet number is displayed in the first line of the output. The fleet test results are displayed within eight separate lines of information:

- The fleet parameters requested by the client program
- The loss rate per test stream in the fleet
- The fleet parameters used by the server program
- The number of context switches detected by the receiver
- The number of packets discarded per stream
- The relative one-way packet delay trend
- The aggregate trend of the fleet
- The state variable updated by the fleet results

At the end of the fleet tests, a final group of results is displayed, showing the estimated available bandwidth of the network link.

Requested Fleet Parameters

The first line of the fleet output displays the fleet parameters that are set for the tests:

```
Fleet Parameter(req):: R=9.57Mbps, L=713B, K=100packets, T=620usec
```

The fleet parameters are:

- The rate of the packets sent during the fleet (R)
- The size of the data packets used in the fleet test (L)
- The number of packets per stream (K)
- The interpacket spacing used for the test (T)

These values are statistically determined at the beginning of the first fleet test, and altered as necessary during successive fleet tests.

Loss Rate per Stream

The second line of the fleet output displays the packet loss during the test:

```
Lossrate per stream :: :0.0:0.0:0.0:0.0:0.0:0.0:0.0:0.0:0.0:0.0:0.0:0.0
```

Since the fleet tests use UDP packets, it is possible that some will not make it from the server to the client hosts on the network. This information shows the loss results from each of the 12 packet streams used within the fleet test. The results are presented as a percentage of lost packets. For heavily loaded networks, this value can become quite large:

```
Lossrate per stream :: :0.0:0.0:0.0:4.0:33.0:0.0:0.0:0.0:0.0:0.0:0.0:7.0
```

This test had one stream that had a fairly large amount of packet loss (33 percent). If only a few streams have packet loss, Pathload will continue with the tests. However, if more than half of the streams have lost packets, Pathload will abort the fleet test and move on to a new fleet test:

```
Lossrate per stream ::
                :18.0:0.0:41.0:19.0:0.0:0.0:3.0:0.0:44.0:0.0:0.0:13.0
Atleast 50% stream were marked as lossy.
```

Server Fleet Parameters

The parameters specified in the request parameters are not necessarily the same parameters that the server will accept for the fleet test. The actual parameters accepted by the Pathload server are presented in the third output line:

```
Fleet Parameter(act):: R=9.57Mbps, L=713B, K=100packets, T=627usec
```

By comparing the accepted parameters with the requested parameters, you can see that the server did not accept the interpacket spacing value requested by the client, but instead used its own value.

Context Switches

The fourth output line in the fleet test identifies the number of context switches that occurred on the server for each test stream (as identified by the client):

```
CS @ sender          ::  [0][0][0][4][2][0][2][2][1][0][0][1]
```

Each bracketed number represents the number of context switches in the fleet test stream. Excessive context switches indicate additional server load, and may affect the results of the Pathload bandwidth estimations.

Packet Discards

The number of packets discarded in the stream due to errors is reported in the fifth output line:

```
Discard[ 0]          ::  [0][0][0][0][0][0][0][0][0][0][0][0]
```

Each bracketed number represents the number of packets discarded within the fleet stream. As with the packet loss item, if a sufficient number of packets are discarded in a test, Pathload will abort the fleet test and start a new one.

Relative One-Way Packet Delay Trend

The relative one-way packet delay trend is shown on the sixth line of the fleet output. It identifies the delay trend for each individual stream in the fleet test:

```
Trend per stream[12]:: UNNNNUNNNNNN
```

Each character represents the trend for an individual stream. The characters used are:

- I (increasing trend)
- N (no trend)
- U (unusable)

The number of streams within the fleet is shown in the brackets (some individual streams may have been aborted within the fleet test due to packet loss or discards).

An increasing delay trend rate indicates that the server is sending data to the client at a higher rate than the network bandwidth can accommodate. The results of the streams within the fleet test are then aggregated for the next output line.

Fleet Aggregate Trend

The seventh output line indicates the overall aggregate delay trend for the fleet test:

```
Aggregate trend     :: NO TREND
```

The possible values for this item are:

- **INCREASING.** The overall fleet test shows an increasing trend of delay times.
- **NOTREND.** The overall fleet test does not show an increasing trend of delay times.
- **GREY.** The individual stream tests were inconclusive.

The three different aggregate trend values are based on the number of individual stream test results within the fleet test:

```
Trend per stream[10]:: IIIUIIIIUI

Aggregate trend     :: INCREASING
```

As seen in this example, if more than half of the stream tests indicate an increasing trend, the fleet test aggregate trend is set to INCREASING, and the R value used in the next fleet test is decreased. Also:

```
Trend per stream[12]:: UNNNNNNNNNNN

Aggregate trend     :: NO TREND
```

If more than half of the stream tests indicate no trend, the fleet test aggregate trend is set to NOTREND, and the R value used in the next fleet test is increased.

```
Trend per stream[12]:: IINIUINIINII

Aggregate trend     :: GREY
```

The GREY aggregate trend indicates that a mix of increasing delay trends and no trends and/or unusable trends appears in the stream tests. Due to the wide mix of results, Pathload cannot determine a clear aggregate value for the fleet test. This can happen with tests performed during bursty network activity, when some streams are affected by high network traffic load, and others aren't.

State Variable Updated

The result of the fleet test is some type of update to one of the variables tracked by Pathload in the statistical analysis of the network bandwidth:

```
Rmin                    :: 9.57Mbps
```

This output shows that the minimum R value should be set to 9.57 Mbps for the next fleet test. This usually indicates that the R value used in the next fleet test will be set to 9.57 Mbps. Table 7.1 shows the values that can be altered by the fleet test.

Don't be confused by the Rmin and Rmax values. The Rmin value represents the maximum bandwidth that produced a NOTREND result, which should be the minimum R value that could be the actual network bandwidth. Pathload calculates the grey region values depending on the network conditions at the time of the test, and modifies them as appropriate, depending on the data results.

Final Test Results

Pathload continues to perform fleet tests until one of two conditions is met:

- Two successive fleet tests produce a bandwidth rate that is within the specified resolution value.

- The bandwidth rate falls within the grey region.

The final output consists of four output lines:

```
Exiting due to user specified resolution
Measurements finished at Wed Oct 30 19:01:13 2002
Measurement latency is 39.46 sec
Available bandwidth range : 9.57-10.76 (Mbps)
$
```

Table 7.1 Pathload State Variables

VARIABLE	DESCRIPTION
Rmin	The maximum rate that produced a NOTREND result
Rmax	The minimum rate that produced an INCREASING trend
Gmax	The maximum rate that produced a GREY result
Gmin	The minimum rate that produced a GREY result

The latency of the network connection is displayed, along with the estimated bandwidth values calculated by Pathload. The first line produces a text message that indicates the reason why the Pathload tests terminated. These values are shown in Table 7.2.

WARNING At the time of this writing, Pathload version 1.0.2 could only determine network bandwidths within the range of 1.5 Mbps to 120 Mbps.

The results from the Pathload test should reflect the approximate network bandwidth available given the current loading conditions of the network.

Summary

This chapter describes the Pathrate and Pathload applications. The Pathrate application can be used to determine the maximum bandwidth capacity between two points on the network. This information is often hard to obtain when you are working with WAN connections, especially on networks that you do not control. The Pathload application allows you to determine the available bandwidth on the network, given the current network traffic load.

Table 7.2   Pathload Termination Messages

MESSAGE	REASON FOR TERMINATION
Exiting due to user specified resolution	The rate of two successive fleet tests was within the resolution value specified by the command prompt parameter.
Exiting due to grey region	The rate estimated by Pathload is within the grey region, indicating that further tests would not produce more precise results.
Exiting with a wider range due to a time interval error	At least one fleet test was unable to use the interpacket spacing requested by the client.
Exiting with a wider range due to a MAX_RATE constraint	The bandwidth rate reached the maximum rate that Pathload can generate.
Exiting with a wider range due to a MIN_RATE constraint	The bandwidth rate reached the minimum rate that Pathload can generate.

Pathrate and Pathload both use packet pairs and packet trains to determine the network speed information. By sending pairs of packets at a known rate, Pathrate can observe the rate at which the packets are received by the remote client, and calculate the network bandwidth. These calculations are performed using statistical methods, determining the range of available network speeds.

By using Pathrate you can determine the maximum network bandwidth that can be attained by a network application. This feature helps you locate network bottlenecks by identifying slower links in the network. Pathload allows you to determine the available bandwidth in links, helping you find overutilized links in the network.

The next chapter discusses the Nettest application, which allows you to perform network bandwidth tests remotely, using a secure network connection.

Nettest

The next network performance tool discussed is the Nettest application. Nettest allows you to perform network tests using a secure connection between the testing hosts, preventing unauthorized users from initiating bandwidth-consuming network tests.

The Nettest application was developed at the Lawrence Berkeley Labs as a secure shell for performing network tests between hosts. Nettest uses the OpenSSL package to provide a secure TCP communication channel between test hosts, while allowing host authentication using digital certificates.

What Is Nettest?

The Nettest application consists of four main parts:

- The main lblnettest application
- Secure certificates and private keys to authenticate and encrypt test connections
- The ACLFile authentication file
- A group of test applications to perform network performance tests

This section describes these parts, and explains how they interact to provide the Nettest application environment.

The lblnettest Application

The main application program for Nettest is the lblnettest program. This program is used as both the client and server program for the test connection. As with other network performance tools, when used in server mode the lblnettest program can be run either in standalone mode or as a background daemon.

NOTE The executable program is called **lblnettest** to distinguish it from the nettest application produced by Cray Research, used to test network performance for Cray systems.

The Nettest application uses three types of hosts for network tests. The master host is used to initiate tests between the test hosts. The master host can be one of the hosts participating in the network test, or it may be a host separate from the test hosts. This is demonstrated in Figure 8.1.

The sender and receiver hosts are the two hosts that participate in the network test. The sender host, obviously, is used to send network traffic to the receiver host. Within a single Nettest test, you can instruct the hosts to switch roles to test network performance in both directions on the connection.

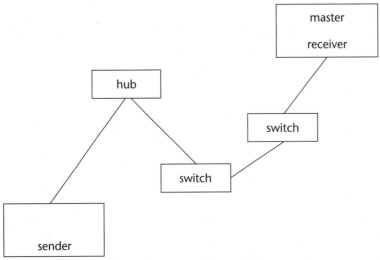

Figure 8.1   A sample Nettest test environment.

Certificates and Keys

Nettest uses OpenSSL to initiate a secure SSL communication channel for the tests. OpenSSL requires a *private key* to encrypt data sent on the network. The private key must be kept secret to ensure the security of the communication.

A *digital certificate* is used to identify and authenticate the host that is requesting the Nettest test. The digital certificate file contains information about the identity of the host, and a digital signature from a certificate authority (CA) verifying the identity. The CA is an organization that customers can trust to ensure that the identity contained in the certificate is valid. For the purposes of Nettest, you can create your own certificate authority, and sign your own digital certificates.

The ACLFile File

Besides using secure communication for the performance tests, Nettest also provides a mechanism for authenticating hosts involved with the test. Only hosts specified in the ACLFile file will be allowed to participate in network performance tests.

The ACLFile file contains the DN of the host (as specified in the certificate file) and the permissions the host has within the Nettest environment. A sample entry from the ACLFile file looks like:

```
name /C=Your_Country/ST=State/L=City/O=Org/OU=Department/CN=CA
rights read, write, execute
```

Each entry in the ACLFile file contains two lines. The first line defines the DN as specified in the certificate used to authenticate the host. The second line defines the rights that the host will have within the Nettest environment. Each host must have at least two entries in the ACLFile file:

- An entry for the CA used to authenticate the host
- An entry for the host DN

Nettest must know the CA used to authenticate the certificate received by the test host. The CA.pem file must also be present with the ACLFile file to identify the CA certificate.

Test Applications

Once the remote host is authenticated, you can perform several different types of tests within the connection. By default, Nettest uses the Iperf performance tool (see Chapter 6, "Iperf") to perform several different types of network performance testing. As described in Chapter 6, the Iperf tool can provide a method for network administrators to test different features of the network, performing a wide array of tests from a single Nettest connection.

Besides the default Iperf tests, Nettest can also incorporate several other tests within its test suite:

- UDP connectivity and response time
- Multicast connectivity and response time
- TCP parameter tuning
- pipechar
- Traceroute

The UDP and multicast tests are included to allow a host to send packets to a receiving host, and determine the round-trip response time for the packets.

NOTE If you are testing multicast packets on a network, remember that any routers between the two test hosts must be configured to forward multicast packets.

The traceroute application is a separate application that shows the router hops between two points on the network. It must be installed as an application on the system before installing Nettest. Many Unix systems include the Traceroute application as part of the standard network functions.

The pipechar network performance tool is also a separate test application that is provided by The Lawrence Berkeley Labs. It can be downloaded from the Web site www-didc.lbl.gov/pipechar/, and installed separately from Nettest.

The OpenSSL Package

The OpenSSL package has become the most popular method used by open source programs to supply SSL functionality. OpenSSL provides an open source set of libraries and utilities that enable a network application to incorporate SSL versions 1.0, 2.0, and 3.0 as well as TLS.

You can download the OpenSSL package from the OpenSSL Project Web site (http://www.openssl.org). At the time of this writing there are two versions of the package that are available for downloading. The main package (openssl-0.9.6g) is used to add SSL capabilities to network applications by supplying a set of C APIs and header files.

Alternately, you can download (openssl-0.9.6g-engine) a package that contains only the OpenSSL engine that can be interfaced to external crypto hardware. The OpenSSL Project expects these two versions to merge when version 0.9.7 is released.

You can also download the latest version of OpenSSL from the OpenSSL FTP server:

```
ftp://ftp.openssl.org/source/
```

At the time of this writing, the latest production version available is openssl-0.9.6g.tar.gz. Once the source code distribution is downloaded, it can be unpacked into a working directory using the tar command:

```
tar -zxvf openssl-0.9.6g.tar.gz
```

This command creates the directory openssl-0.9.6g and places the source code there. You must change to the working directory to complete the rest of the installation.

As with other open source packages, the first step is to run the config program. The config program determines the operating environment of your Unix system and prepares the necessary makefiles for the make program.

By placing parameters on the config command line, you can configure special features and modify default values of the OpenSSL program. Table 8.1 lists the options that can be used with the config program.

Once you determine which (if any) options are required for your environment, you can run the config program:

```
./config
```

Table 8.1 OpenSSL Config Options

OPTION	DESCRIPTION
--prefix=DIR	This option defines the directory of the OpenSSL libraries, binary files, and certificates (default = /usr/local/ssl).
--openssldir=DIR	Defines the directory for the OpenSSL certificates. If no prefix is defined, library and binary files are also placed here (default = /usr/local/ssl).
no-threads	Don't include support for multithreaded applications.
threads	Include support for multithreaded applications.
no-shared	Don't create shared libraries.
shared	Create shared libraries.
no-asm	Don't use assembler code.
386	Use the 386 instruction set code only (default = 486 code).
no-cipher	Do not include support for specified encryption type.

The config program attempts to automatically determine the type of Unix system you are compiling OpenSSL on, and creates the OpenSSL makefiles accordingly. If for some reason the config program has difficulty determining your Unix system type, you can manually define it, using the Configure program.

The Configure program performs the same function as the config program, but it also allows you to manually define your Unix system from a long list of possibilities. You can run the Configure program with no parameters to see the system types defined.

After running the config (or Configure) program, you can use the make program to create the binary files and libraries, the make test program to test the created files, and the make install program to install the OpenSSL files in the location specified in the config program.

WARNING You must have root privileges to run the make install command to install OpenSSL in the appropriate directories.

Downloading and Installing Nettest

The Nettest application home page is located at http://www-itg.lbl.gov/nettest/. The Nettest Web site contains information about Nettest, along with links to other network projects at Lawrence Berkeley Labs. This section describes how to download, compile, and install the Nettest application on a Unix system.

Downloading Nettest

The Nettest source code distribution can be found in the Downloads link on the Nettest home page. At the time of this writing, the current version of Nettest is 0.2b1, and can be downloaded from the URL:

```
http://www-itg.lbl.gov/nettest/download/files/nettest-src-V0.2b1.tar.gz
```

As usual, the distribution file must be uncompressed and untarred into a working directory before you can begin compiling. This can be done using the gunzip and tar programs, or on some systems, just the tar command with the -z option:

```
tar -zxvf nettest-src-V0.2b1.tar.gz
```

This creates a working directory of nettest, and places the source code in subdirectories under the nettest directory.

Before Compiling

The Nettest application relies heavily on the Domain Name System (DNS) when specifying hostnames used as test hosts. It expects all test hosts to be registered within DNS for the tests to work properly. When performing tests on networks that do not use DNS (or when using test machines that are not registered within the company DNS database), you first must do some tricks to fool Nettest. This section describes the tasks that I had to perform to get Nettest to work on my non-Internet network.

Define All Test Hosts

Since Nettest expects to use DNS hostnames for all test hosts, things can get sticky for standalone networks (as was the case in my test network). Even when you specify all IP addresses as test hosts, Nettest attempts to resolve the IP addresses to hostnames, and complains if it can't. If your test systems are not registered in the DNS system, you must ensure that each test system knows all of the other test systems by both name and address.

The way to do this is the /etc/hosts file. This file allows you to specify a list of IP addresses and hostnames that are frequently used by the system. Each line on the /etc/hosts file represents a single host entry. The format of the entry is:

```
IPaddress       hostname [alias]
```

The IPaddress field represents the numeric IP address (also called the quad dotted address). The hostname must be separated from the IP address by at least one tab. Following the hostname, one or more host aliases can be listed.

There should already be two entries in the /etc/hosts file for your own system. You must add entries for all of the test hosts used for Nettest. A sample /etc/hosts file looks like:

```
127.0.0.1       localhost.localdomain localhost
192.168.1.2     shadrach.ispnet1.net shadrach
192.168.1.100   meshach.ispnet1.net meshach
192.168.1.6     abednago.ispnet1.net abednago
```

The first line defines the special localhost address, which is often used for TCP/IP communications within the same host. The second line identifies the actual hostname and IP address of the local host. Subsequent lines are used to define other hosts on the local network.

After the test hosts have been defined for each host used in the Nettest tests, you must also ensure that the /etc/hosts file will be used by the Unix system. For Linux systems, this is determined by the /etc/host.conf file. This file defines how the system will perform hostname lookups.

There are several lines that may be present in the /etc/host.conf file. To ensure that the system will use the /etc/hosts file, the pertinent /etc/host.conf line is:

```
order hosts,bind
```

The order line defines how hostname lookups will be performed, and in what order the methods will be tried. The hosts entry instructs the system to perform hostname lookups from the /etc/hosts file first, then use the DNS system (bind) if the hostname is not found in the /etc/hosts file.

Modify the Source Code

Unfortunately, the Nettest source code uses the Unix gethostbyaddr() function to find the host's hostname based on its IP address. On my Linux system, even though I had the information in the /etc/hosts table, this function produced an error, and the Nettest application failed.

NOTE This section pertains to a change I made in the source code for Nettest to work properly in my Linux environment (kernel 2.4.3). If you are using Nettest on a Sun server, you may or may not experience similar problems. The Nettest source code modified in this section uses different function calls for Sun systems.

To solve this problem, you must modify one source code file in the Nettest distribution package. The file is network.cc, located under the src directory of the working directory:

```
nettest/src/common/network.cc
```

First, it's a good idea to copy the original file to a backup file:

```
$ cp network.cc network.cc.org
```

Next, you can use the Unix editor of your choice, and modify the network.cc file. The gethostbyaddr() function is used on line 143 of the source code; you can find it by searching for the function, or going directly to the source code line—whichever is easier in your editor.

After finding the line, comment it out by placing two forward slashes on the start of the line. Since the line is broken into two lines, you will have to comment out the second line as well. When you are done, it should look like this:

```
//    local_host_p = gethostbyaddr( (const char*)&local_name.sin_addr,
//                              sizeof(local_name.sin_addr), AF_INET);
```

In place of this function call, I used the Unix gethostbyname() function, and specified the full test hostname of the host system:

```
local_host_p = gethostbyname("shadrach.ispnet1.net");
```

This new function call specifically states the hostname of the local host without using any type of hostname lookup system.

After saving the changes, you can proceed with the normal installation instructions.

Compiling and Installing Nettest

After downloading and modifying the necessary Nettest files, you can begin compiling the source code to produce the executable program. Unlike the other software installation packages covered so far in this book, Nettest does not provide a standard configure script to run. Instead, it uses the autoconf program to produce the configure script.

Change to the src subdirectory of the distribution working directory, and run the autoconf program:

```
[rich@shadrach src]$ autoconf
```

On my Linux system, when I ran the autoconf program, I saw several warning messages on the screen:

```
configure.in:526: warning: AC_TRY_RUN called without default to allow

cross compiling
```

This did not appear to affect the outcome of the Nettest compile. When the autoconf program is finished, it produces the configure script that you can run to prepare for compiling. Before running the configure program, you should change to the build directory for your platform:

```
$ cd ../build/linux

$ ../../src/configure
```

When in the build directory, you must reference the configure script located in the src directory, using the standard Unix notation. The configure script checks the settings for the system you are trying to build Nettest on, and also asks you a few questions about the Nettest environment you want to create. The first two questions relate to the location of the Nettest binary, and the location of the OpenSSL installation on the system:

```
Where is the install location? [/usr/local/bin]

Where is the top of your SSL installation? [/usr/local/ssl]

openssl libs are at: /usr/local/ssl/lib
openssl headers are at: /usr/local/ssl/include/openssl
```

You can press the Enter key to accept the default values shown in the brackets, or enter new information and press Enter. The next question may be somewhat confusing:

```
Configure Nettest to support Sender-Only tests? [no]
```

It is asking if you want to include any of the other tests besides the standard Iperf network tests in the Nettest installation. If you answer Yes, it asks you which other tests to include, along with the directory where they can be found:

```
Select Optional SO Method Tests:
   If you select a test you'll need to provide nettest with the location
of the binary.
   These tests are run as separate processes.

Use traceroute? [no]
Yes
Path to traceroute binary? [/usr/local/bin/traceroute]
/usr/sbin/traceroute
Use pipechar? [no]
Is this the configuration you want? [yes]
```

At the end of the questions, the configure program allows you to redo any answers, and then proceeds with the rest of the configure process.

When this is completed, you can create the executable file by running the make program with the all option:

```
$ make all
```

After this finishes, you can install the lblnettest executable file into the installation directory specified in the configure process by changing to the root user and running the make program with the install option.

Creating Certificates and Keys

After installing Nettest, you must prepare for your Nettest environment. To do this you must either create your own certificates and keys to use, or obtain them from a commercial CA company. The OpenSSL application provides a way for you to create your own certificates and keys that can be used in Nettest. This section describes how to use OpenSSL to create the proper certificates and keys to use for the Nettest hosts on your network.

Creating a Certificate Authority

First, you must establish a CA certificate and key that will be used to validate your actual certificates and keys used for Nettest. This is done using the req option in OpenSSL:

```
$ openssl req -out CA.pem -new -x509 -days 3650
```

This command instructs OpenSSL to create a new X.509 certificate, called CA.pem, and allows it to be valid for 10 years (the default is 30 days). By default, OpenSSL will also create the private key in the file privkey.pem.

When the process starts, OpenSSL will ask you for a pass phrase to be associated with the certificate. By entering in a secret phrase, you can prevent others from using the certificate without authorization.

WARNING It is extremely important to remember the pass phrase you use when creating keys and certificates. If you forget them, you will not be able to use the keys or certificates, and will have to create new ones.

While it creates the certificate and key, OpenSSL asks several questions that will be used to identity the CA. You don't necessarily have to provide useful information for the questions, but it helps to provide information pertinent to your environment:

```
Country Name (2 letter code) [AU]:US
State or Province Name (full name) [Some-State]:Indiana
Locality Name (eg, city) []:Indianapolis
Organization Name (eg, company) [Internet Widgits Pty Ltd]:NetworkTest
Organizational Unit Name (eg, section) []:Chapter8
Common Name (eg, YOUR name) []:CA
Email Address []:
```

This information identifies the CA entity used to sign all of the certificates and keys used in the Nettest tests. This information must also be entered into the ACLFile file in Nettest (as explained later in the *Creating the ACLFile File* section).

You can use the OpenSSL verify option to test the certificate:

```
$ openssl verify -CAfile CA.pem CA.pem
CA.pem: OK$
```

The Openssl verify option tests the CA.pem file against the CA.pem CA (which should obviously work). This test will be more useful for the other certificates you generate in the next steps.

Creating the Client Certificate and Key

After creating the CA certificate and private key, you can create the certificate and key used on the client Nettest host. Again, this is done using OpenSSL.

The first step is to create the key used on the client host:

```
$ openssl genrsa -des3 -out client.key 1024
```

This command generates a new 1,024-bit private key for the client host. Again, you must enter a pass phrase when creating the key. It is extremely important to remember the pass phrase used to create the client key, as you will need to use it within Nettest to access the key.

Once the client key is created, you can use it to create the client certificate:

```
$ openssl req -key client.key -new -out client.req
```

To create the certificate, you must first enter the pass phrase that was used to create the client key. Next, OpenSSL asks the standard questions again to identify the organization that the certificate represents. Again, you do not need to answer these questions accurately, but it helps when identifying the client host. This information will also have to be configured into the ACLFile file for Nettest.

After creating the client certificate, you must sign it using the CA certificate and key. Before you can do this, you must create a serial file that keeps track of the number of certificates signed by the CA. This can be done using the command:

```
$ echo 00 > cert.srl
```

The client certificate can now be signed by the CA:

```
$ openssl x509 -req -in client.req -CA CA.pem -CAkey privkey.pem -
CAserial cert.srl -out client.pem
Signature ok
subject=/C=US/ST=Indiana/L=Indianapolis/O=NetworkTest/OU=Chapter8/
CN=client
Getting CA Private Key
Enter PEM pass phrase:
$
```

OpenSSL will display the certificate subject, which should be the information you entered when creating the client certificate. Next, you must enter the pass phrase for the CA certificate. The output file is the completed client certificate, signed by the CA.

The client.key, client.pem, and CA.pem files must be transferred to the client Nettest host. By default, Nettest uses the certificate file nettest.pem, and the key file key.pem. To make life easier, you can rename the files to these default values:

```
$ cp client.pem nettest.pem
$ cp client.key key.pem
```

The files must be placed in the directory from which you plan to run Nettest.

WARNING Don't forget to copy the CA.pem file to the directory where you will be running Nettest. Nettest will not work if you don't.

Creating the Server Certificate and Key

Next, you can create the server Nettest certificate and private key files, using the same technique as for the client files:

```
openssl genrsa -out server.key 1024
openssl req -key server.key -new -out server.req
openssl x509 -req -in server.req -CA CA.pem -CAkey privkey.pem -CAserial
cert.srl -out server.pem
```

As with the client certificate, you must enter a pass phrase when creating the server key, and you must enter your organization information to identify the server entity. This information will be shown when you create the signed server.pem file:

```
subject=/C=US/ST=Indiana/L=Indianapolis/O=NetworkTest/OU=Chapter8/
CN=server
```

After creating the server certificate (server.pem) and key (server.key), you can copy them to the appropriate directory on the Nettest server host, and rename them to nettest.pem and key.pem if you wish. Don't forget to put a copy of the CA.pem file in the directory as well. You are now ready to modify the ACLFile file for the Nettest installation.

Creating the ACLFile File

The ACLFile file defines which hosts are allowed access to Nettest, and what type of access they are allowed. The ACLFile file must be created in the directory where you are running the lblnettest application.

The first entry defines the CA certificate that was used to certify the client and server certificates:

```
name /C=US/ST=Indiana/L=Indianapolis/O=NetworkTest/OU=Chapter8/CN=CA
rights read, write, execute
```

The first line defines the DN of the CA, as defined when you created (or received) the CA certificate. You can see this value by using the -text option in OpenSSL:

```
$ openssl x509 -text -in CA.pem
Certificate:
    Data:
        Version: 3 (0x2)
        Serial Number: 0 (0x0)
        Signature Algorithm: md5WithRSAEncryption
        Issuer: C=US, ST=Indiana, L=Indianapolis, O=NetworkTest,
                OU=Chapter8, CN=CA           Validity
            Not Before: Nov  7 18:04:36 2002 GMT
            Not After : Nov  4 18:04:36 2012 GMT
        Subject: C=US, ST=Indiana, L=Indianapolis, O=NetworkTest,
OU=Chapter8, CN=CA
```

The Subject: line defines the DN of the certificate. This must match the entry in the ACLFile file (using slashes instead of commas in the DN).

The rights that are assigned to the host are listed after the DN. To grant all rights to a test host, you must specify the read, write, and execute attributes.

After the CA is defined, the DN for the remote host is defined. On the server host, you must define the client certificate, and vice versa. Again, you can use the OpenSSL -text option to view the actual DN in the certificate, to use the proper definition in the ACLFile file.

Using Nettest

Now that Nettest is installed and configured, you are ready to test it out. The lblnettest program is used on both the client and server hosts. The lblnettest operation is controlled by command-line parameters. Table 8.2 defines the parameters that are available.

Table 8.2   lblnettest Command-Line Parameters

PARAMETER	DESCRIPTION
-h *hostname*	Define the master host for the test.
-c *cert*	Define the client certificate file to use if not using the default nettest.pem file.

Table 8.2   *(continued)*

PARAMETER	DESCRIPTION
-k *key*	Define the client key file to use if not using the default key.pem file.
-a *phrase*	Define the client pass phrase required for the connection.
-b *phrase*	Define the local nettest.pem and key.pem pass phrase.
-s	Place Nettest in server mode, waiting for new connection attempts.
-d	Run Nettest as a daemon process.
-D *debug*	Define a debug level for more verbose output.

The following sections describe how to use the Nettest application in a testing environment.

Starting a Nettest Session

Any remote host participating in the Nettest test must have the lblnettest program running in server mode, either as a standalone application or as a daemon. To start Nettest in standalone mode, you can use the following command:

```
$ ./lblnettest -s
Nettest Nov  6 2002 00:20:06
For Client cert/key pair ( entered on Command Line ):
        Enter a Passphrase to decrypt private key:
For nettest.pem, key.pem :
        Enter a Passphrase to decrypt private key:

### Waiting for a connection
```

When the lblnettest program starts in server mode, it first asks for the pass phrases used for both the clients and the local nettest.pem file (this is the pass phrase you used when creating the key files). After you enter the proper pass phrases, lblnettest begins listening for remote connections.

One host in the test must define the master host, which is used to control the tests. The master can be any host that is placed in server mode. If you are using only two hosts for the tests, then the master will be the server host. To initiate the tests, on the client host enter the command:

```
$ ./lblnettest -h 192.168.1.100
Nettest Nov  6 2002 00:22:26
For Client cert/key pair ( entered on Command Line ):
        Enter a Passphrase to decrypt private key:
For nettest.pem, key.pem :
```

```
        Enter a Passphrase to decrypt private key:

Select an option
        u = udp connectivity and round trip time
        m = multicast connectivity and round trip time
        i = tcp throughput (iperf test)
        w = traceroute
        p = pipechar
        t = tuned tcp (determine optimal tcp parameters)
        c = change Test Master
        o = change Requester's result reporting (printing to stdout)
        D = change Debug Level
        q = quit
```

The -h command-line option is used to define the hostname or IP address of
the remote Nettest server that will be used as the master. As with server mode,
lblnettest first asks for the correct pass phrases for the client and local keys.
After you enter the pass phrases, a menu is displayed showing the options that
can be used in the program.

Performing Tests

You can select the desired test from the client menu presented by Nettest
(some items may not be available if the application has not been installed, such
as pipechar).

After you select a menu option to start a test, a series of questions is presented, allowing you to define the hosts and parameters used for the test. After
the questions are answered, the test begins, and the test results are displayed
at both test hosts. A sample UDP RTT test looks like:

```
U

  ---------------------------------------------------------------
    Enter test Receiver and Sender Names
    or Return[] for Default


  ---------------------------------------------------------------

Who is the Sender? []  192.168.1.6

Who is the Receiver? []  192.168.1.100

        Sender  : abednago.ispnet1.net
        Receiver: meshach.ispnet1.net
Number of RTT tests? [10]
Port number? [3642]
```

Nettest provides some default values that you can use for the tests. To accept the defaults, just press Enter. To use different values, enter the value at the prompt.

NOTE Notice that, even though the test hosts were defined by address, Nettest converted the address to hostnames. This is why it is important to include the hostnames in the /etc/hosts file (or have them defined in DNS).

When you have finished answering the questions, Nettest displays the test connection string it will send to the master host, and asks if you want to continue with the test:

```
*****************************************
    *** Sender-Recv TEST  REQUEST ***

Debug / Test /  master  /  sender  /   receiver   /   parameters

0/udpping/abednago.ispnet1.net/abednago.ispnet1.net/meshach.ispnet1.net/
-n 10 -p 3642


*****************************************

        Continue? [y]-yes []-no : y
```

The test connection string defines the values used in the test to the master host, allowing it to perform the test automatically. If you need to change any of the values, you can select the -no option and redefine the values. If you select -yes, to continue with the test, Nettest displays the test environment values.

After the test environment values have been displayed, Nettest starts the test. Unfortunately, the test selection menu appears before the test results are displayed. When the test is complete, the results are shown in the defined output (the standard output by default) on both test hosts:

```
Unicast RTT (msec) to abednago.ispnet1.net
        Test       : -n 10 -p 3642
        Average RTT: 0.560125
        Maximum RTT: 0.648
        Minimum RTT: 0.528
        Last   RTT: 0.551
```

You can then select another test to perform, or quit the application by selecting the q option. If you select the i option to perform Iperf tests, you must select the Iperf command-line parameters used for the test from the supplied menu.

NOTE   At the time of this writing, Nettest version 0.2b1 included Iperf version 1.2, which is older than the current Iperf version shown in Chapter 6. The available Iperf tests are slightly different in this version than in the current version, so be careful when selecting the Iperf test option in Nettest.

Summary

The Nettest application allows you to perform network tests in a secure environment. This is done using the OpenSSL SSL package, which encrypts network sessions.

The Nettest application not only uses encrypted sessions, but also requires hosts participating in the network tests to authenticate themselves before granting them access to the test. This prevents unauthorized participants from initiating bandwidth-intensive tests. Each host participating in the network test must be assigned a certificate, and the master host must identify the certificate and grant the host rights.

Once the network hosts have been authenticated, you can perform several different types of network tests using Nettest, including tests contained in the Iperf network performance tool. This allows you to perform many different tests from a single network connection, without having to reconnect to remote test hosts for each test.

The next chapter describes another product of Lawrence Berkeley Labs, the Netlogger application. Netlogger allows you to perform detailed end-to-end analysis of distributed network applications, providing a graphical tool that can assist in determining network and application performance.

NetLogger

So far, all of the network performance tools discussed in this book have directly measured network bandwidth. The NetLogger application differs from the others in the way it is used to indicate performance. Instead of measuring network activity, NetLogger does what its name says, it logs network (and other) actions into a log file. You can analyze the log file after the testing to look for problems and trends. This chapter describes the NetLogger application, explains how to install it, and demonstrates how to use it to watch network application behavior on your network.

The NetLogger application is another product of the Lawrence Berkeley Labs, and was developed to help provide a method to monitor distributed network applications. When distributed network applications suffer performance problems, it is often difficult to determine the cause of the slowness. The problem could be network loading, host loading, poor disk access times, or a host of other problems. The NetLogger application allows you to place monitoring points within network applications to timestamp and log activities within the program. After the program has finished, you can use a graphical analysis tool provided with NetLogger to analyze the trends in the log data.

What Is NetLogger?

The NetLogger application contains a whole suite of programs, scripts, and APIs that are used to assist you in monitoring distributed network applications. This section describes the various pieces and parts of the NetLogger application.

NetLogger APIs

The core of NetLogger is not a program, but a set of programming libraries. The NetLogger application provides several libraries of NetLogger methods for interfacing within application programs. The NetLogger distribution includes APIs that can be used in the following languages:

- C
- C++
- Fortran
- Java
- Perl
- Python

Each API contains methods for creating and opening a NetLogger session, and for writing event entries into the NetLogger session.

> **NOTE** At the time of this writing (NetLogger version 2.0.12), all of the NetLogger APIs rely on the core C language API. This means that, although there are APIs for generic languages such as Java, the NetLogger APIs will only work on a Unix platform. It is anticipated that future versions of NetLogger will work on other computer platforms.

NetLogger Host and Network Monitoring Tools

While it is extremely useful to have the NetLogger APIs to help monitor network applications, not everyone has the luxury of being able to plug monitoring methods into source code. The NetLogger application also contains some canned scripts that allow you to monitor standard host and network features without having to modify applications.

One of the canned applications is nl_tcpdump. This program modifies the original tcpdump program (see Chapter 2, "Watching Network Traffic") to output network traffic events in NetLogger log file format. This enables you to easily detect errors in network connections without having to pore over lots of lines of tcpdump output. You can also graphically analyze the tcpdump output from a network trace, using the NetLogger nlv program (discussed in the *NetLogger Graphical Tool* section).

Besides the tcpdump program, NetLogger also has versions of the common vmstat and netstat Unix programs that are used to monitor system resources. By performing the vmstat or netstat commands at constant intervals, and sending the output to a log file, you can analyze trends in system and network usage and performance.

NetLogger Log File

As mentioned, the NetLogger APIs send monitored events to a log file. NetLogger uses two special file formats for logging events received from applications. One format uses a standard text log entry format called *Universal Logging Message* (ULM). The ULM format contains both NetLogger core information and user-defined event information specific to the application being monitored. The core information includes:

- A timestamp in the format YYYYMMDDhhmmss.ssssss (using Universal Time Coordinates, or UTC)
- The host name of the originating host
- The program name of the originating program
- A security level (Emergency, Alert, or Usage)
- An event name defined in NetLogger

Each field in the log entry is prefaced by the field name, followed by an equal sign, and then the field value:

```
DATE=20021115194512.033423
```

The fields within the log entry are separated by blank spaces:

```
DATE=20021115194525.321690 HOST=shadrach.ispnet1.net PROG=test_prog
LVL=Usage NL.EVNT=event
```

After the core information, additional user-defined fields may be added to define values present in the event being monitored. The user-defined fields should store data that can be used for analyzing the log file after the application has finished. The format of the user-defined fields is:

```
PROGRAM.FIELD
```

Where PROGRAM is the program name, and FIELD is the field identifier. The PROGRAM and FIELD names can contain up to four characters each.

The NetLogger session can store log files in several different methods:

- As a text or binary file on the local host
- Using the netlogd program running on the local or a remote host to write to a text file
- Using the standard Unix syslogd logging facility on the local or a remote host
- Using the netarchd program, which interfaces with a database file, on the local or a remote host

NetLogger Graphical Tool

The NetLogger application includes the nlv program for graphically analyzing log files. The nlv program analyzes a single NetLogger log file and displays the timestamped events in a graphical environment. Displaying the events often makes it easier to see problems, especially problems concerning timing issues, such as excessive network transmission times.

The NetLogger application also contains tools that can be used to merge multiple log files into a single log file, allowing you to display the results from multiple tests in a single nlv graph. This feature allows you to compare tests, and helps identify bottlenecks and other performance problems.

Downloading and Installing NetLogger

The main Web page for NetLogger is maintained at http://www-didc.lbl.gov/NetLogger. This page contains information about NetLogger, as well as the download link for current versions of NetLogger. There are three separate distribution files that are used for each version of NetLogger:

- A source code file for any Unix platform
- A Linux binary distribution file
- A Solaris binary distribution file

This section describes how to download and install NetLogger using the different distribution files.

Source Code Distribution File

The source code file can be downloaded and built on most Unix platforms. At the time of this writing, the most current version is version 2.0.12, and can be downloaded at the URL:

```
ftp://george.lbl.gov/pub/NetLogger/netlogger-2.0.12.src.tar.gz
```

If you plan on compiling the nlv program, you must also have three separate library files:

- TCL version 8.1
- Tk version 8.1
- Tk BLT widgets version 2.4.i

You must have the correct versions of these libraries for the NetLogger application to compile properly on the system. The NetLogger download Web page includes two distribution files for these libraries—one for Linux systems, and one for Solaris systems:

```
ftp://george.lbl.gov/pub/NetLogger/netlogger-nlv.libs.linux.tar.gz

ftp://george.lbl.gov/pub/NetLogger/netlogger-nlv.libs.solaris.tar.gz
```

These distributions files contain the necessary libraries to compile the nlv program included in the NetLogger source code distribution file.

Before beginning the compile process, you must first create a couple of directories, and move the nlv library files into the work area. After changing to the working directory, you must create a build directory where all of the work will be done:

```
[rich@shadrach netlogger-2.0.12.src]$ mkdir build
[rich@shadrach netlogger-2.0.12.src]$ cd build
[rich@shadrach build]$ mkdir lib
```

After you create the build directory, a lib directory is created to hold the libraries required for nlv. These can be obtained from uncompressing the library distribution file:

```
tar -zxvf netlogger-nlv.libs.linux.tar.gz -C netlogger-
2.0.12.src/build/lib
```

Now that the source code and library files are extracted and in the proper place, you can start the compile process to create the executable files. From the build directory, you must run the configure program located in the root of the working directory:

```
[rich@shadrach build]$ ../configure
```

The configure program performs the usual process of determining which elements are required to compile the programs, and creating the necessary makefile for the compile process. At the end of the process, a summary is displayed, showing the configure results.

After the configure program finishes, you can use the make command to build the executable and library files.

Binary Distribution File

The NetLogger application has prebuilt binary distributions for both the Linux and Solaris platforms. At the time of this writing, the most current binary distribution file available can be downloaded from the URLs:

```
ftp://george.lbl.gov/pub/NetLogger/netlogger-2.0.12.bin.linux.tar.gz
ftp://george.lbl.gov/pub/NetLogger/netlogger-2.0.12.bin.solaris.tar.gz
```

NOTE If you download the binary distribution file, you do not need to download the nlv library files.

After downloading the binary distribution file, you can extract it to a working directory, using the standard tar command. The complete NetLogger application is contained within the binary distribution, including the API libraries and the nlv program. You must still use the make install command to install the NetLogger libraries into the proper place on your system.

Using the APIs

The core of NetLogger is the ability to add monitoring functions within applications. The API functions provide a way to insert monitoring points within applications, to log events as they happen in the program. This section describes the API functions, and explains how to use them within applications.

Functions

The NetLogger APIs contain methods that are used to control how and where NetLogger events are logged. While different languages use different method names, each of the basic methods contains the same format. This section describes the basic format of the NetLogger APIs.

Open

The Open API initiates the connection from the application to the NetLogger log file. Only one connection to a NetLogger log file can be open per Open statement. To log events to multiple logs, you must have multiple Open statements, one for each log file connection.

The standard format of the Open API is:

```
Open(URL, [host], [prog], [flags])
```

The only required field in the Open API is the URL. The URL points to the location of the NetLogger log file. There are three different schemes that can be used for the URL:

- x-netlog://host[:port] specifies a netlogd host at address *host* and optional port *port*.
- x-syslog:// specifies the syslog logging facility on the local host.
- file:// specifies using a local file.

The *host* field defines an option hostname or IP address to use as the HOST field in the event log. By default, NetLogger uses the local hostname of the system. The *prog* field defines the program name used in the PROG field in the event log. By default the word unknown is used as the program name. You can replace this value with the name of the application being monitored.

The *flags* field indicates the output option that is being used to log the event. Table 9.1 shows the flag values that can be used.

The ENV flag is extremely useful in test environments. Instead of hard-coding the URL in the application, you can use the ENV flag to set the URL of the logging method in an environment variable on the system. This provides great flexibility by allowing you to easily change the logging location. Besides the URL value, a switch is also defined, NETLOGGER_ON. When this environment value is false, the NetLogger API will not log events to the log file. When it is set to true (or not defined), the NetLogger API sends events to the log file defined in the NETLOGGER_DEST environment variable. This variable must have the same format as the URL field in the Open API.

Table 9.1   Open Flag Values

VALUE	DESCRIPTION
ULM	Use ULM text entries in the event log.
BIN	Use binary messages in the event log.
XML	Use XML-formatted entries in the event log.
ENV	Override the URL value with system environment setting NETLOGGER_DEST.
FLUSH	Flush each message as it is written to the log file.
STREAM_FILE	When in BIN mode, this value instructs NetLogger to write messages to the log file similar to a network socket.
ANNOUNCE	Write an NL_START event before the logged event, and write an NL_END event after the logged event.

The output of the Open API method is a handle to the log file device. This must be used in calls to the Write API to indicate which log file to write events to.

A sample Open statement from the C API methods is:

```
NetLoggerOpen("x-netlog://shadrach.ispnet1.net");
```

This statement opens the log file from the netlogd host shadrach.ispnet1.net, logging events as ULM text messages.

Write

To send events to the log file you must use the Write API. The Write API sends information to the event log, using the format selected in the Open statement. The Write format is:

```
Write(handle, level, event_name, format_string, value_list)
```

The *handle* field identifies the open log file device as returned by the Open API function call. The *level* field defines the logging level that is used to identify the event. This level is an integer field, with 0 being the lowest level, and 255 being the highest.

The *event_name* field identifies the name of the NetLogger event that is used to log the events. A single event name can be used to identify the same type of events logged within an application. Events logged with the same event name will be easier to identify within the log file, especially if you are logging different types of data (such as disk access times and network access times). Each event name used must use a unique format string.

> **WARNING** Do not use different format strings with the same event name in the Write method (called *overloading*). If you need to log different information from the same application, use separate event names for the different information formats. If you overload an event name, unpredictable results will occur.

The *format_string* field defines the user-defined event log fields that are sent to the log file. The format of the format string is:

```
"name=format_code name=format_code name=format_code..."
```

The *name* field defines the name of the user-defined field. As mentioned in the *NetLogger Log File* section, the user-defined fields should follow a set pattern of PROGRAM.FIELD, where PROGRAM is the program name, and FIELD is the parameter to monitor. Each field should be four or fewer characters.

The *format_code* field identifies the type of data that will be placed in the field. Table 9.2 shows the data types that can be used.

Table 9.2 Write Method Format Codes

CODE	DESCRIPTION
%s	A string value of up to 255 characters
%d	A 32-bit integer value
%f	A 32-bit floating-point value
%ld	A 64-bit integer value
%lf	A 64-bit floating-point value

The format code is used similarly to the C language printf formats. It is a placeholder that defines the type of data that is identified in the *value_list* field. For example, a sample C language Write API would look like:

```
NetLoggerHandle nlh;
int ret;

nlh = NetLoggerOpen("x-netlog://shadrach.ispnet1.net");
ret = NetLoggerWrite(nl, 0, "NetworkData", "recv=%d sent=%d errors=%d",
recv, sent, errors);
```

This code snippet opens a connection to the netlogd server on host shadrach.ispnet1.net, and logs an event message called NetworkData. The event message includes three user-defined fields, indicating three different data points within the application program.

Close

To properly terminate a NetLogger session, you must call the Close API method. This method properly disconnects the application from the log file device:

```
Close(handle)
```

The *handle* field identifies the log file device opened using the Open API method call. The Close call flushes any unwritten events to the log file before closing the device. The C API function call looks like:

```
NetLoggerClose(nlh);
```

For log files that are cached, such as a database log file using netarchd, it is crucial that any unwritten events be flushed from the queue. If you need to perform this task without closing the log file device, you can use the Flush API method:

```
Flush(handle)
```

Libraries

The NetLogger APIs have been created for several different programming languages. This section describes how to use the libraries and function calls available for the C programming language.

The NetLogger C APIs are provided in the shared library file libnetlogger.so. If you run the standard install make option, this file is installed in the directory /usr/local/lib. To run applications that use NetLogger APIs, you must ensure that the libnetlogger.so file is in your library path.

Table 9.3 shows the main C NetLogger API function calls that are available.

Table 9.3   Main NetLogger C Functions

FUNCTION	DESCRIPTION
NetLoggerOpen()	Opens a new handle to a NetLogger file
NetLoggerOpenWithTrigger()	Opens a new handle that uses a trigger configuration file
NetLoggerWrite()	Writes an event to the open NetLogger handle
NetLoggerWriteList()	Writes a list of events to an open NetLogger handle
NetLoggerGTWrite()	Writes an event using a user-defined timestamp
NetLoggerGTWriteList()	Writes a list of events using a user-defined timestamp
NetLoggerWriteMessage()	Writes a message to the open NetLogger handle
NetLoggerFlush()	Flushes any unwritten events to the log file
NetLoggerClose()	Closes an open NetLogger handle

To compile C programs that use the NetLogger APIs, you must link them with the libnetlogger.a library file, and use the header file /usr/local/include/netlogger.h. These files provide the NetLogger API functions for programming C applications. A sample C application that uses the NetLogger APIs is shown in Figure 9.1.

To compile this program, you must use the following command:

```
$ cc -o test test.c -L/usr/local/lib -lnetlogger
```

This command produces the program file test, which can be run to produce the NetLogger file test.log in the current directory.

WARNING To run C programs that use the NetLogger APIs, the location of the NetLogger shared library must be defined. The easiest way to do this is to specify the directory location in the LD_LIBRARY_PATH environment variable.

```
#include <stdio.h>
#include "/usr/local/include/netlogger.h"

int main()
{
    NetLoggerHandle nlh;
    int ret;

    nlh = NetLoggerOpen("file://test.log", "shadrach.ispnet1.net",
                        "TestProgram", 0);
    if (!NetLoggerIsValid(nlh))
    {
        fprintf(stderr, "Improper NetLogger file device");
        return 1;
    }
    ret = NetLoggerWrite(nlh, 0, "TestData", "test=%d", 100LL);
    NetLoggerClose(nlh);
    return 0;
}
```

Figure 9.1   Sample C NetLogger program.

The following is the output from the test program:

```
$ LD_LIBRARY_PATH=/usr/local/lib ; export LD_LIBRARY_PATH
$ ./test
$ cat test.log
DATE=20021114144648.237137 NL.EVNT=TestData HOST=shadrach.ispnet1.net
PROG=TestProg LVL=0 test=100
$
```

The test.log log file contains an entry from the NetLoggerWrite command in the test program. Notice how the individual fields in the entry were created using the data from the NetLoggerOpen and NetLoggerWrite function calls.

Using nlv

The nlv application is possibly the most valuable, but also the most complicated, NetLogger application. This section describes how to configure and use nlv to help analyze NetLogger log files.

Types of nlv graphs

Before diving into the nlv configuration files, it is a good idea to see what nlv does. The nlv program can read a NetLogger log file, and graph events on a timeline, showing when events occurred in relation to one another. This is an excellent technique to use for watching host and network performance issues, such as how long a data transfer took reading data from the disk, versus how long it took sending the data across the network.

nlv uses three different types of graphs to display event data:

- **point.** Displays individual data points within an event on a timeline
- **load-line.** Uses a line to connect individual data points within an event, forming a simple graph
- **life-line.** Displays a set of events as a single line, showing the path between events

The point graph is the simplest way to show data in nlv. It is used to show occurrences of individual events against the timeline. This graph is used to show events that have no specific value, but are worth seeing when they trigger.

The load-line graph takes the point graph one step further. The load-line graph is used to graph events that can have multiple values, such as the utilization of a system.

The life-line graph is where nlv can really show its usefulness. Often when analyzing a process it is desirable to see which events within the process took the longest time. This is where the life-line graph comes in. By using a timeline to map out the times when monitored events occurred, you can see how much time each event required, relative to the other events in the process. This is shown in Figure 9.2.

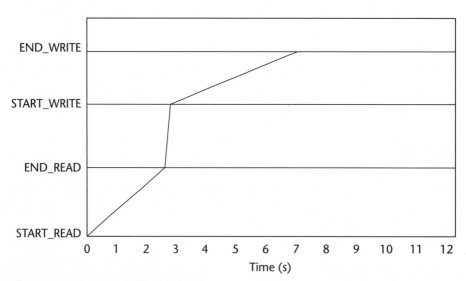

Figure 9.2   Sample nlv life-line graph.

By analyzing the graph in Figure 9.2, you can see that the disk read process took longer than the network write process, indicating a disk bottleneck for this system.

The trick to converting the raw NetLogger log files into pretty graphs is all in the nlv configuration files. The next section describes how to configure nlv to graphically display your data.

Configuring nlv

There are three configuration files that are required to use nlv to analyze a log file:

- bltGraph.pro
- nlv-main.cfg
- nlv-keys.cfg

This section describes what these configuration files are, and how to build each of them to analyze a log file.

The bltGraph.pro File

The bltGraph.pro file controls how nlv prints graphs. It maps the graphical coordinates of the graphs produced in nlv to Postscript coordinates for printing. The nice thing about the bltGraph.pro file is that it never changes. It is provided in the NetLogger distribution and can be used as is. The location of the bltGraph.pro file in the distribution working directory is:

```
nlv/cfg/bltGraph.pro
```

To use this file, you must put it in one of three locations:

- $NLHOME
- $NLHOME/etc
- the current directory when running nlv

The $NLHOME environment variable points to the location where you want to keep the NetLogger files. This can be any directory on the host, and does not have to be (and probably shouldn't be) the NetLogger working directory.

The nlv-main.cfg File

The nlv-main.cfg file is used to define configuration parameters for how the nlv program operates. It defines settings for the nlv window, icons, graphs, and printing. A sample nlv-main.cfg file is located in the distribution working directory in the nlv/cfg subdirectory. In most cases you can use this sample nlv-main.cfg file without modification. Like the bltGraph.pro file, it must be located in either the current directory, or in either the $NLHOME or $NLHOME/etc directory.

The nlv-main.cfg file is a text file that contains one nlv option per line. There are two formats that are used for the options. The first format:

```
option parameter
```

defines a single parameter for an option, such as:

```
AutoResize 0
```

which indicates that the nlv window will not automatically resize if the graph becomes larger. For options that require more than one parameter, the format is:

```
option list parameter1, parameter2, ...
```

Using the list keyword lets nlv know that there is more than one parameter associated with the option. An example of this would be:

```
color-ip    list #f00 #0f0 #99f #aa0 #0aa #a0a #b23 #23b
```

There are lots of options that can be used to customize the look and feel of the nlv window. Table 9.4 shows some of the more common options that can be used in the nlv-main.cfg file.

Table 9.4 nlv-main.cfg Options

OPTION	DESCRIPTION
AutoLegendRefresh	Command used to refresh display when legend entry buttons are clicked (default: 1)
AutoResize	Command used to enlarge the window if the graph expands (default: 1)
Color-ip	Color map used for displaying individual graphs
Color-winbg	Window background color
Color-graphbg	Graph background color
Lpr	Command used to print a postscript file (default: lpr)
Lpropts	Additional options used to print a postscript file (default: -h)
MaxGraphElements	Number of graphical elements viewable at once (default: 2,500)

Table 9.4 *(continued)*

OPTION	DESCRIPTION
Printers	Names of available printers
StartMode	Mode to display the graphs in (can be either Play or Pause) (default: Pause)
TimeUnit	The unit of time used on the X axis (default: milliseconds)

You can look at the sample nlv-main.cfg file provided with the NetLogger distribution, and modify the options necessary to run nlv on your system.

The nlv-keys.cfg File

The nlv-keys.cfg file defines how the log information will be displayed in nlv. This file is crucial to displaying the monitored data. It defines which events are graphed, and how they are graphed. Since the nlv-keys.cfg file is specific to an individual log file, it should be kept in the same directory as the log file.

The basic unit within the nlv-keys.cfg file is the *eventset*. An eventset defines one or more specific event types that are graphed within nlv. All events in the log with the defined event values are contained within the eventset for display. How the events are displayed is defined within the eventset definition. You can specify multiple eventsets within a single nlv-keys.cfg file, to graph more than one event at a time.

The eventset definition contains keywords that are used to define the parameters used to graph the event. Table 9.5 shows the keywords used.

Table 9.5 net-keys.cfg Eventset Keywords

KEYWORD	DESCRIPTION
eventset	Defines the NetLogger event to graph
annotate	Lists the fields used for annotating events
events	List of the events contained in the eventset
group	List of fields used for grouping events
groupalias	Aliases to use for hostnames
id	List of fields to use for identifying connected events
rotateclients	Indicates if ids will continually change during program execution
type	Defines the type of graph
val	Scaled value used for point or load-line graphs

The easiest way to describe the nlv-keys.cfg file is to show a few examples and walk through them. The first example shows a simple life-line graph for a series of events logged in a log file:

```
# Sample eventset
eventset +SEND_DATA {
  {type line}
  { events {+START_READ +END_READ +START_SEND +END_SEND} }
}
```

The first line in the configuration file starts with the pound sign, indicating that it is a comment. Since each nlv-keys.cfg file is unique for a set log file, it is best to identify the associated log file within the comments.

The second line defines the name of the eventset. Notice that there is a plus sign before the name. This is used to indicate that the eventset will be displayed by default on the nlv graph. If you do not want the eventset displayed, you can use a minus sign. The entire eventset is contained within braces. Individual options within the eventset are also contained with braces, and when multiple values are used for an option, they are also contained within braces.

After the eventset is declared, the type of graph used is defined, using the type statement. The three graph types are defined using the keywords:

- line (for a life-line graph, the default if no type statement is present)
- load (for a load-line graph)
- point (for a point graph)

After the type of graph is declared, the list of events graphed must be defined. In this case, the graph will show the time elapsed between specific events, so the events to display are listed. As with the eventset, a plus sign is used to indicate which events will be displayed on the graph, and a minus sign is used to hide events when the graph is drawn.

To show multiple graphs based on a value within the event, you can use the id option. The id option defines which field within the event log will be used to distinguish graphs. You can use user-defined fields to separate the graphs—for example, defining separate reads and writes to separate data files. An example of this would look like:

```
# multiple graph config file
eventset +SEND_DATA {
{ id FILE.READ }
{ type line }
{events { +START_READ +END_READ +START_SEND +END_SEND } }
}
```

This nlv-keys.cfg file uses the user-defined field FILE.READ, which is used to identify the read/write session to track. To test this environment, you can create a sample program to generate the logfile. Figure 9.3 shows the sample.c program, which generates these events.

After creating the sample.c program, compile and run it to generate the sample.log NetLogger log file with the appropriate entries. The log file output should look like this:

```
DATE=20021115180028.465153 NL.EVNT=START_READ HOST=shadrach.ispnet1.net
PROG=TestProg LVL=0 FILE.READ=1
DATE=20021115180028.465511 NL.EVNT=START_READ HOST=shadrach.ispnet1.net
PROG=TestProg LVL=0 FILE.READ=2
DATE=20021115180030.467402 NL.EVNT=END_READ HOST=shadrach.ispnet1.net
PROG=TestProg LVL=0 FILE.READ=1
DATE=20021115180030.467561 NL.EVNT=START_SEND HOST=shadrach.ispnet1.net
PROG=TestProg LVL=0 FILE.READ=1
DATE=20021115180031.477400 NL.EVNT=END_READ HOST=shadrach.ispnet1.net
PROG=TestProg LVL=0 FILE.READ=2
DATE=20021115180031.477444 NL.EVNT=START_SEND HOST=shadrach.ispnet1.net
PROG=TestProg LVL=0 FILE.READ=2
DATE=20021115180033.487401 NL.EVNT=END_SEND HOST=shadrach.ispnet1.net
PROG=TestProg LVL=0 FILE.READ=2
DATE=20021115180034.497400 NL.EVNT=END_SEND HOST=shadrach.ispnet1.net
PROG=TestProg LVL=0 FILE.READ=1
```

As expected, each event is logged with the appropriate event name, and the FILE.READ user-defined field value. Now, you can run the nlv program using the sample.log log file and the nlv-keys.cfg configuration file. Figure 9.4 shows the output generated from this test.

```c
#include <stdio.h>
#include "/usr/local/include/netlogger.h"

int main()
{
    NetLoggerHandle nlh;
    int ret;

    nlh = NetLoggerOpen("file://sample.log", "shadrach.ispnet1.net",
                        "SampleProgram", 0);
    if (!NetLoggerIsValid(nlh))
    {
        fprintf(stderr, "Improper NetLogger file device");
        return 1;
    }
    ret = NetLoggerWrite(nlh, 0, "START_READ", "FILE.READ=%d", 1LL);
```

Figure 9.3   The sample.c program. *(continued)*

```
      ret = NetLoggerWrite(nlh, 0, "START_READ", "FILE.READ=%d", 2LL);
      sleep(2);
      ret = NetLoggerWrite(nlh, 0, "END_READ", "FILE.READ=%d", 1LL);
      ret = NetLoggerWrite(nlh, 0, "START_SEND", "FILE.READ=%d", 1LL);
      sleep(1);
      ret = NetLoggerWrite(nlh, 0, "END_READ", "FILE.READ=%d", 2LL);
      ret = NetLoggerWrite(nlh, 0, "START_SEND", "FILE.READ=%d", 2LL);
      sleep(2);
      ret = NetLoggerWrite(nlh, 0, "END_SEND", "FILE.READ=%d", 2LL);
      sleep(1);
      ret = NetLoggerWrite(nlh, 0, "END_SEND", "FILE.READ=%d", 1LL);
      NetLoggerClose(nlh);
      return 0;
  }
```

Figure 9.3 *(continued)*

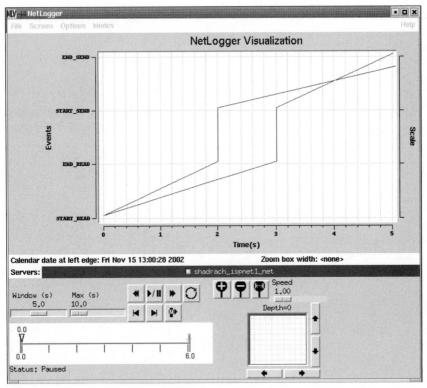

Figure 9.4 nlv output for sample.log.

You can see the two separate graphs generated, one for each FILE.READ event series. From this graph you can see the time that elapsed for each monitored event.

Summary

The NetLogger application can help you watch system and network events as they play out within application programs. The NetLogger package includes APIs that can be added to programs to log specific events as they occur within the program. This provides great flexibility in creating your own monitoring environment.

Besides the API functions, NetLogger also includes some scripts that can be used to monitor standard system and network performance, such as the vmstat and netstat statistics from the system, and network retransmissions and window sizes from the tcpdump output. This information can be saved in NetLogger format for analysis.

You can point multiple hosts to the same log file using the netlogd and netarchd programs. The netlogd program listens to TCP port 14830 for incoming events, and stores them in a standard NetLogger log file. The netarchd program performs the same function, but interfaces with a mySQL or postgresql database to store the events in a database format. These programs provide the functionality of enabling multiple hosts to generate events within a single log file. This enables you to watch distributed network applications from all points of interest.

The nlv program is a great tool within NetLogger for graphically displaying the data within the log files. Presenting the information graphically often makes it easier to detect trends, and compare response times between events in the application.

The next chapter discusses the tcptrace application. The tcptrace program can extract information from standard tcpdump files to help you see problems occurring within the existing network traffic. This can be a valuable tool for determining host problems on the network.

tcptrace

The tcptrace application does not perform network tests itself. Instead, it is used to analyze network traces performed with tcpdump, and a few other similar packet-capturing applications. This chapter describes how to use tcptrace, along with the xplot and jPlot graphical programs used to produce graphs with tcptrace data.

The tcptrace application was developed by Shawn Ostermann at Ohio University as a method of analyzing TCP sessions captured with the tcpdump application. tcptrace can be used to analyze network throughput, packet round-trip times, sequences, retransmissions, window sizes, and other TCP features of network sessions. This information can then be plotted, using the xplot or jPlot programs, to produce graphical information about network sessions.

What Is tcptrace?

The tcptrace application is an extremely useful tool for finding network problems by analyzing TCP sessions on the network. Often, network problems appear as quirks within TCP sessions, such as retransmitted packets or poor round-trip times.

The tcptrace application can analyze TCP sessions captured from several different applications:

- tcpdump
- WinDump
- snoop
- etherpeek
- HP NetMetrix

The tcpdump and WinDump applications were both described in Chapter 2, "Watching Network Traffic," and will be used to produce the examples in this chapter. The snoop application can be found on Sun Solaris workstations and servers, while the etherpeek application is a commercial Windows network-monitoring product.

The tcptrace application can be run in two modes. In console mode, information from the TCP sessions is displayed in a text format on the terminal, showing each session found in the dump file, and some basic information about the session. In graphical mode, session information is placed in separate files that can be used by the xplot or jPlot applications to produce graphs showing trends and features of the TCP sessions.

Console Mode

When run in console mode, tcptrace decodes the trace file and shows varying levels of information regarding the sessions found in the trace. By default, the sessions and their status are identified, along with the total number of packets sent between the hosts:

```
$ tcptrace test1
1 arg remaining, starting with 'test1'
Ostermann's tcptrace -- version 6.2.0 -- Fri Jul 26, 2002

6828 packets seen, 6828 TCP packets traced
elapsed wallclock time: 0:00:00.819992, 8326 pkts/sec analyzed
trace file elapsed time: 0:01:56.243460
TCP connection info:
*** 6 packets were too short to process at some point
        (use -w option to show details)
  1: 192.168.1.2:1027 - 192.168.1.1:23 (a2b)      2>     1<
  2: 192.168.1.2:1028 - 192.168.1.1:23 (c2d)    161>   161<  (complete)
  3: 192.168.1.2:1029 - 192.168.1.1:21 (e2f)     34>    27<  (complete)
  4: 192.168.1.1:1051 - 192.168.1.2:113 (g2h)      1>     1<  (reset)
  5: 192.168.1.1:20 - 192.168.1.2:1030 (i2j)       6>     4<  (complete)
  6: 192.168.1.1:20 - 192.168.1.2:1031 (k2l)    1070>   688<  (complete)
```

```
7: 192.168.1.1:20 - 192.168.1.2:1032 (m2n)   1409>   932<  (complete)
8: 192.168.1.1:20 - 192.168.1.2:1033 (o2p)      6>     4<  (complete)
9: 192.168.1.1:20 - 192.168.1.2:1034 (q2r)   1394>   927<  (complete)
$
```

The tcptrace output shows each detected session, and assigns a unique label to each session. In this example, the first session detected was between hosts 192.168.1.2 port 1027 and 192.168.1.1 port 23. This session is labeled as session a2b. The second session is labeled c2d, the third, e2f, and so on. These session labels are important when you are using tcptrace in graphical mode, as this is how the session graph files are labeled.

Graphical Mode

One of the best features of tcptrace is the ability to produce TCP session information in a graphical form. When you store the TCP session information in xplot formatted files, you can use tcptrace to produce xplot graphs of the session information. Figure 10.1 shows a sample xplot graph of tcptrace session data.

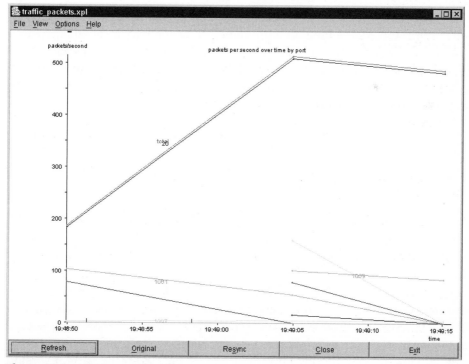

Figure 10.1   tcptrace session data.

This sample graph shows the packets per second of the captured network traffic, separated by TCP port number. Using this information you can quickly see where the majority of the network traffic originated (in this example, an FTP session on port 20). tcptrace can graph several different types of TCP information:

- Throughput
- Round-trip time values
- Time sequence plots
- Outstanding data
- Segment size

This information can be plotted for each session detected by tcptrace in the trace file. This can produce lots of graphs from a single trace file, so tcptrace also includes features that allow you to plot individual parameters for each session.

Downloading and Installing tcptrace

The tcptrace Web site is located at http://irg.cs.ohiou.edu/software/tcptrace/ index.html. It contains links to various help pages for tcptrace, along with a link to the download area. In the download area, you can download the source code distribution of tcptrace, a Linux binary distribution package, or a Windows binary package. At the time of this writing, the current version of tcptrace is version 6.2.0, and can be downloaded from the URLs:

```
http://irg.cs.ohiou.edu/software/tcptrace/download/tcptrace-6.2.0.tar.gz
http://irg.cs.ohiou.edu/software/tcptrace/download/tcptrace-
6.2-0.i386.rpm
http://irg.cs.ohiou.edu/software/tcptrace/download/win_tcptrace-
6.2.0.zip
```

The first download URL is for the complete source code distribution for Unix platforms. The second download URL is the Linux binary distribution package using the RPM package installer. The last download URL is the Windows binary distribution package, using the ZIP package installer.

The most versatile installation option is to compile tcptrace directly from the source code distribution. This method has been known to work on several different Unix platforms. As usual, you must uncompress and expand the source code distribution file into a working directory, using the gunzip and tar commands. This creates a working directory tcptrace-6.2.0 (for the current version of tcptrace). All of the source code files are located under this structure.

To build the executable file, you must change to the working directory, and use the configure and make commands, as usual:

```
$ ./configure

$ make
```

NOTE To build the tcptrace program, you must have the libpcap library installed on your Unix system. If you have installed tcpdump on your system, this should already be present. The process of downloading and installing the libpcap library was described in Chapter 2.

If you want to install tcptrace into a common location on the system, you can run the make install script, which places the tcptrace executable file in the /usr/local/bin directory. tcptrace does not require any special privileges to run on the system, as it does not interact directly with the network interfaces. It just needs to read saved tcpdump trace files.

Using tcptrace in Console Mode

After installing tcptrace using one of the install methods, you can begin analyzing tcpdump files. Remember, the application is called tcptrace because its main purpose is to analyze TCP sessions. It has limited UDP capabilities. This section describes how to use the various command-line options for displaying session information in standard text format on the console.

Using Basic Command-Line Options

By default, tcptrace produces information directly on the console. There are many command-line options that can be used to modify the display results.

Standard Session Output

There are 18 command-line options that can be used to modify the format of the tcptrace output sent to the console. Table 10.1 lists these options.

Table 10.1   tcptrace Console Mode Options

OPTION	DESCRIPTION
-b	Show a brief listing of the TCP sessions (the default output).
-d	Debug mode. Display additional information while processing.

(continued)

Table 10.1 *(continued)*

OPTION	DESCRIPTION
-D	Display all values in decimal.
-e	Extract data contents of each TCP session to a file.
-l	Show a detailed listing of the TCP sessions.
-n	Don't attempt to resolve hostnames.
-O*file*	Dump matching packets to a separate tcpdump dump file.
-p	Display packet information for each packet.
-P	Display packet information for specific packets.
-r	Show round-trip time statistics.
-s	Use short (unqualified) hostnames.
-t	Show progress by displaying packet numbers while calculating.
-u	Perform minimal UDP packet processing.
-w	Display any warning messages while analyzing packets (default is don't display warnings).
-W	Show estimated congestion window values.
-q	Show no output (used when using modules or producing graph files).
-X	Display all values in hexadecimal.
-Z	Dump raw round-trip times to file.

The -l option shows detailed information about each TCP session detected in the dump file. A sample session detailed listing looks like:

```
TCP connection 9:
        host q:        192.168.1.1:20
        host r:        192.168.1.2:1034
        complete conn: yes
        first packet:  Tue Nov 19 07:18:32.319212 2002
        last packet:   Tue Nov 19 07:18:33.164690 2002
        elapsed time:  0:00:00.845478
        total packets: 2321
        filename:      test1
    q->r:                          r->q:
      total packets:      1394       total packets:      927
      ack pkts sent:      1393       ack pkts sent:      927
      pure acks sent:        2       pure acks sent:     925
```

```
sack pkts sent:              0          sack pkts sent:            0
max sack blks/ack:           0          max sack blks/ack:         0
unique bytes sent:     1979018          unique bytes sent:         0
actual data pkts:         1390          actual data pkts:          0
actual data bytes:     1979018          actual data bytes:         0
rexmt data pkts:             0          rexmt data pkts:           0
rexmt data bytes:            0          rexmt data bytes:          0
zwnd probe pkts:             0          zwnd probe pkts:           0
zwnd probe bytes:            0          zwnd probe bytes:          0
outoforder pkts:             0          outoforder pkts:           0
pushed data pkts:          367          pushed data pkts:          0
SYN/FIN pkts sent:         1/1          SYN/FIN pkts sent:       1/1
req sack:                    Y          req sack:                  Y
sacks sent:                  0          sacks sent:                0
urgent data pkts:            0 pkts     urgent data pkts:     0 pkts
urgent data bytes:           0 bytes    urgent data bytes:  0 bytes
mss requested:            1460 bytes    mss requested: 1460 bytes
max segm size:            1460 bytes    max segm size:      0 bytes
min segm size:              72 bytes    min segm size:      0 bytes
avg segm size:            1423 bytes    avg segm size:      0 bytes
max win adv:             32120 bytes    max win adv:     8760 bytes
min win adv:             32120 bytes    min win adv:      164 bytes
zero win adv:                0 times    zero win adv:      63 times
avg win adv:             32120 bytes    avg win adv:     5812 bytes
initial window:           2920 bytes    initial window:     0 bytes
initial window:              2 pkts     initial window:     0 pkts
ttl stream length:     1979018 bytes    ttl stream length: 0 bytes
missed data:                 0 bytes    missed data:        0 bytes
truncated data:        1959558 bytes    truncated data:     0 bytes
truncated packets:        1390 pkts     truncated packets:  0 pkts
data xmit time:          0.842 secs     data xmit time:  0.000 secs
idletime max:             47.5 ms       idletime max:      47.1 ms
throughput:            2340709 Bps       throughput:         0 Bps
```

Each TCP session is shown, along with the pertinent TCP information for each side of the connection (in this example, from host q to host r, and from host r to host q). Since this is an FTP session, the numbers are somewhat one-sided. Most of the information presented in the detailed listing is self-explanatory.

If you would like to see the actual packets in a session, you can use the -p option. This prints out a short description of each packet:

```
Packet 2992
        Packet Length: 1514 (saved length 68)
        Collected: Tue Nov 19 07:18:00.122965 2002
        ETH Srce: 00:e0:7d:74:df:c7
        ETH Dest: 00:e0:7d:75:3e:6d
            Type: 0x800 (IP)
        IP  VERS: 4
        IP  Srce: 192.168.1.1
```

```
IP  Dest: 192.168.1.2
       Type: 0x6 (TCP)
       HLEN: 20
        TTL: 64
        LEN: 1500
         ID: 2340
      CKSUM: 0xa89c
     OFFSET: 0x4000   Don't Fragment

TCP SPRT: 20
       DPRT: 1032
        FLG:    -A---- (0x10)
        SEQ: 0x1be7dc33
        ACK: 0x00051582
        WIN: 32120
       HLEN: 20
      CKSUM: 0x4527
       DLEN: 1460 (only 14 bytes in dump file)
       data: 1460 bytes
```

The packet information shows header information for the Ethernet, IP, and TCP layers. The -p option displays information for all of the packets in all of the captured sessions. You can use the -P option to limit the packets displayed. When you want to limit the packets displayed, there are additional command-line options that must be used to define the packet or session ranges to analyze. Table 10.2 shows these options.

By using the -o option, you can analyze a single TCP session in the dump file. The command:

```
tcptrace -P -o3 test1
```

prints the packet header information for packets contained in session 3 within the test1 dump file.

Table 10.2   tcptrace Packet-Limiting Options

OPTION	DESCRIPTION
-iN	Ignore packets contained in session N.
-oN[-M]	Include packets contained in sessions N through M.
-c	Ignore packets in incomplete sessions.
-BN	Start the analysis at segment N.
-EN	Stop the analysis at segment N.

tcptrace Filters

While the -o option can be used to limit the analysis to one or more sessions, this still can produce lots of unwanted packets. You can fine-tune the display of sessions in tcptrace output by using the -f filter option to select specific types of packets to analyze.

The -f option allows you to create filter expressions that will be compared against each packet in the dump file. Only sessions that contain one or more packets matching the filter expression will be processed.

NOTE The filter expression does not limit the output to individual packets, only to sessions. If one packet in a session matches a filter expression, the entire session is analyzed.

The filter expressions can be as simple or as complex as you require, using arithmetic and Boolean operations to check values. For example, to see only sessions that had a throughput higher than 10,000 Bps, you could use the command:

```
$ tcptrace -f'thruput>10000' test1
```

The output of this command shows the sessions that match the criteria. You can then combine the filter with other command-line options (including modules) to limit the sessions used in the analysis.

There are lots of variables that can be used to filter packets in the sessions. The complete filter list can be seen by using the -hfilter command-line option for tcptrace. Table 10.3 shows a few of the more popular values that can be used.

Table 10.3 Some tcptrace Filter Variables

VARIABLE	DESCRIPTION
bad_behavior	Bad TCP packet within the session
data_bytes	Bytes of data within the packet
data_segs	Segments (packets) of data
data_segs_push	Packets with the TCP PUSH flag set
Hostadr	The host IP address
Hostname	Full hostname
Mss	Maximum segment (packet data) size

(continued)

Table 10.3 *(continued)*

VARIABLE	DESCRIPTION
out_order_segs	Out of order packets
Portname	Service name of the port number (as seen in the /etc/services file)
retr_max	Maximum number of retransmissions of a single packet
rexmit_bytes	Total number of retransmitted bytes in the session
reset_count	Number of packets containing a TCP RESET flag
rtt_min	Minumum round-trip time value
rtt_max	Maximum round-trip time value
Thruput	Session throughput value
unique_bytes	Non-retransmitted bytes
urg_data_bytes	Number of bytes within packets with TCP URGENT flag set
urg_data_pkts	Number of packets with TCP URGENT flag set
win_max	Maximum TCP window size advertisement
win_min	Minimum TCP window size advertisement
win_zero_ct	Number of packets with the TCP window size set to zero

By default, each variable specified applies to both hosts in the TCP session. To further define each variable, you can add a prefix of c_ to specify only client values, and s_ for only server values. Thus, to see the sessions that have a zero window size value for the server host, you would use the command:

```
tcptrace -f's_win_zero_ct>0' test1
```

Using the command:

```
tcptrace -f'win_zero_ct>0' test1
```

allows sessions with either client or server zero window sizes. This would be equivalent to the filter:

```
tcptrace -f((c_win_zero_ct>0)OR(s_win_zero_ct>0)) test1
```

Using Module Options

Besides performing normal packet decoding, tcptrace includes special modules that are programmed to produce specialized formatted output for specific types of TCP sessions, or for specific session information. Table 10.4 shows the modules that are included in tcptrace version 6.2.0.

Each of these modules can be used to produce useful information about the TCP connections contained in the dump file. To specify a module, you must use the -x option and the module name:

```
tcptrace -xrealtime test1
```

Some modules also contain options that can be used to further define how the module uses and outputs data. To separate the module options from the command-line options, the module options should be enclosed in double quotes immediately after the module name:

```
tcptrace -xcollie"-n" test1
```

This command uses the collie module, but specifies the -n option, which does not display the heading labels for the data. Some modules have lots of options, while others have none. To view a listing of all the modules and their options, you can use the -hxargs option of tcptrace:

```
tcptrace -hxargs
```

Table 10.4 tcptrace Modules

MODULE	DESCRIPTION
collie	Displays general information about each connection detected
HTTP	Displays specific information on HTTP sessions
realtime	Displays connection information in time-order
rttgraph	Displays information about round-trip times
slice	Generates traffic information by time slice
tcplib	Generates a tcplib formatted data file
traffic	Creates information about overall traffic statistics

You can use the collie module to display information about each individual session in a dump file:

```
Session Start: Tue Nov 19 07:17:59.197779 2002
Session End: Tue Nov 19 07:18:01.342226 2002
Source IP address: 192.168.1.1
Source Port: 20
Source Fully Qualified domain name: 192.168.1.1
Destination IP address: 192.168.1.2
Destination Port: 1032
Destination Fully Qualified domain name: 192.168.1.2
Bytes Transferred Source to Destination: 1979018
Bytes Transferred Destination to Source: 0
Packets Transferred Source to Destination: 1409
Packets Transferred Destination to Source: 932
```

To see the overall statistics of the sessions, you can use the slice and traffic modules. Both of these modules produce separate data files that contain the output information. The slice module produces the file slice.dat, which looks like this:

```
date              segs    bytes   rexsegs  rexbytes      new     active
--------------   ------- -------- -------- --------    -------- --------
07:16:59.206839    59      2663      0        0          2         2
07:17:14.206839   172     37882      0        0          1         1
07:17:29.206839     3       136      0        0          1         1
07:17:44.206839    32      4200      0        0          1         3
07:17:59.206839  1772   1584382      0        0          2         3
07:18:14.206839  2388   2080318      0        0          0         3
07:18:29.206839    68      8080      0        0          1         3
07:18:40.450300  2334   2072607      0        0          1         2
```

The slice data shows, by time slice, the number of new sessions started, the number of active sessions detected, and information about the individual packet segments seen. The traffic module produces two data files:

- traffic_byport.dat shows traffic information sorted by TCP port.

- traffic_stats.dat shows overall traffic statistics.

The traffic_byport.dat file shows general information per port:

```
Overall totals by port
TOTAL         bytes: 5790268  pkts:   6828  conns:   9  tput: 4916 B/s
Port    20    bytes: 5733948  pkts:   6440  conns:   5  tput: 49430 B/s
Port    21    bytes:    3554  pkts:     61  conns:   1  tput:   30 B/s
Port    23    bytes:   52666  pkts:    325  conns:   2  tput:  454 B/s
Port   113    bytes:     100  pkts:      2  conns:   1  tput:    0 B/s
Port  1027    bytes:     148  pkts:      3  conns:   1  tput:    1 B/s
Port  1028    bytes:   52518  pkts:    322  conns:   1  tput:  452 B/s
```

This table can be used to analyze which TCP port (application) produced the most traffic within the dump file, and the average throughput of the traffic. The overall statistics for all the sessions in the dump file are stored in the traffic_stats file:

```
Overall Statistics over 116 seconds (0:01:56.243460):
5790268 ttl bytes sent, 49916.103 bytes/second
5790268 ttl non-rexmit bytes sent, 49916.103 bytes/second
0 ttl rexmit bytes sent, 0.000 bytes/second
6828 packets sent, 58.862 packets/second
0 connections opened, 0.000 conns/second
1 dupacks sent, 0.009 dupacks/second
0 rexmits sent, 0.000 rexmits/second
average RTT: 67.511 msecs
```

Graphical Programs

An excellent feature of tcptrace is that it can produce graphs showing the information displayed in the console mode options. Actually, saying that tcptrace produces graphs is a bit of a misnomer. In reality, it produces data files that can be used to produce graphs. To view the tcptrace graphs you must have either the xplot or jPlot program. Both of these applications can read the data in the tcptrace graph files and produce graphs showing the session information.

This section describes how to download and install both the xplot and jPlot applications.

xplot

The xplot application was developed by Tim Shepard at MIT for plotting information generated from the tcpdump application. The xplot application reads text files containing graphing instructions, and plots the necessary points, lines, and axis to visualize the graph.

WARNING xplot uses X-Windows to display the graphs. Both the X-Windows operating environment and the X-Window development library must be installed on the host system before compiling xplot. Most Unix systems install the X-Windows environment by default, but the development libraries must be installed separately. Consult your particular Unix distribution information regarding these files.

The main xplot Web site is located at http://www.xplot.org. At the time of this writing, the current xplot release was version 0.90, but an interim patch was released to fix a color problem that appears on some Unix systems. The interim release can be downloaded from the URL:

```
http://www.xplot.org/xplot/xplot-0.90.7.tar.gz
```

The xplot source code distribution file must be uncompressed and expanded into a working directory. As usual, you must run the configure program so the makefile will be created with the pertinent information for your system (including the specific location of the X-Window library files on the system). After the configure program finishes, you must run the make program to build the xplot executable file.

jPlot

The jPlot application was also developed at Ohio University as a Java version of xplot. It incorporates the features of xplot, including the ability to read xplot graph files. This allows jPlot to read and graph the xplot output files generated by tcptrace. Since it is a Java application, it can be used on any platform that supports Java. This enables you to view tcptrace files from almost any host platform.

NOTE At the time of this writing, the jPlot authors recommend using Java version 1.3 when using jPlot. Future versions of jPlot are expected to be compatible with newer versions of Java.

JPlot can also be downloaded from the tcptrace Web site. There is a separate link called Useful Companion Programs, that contains the links for downloading jPlot. There are two separate download files: one is a .tar.gz distribution for Unix platforms, and the other is a .zip distribution for Windows platforms:

```
http://irg.cs.ohiou.edu/software/tcptrace/jPlot/download/jPlot.1.0.0beta
.tar.gz
```

```
http://irg.cs.ohiou.edu/software/tcptrace/jPlot/download/jPlot.1.0.0beta
.zip
```

Both distributions include the same files. The jPlot distribution files contain all of the Java source code used to create the application, as well as a premade jar file that contains all of the compiled classes. With the jar file, you do not need to compile the source code; just use the jPlot.jar file to use the application.

To run jPlot, you must specify the jPlot.jar file in the -classpath command-line option, along with the jPlot application name:

```
java -classpath jPlot.jar jPlot file
```

Using tcptrace in Graphical Mode

After installing xplot or jPlot, you are ready to start graphing information contained in the captured sessions. This section describes how to produce graphs showing network performance features.

Standard Graphs

There are several command-line options that can be used to generate standard TCP information graphs from tcptrace. Table 10.5 lists the options.

The tcptrace graphing options behave differently than the console mode options. Instead of directly creating and displaying the graph, tcptrace creates data files used by xplot or jPlot to display one or more graphs. When you use the graphing options, by default, graphs are generated for all of the sessions contained in the dump file, two files for each session (one for each direction of the session). If there are lots of sessions in the dump file, this will create lots of graphs.

Throughput Graph

The -T option produces graphs showing the throughput of each session in the dump file. Each graph is identified by the session label (such as a2b), along with the tput identifier (indicating that it is a throughput graph), followed by an extension of .xpl:

```
$ tcptrace -T -o6 test1
1 arg remaining, starting with 'test1'
Ostermann's tcptrace -- version 6.2.0 -- Fri Jul 26, 2002

6828 packets seen, 6828 TCP packets traced
elapsed wallclock time: 0:00:00.241991, 28215 pkts/sec analyzed
trace file elapsed time: 0:01:56.243460
TCP connection info:
*** 1 packets were too short to process at some point
        (use -w option to show details)
  6: 192.168.1.1:20 - 192.168.1.2:1031 (k21) 1070>  688<  (complete)
$ ls -al *.xpl
-rw-r--r--    1 rich     rich        61401 Nov 21 09:35 k21_tput.xpl
-rw-r--r--    1 rich     rich          112 Nov 21 09:35 12k_tput.xpl
$
```

Table 10.5 Standard Graphs

OPTION	GRAPH
-T	Throughput
-R	Round-trip time
-S	Time sequence
-N	Outstanding data
-F	Segment size
-G	All graphs

As can be seen, you can use the -o option to limit the graphs produced to a specific session (or group of sessions). The tcptrace command shows the sessions that are graphed, along with the session label (k2l in this example). The graphs produced are k2l_tput.xpl and l2k_tput.xpl. Depending on the type of connection, one graph may have more useful information than the other (such as in an FTP transfer where the bulk of the information is being sent one way).

You can use the xplot or jPlot application to display either an individual session graph, each graph separately, or each graph in the same graph window. Figure 10.2 shows a sample throughput graph generated from a TCP session.

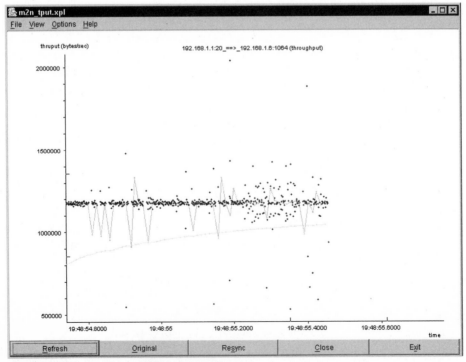

Figure 10.2 Sample throughput graph.

The throughput graph shows three types of data. The dots (shown in yellow, if in color) each represent the calculated throughput for each individual segment. This is calculated from the formula:

```
(segment size)/((end time of segment)-(end time of previous segment))
```

The varying line (shown in red, if in color) represents the throughput average over a set number of dot data points. By default, tcptrace uses the previous 10 data points to produce the average throughput. You can change this value using the -A command-line option, along with the number of data points to use in the average:

```
tcptrace -T -A5 test1
```

This command calculates the throughput average after every five data points. The curved line (shown in blue, if in color) shows the third type of data. This is the throughput average calculated from the start of the session up to the calculation point. This value will show the more consistent throughput value.

Both xplot and jPlot also allow you to zoom in on the graph to see more detail. As you can see in Figure 10.3, the data plotted produced a graph with a wide range of values. By selecting the more active area of the graph and zooming in, you can see more detail.

Time Sequence Graph

The -S option produces a time sequence graph. This graph is one of the most useful graphs for troubleshooting network problems. It shows the time sequence of how packets are sent, and how the receiving host acknowledges them. Lots of additional features are included in the time sequence graph, such as retransmitted packets and zero TCP window sizes. Figure 10.3 shows a sample time sequence graph of a single FTP session.

There are several different lines, shapes, and letters that appear on the time sequence graph. Table 10.6 describes what the different lines in the graph represent.

Table 10.6 Time Sequence Graph Lines

OBJECT	DESCRIPTION
Yellow line	The receive window size as advertised by the receiver
Green line	The ACK values returned by the receiver
Green ticks	Duplicate ACKS detected
Yellow ticks	Duplicate receive window size advertised

(continued)

Table 10.6   *(continued)*

OBJECT	DESCRIPTION
White arrows	Sent packet segment, showing the SEQ numbers contained in the packet
Red Arrow	Duplicate (retransmitted) packet segments
White diamond	A packet segment that contained the TCP PUSH flag

By observing the lines in the graph, you can see the characteristics of the session. Under normal conditions, the slopes of the lines should mirror each other, and represent the throughput of the packets. You can zoom in on a section of the graph to see how the packet segments are sent to the receiver. There should be multiple packets sent to the receiver, up to the next window-size level (the yellow line). When the packet segments match the window size, you should see the ACK value reach the window size, and a new window size is generated. This cycle continues until all of the data has been transmitted.

Besides the plotted lines, you may see several different characters appear on the graph. Table 10.7 describes what these characters represent.

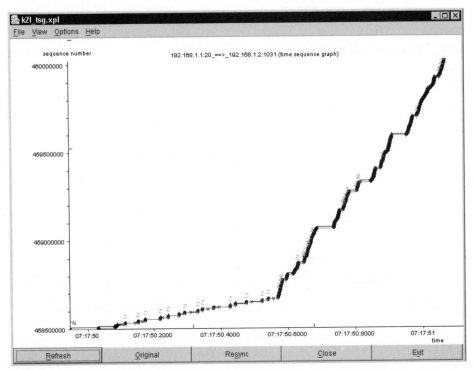

Figure 10.3 Sample time sequence graph.

Table 10.7   Time Sequence Graph Characters

CHARACTER	DESCRIPTION
SYN	A TCP SYN flag detected (indicating the start of a session)
R	A retransmitted segment (shown by the red arrow line)
3	A triple duplicate ACK of a segment
HD	A hardware duplicate address detected
P	A zero window size probe packet
U	A TCP URGENT flag detected (indicating special data)
S	A selective ACK (ACKing packets before the window size reached)
O	An out-of-order packet
Z	A zero window size advertisement by the receiver
CE	Congestion experienced
CWR	Congestion window reduced

You can use these objects to determine the flow of the session, and see if a device is sending lots of zero window size packets.

Traffic Module Graphs

Besides the standard command-line options for generating graphs, the traffic module contains several options for producing graphs of its own. Each graph is identified by an option under the -xtraffic command-line option. As mentioned in the *Using Module Options* section, you must enclose module options in single quotes after the module name:

```
tcptrace -xtraffic'-A' test1
```

Lots of different types of graphs can be generated from the traffic module. Table 10.8 lists the graphs that are available, and their option names.

Table 10.8   Traffic Module Graphs

OPTION	FILENAME	DESCRIPTION
-A	traffic_active.xpl	Active connections
-B	traffic_bytes.xpl	Bytes per second
-C	traffic_openclose.xpl	Open and Closed session totals

(continued)

Table 10.8 *(continued)*

OPTION	FILENAME	DESCRIPTION
-H	traffic_halfopen.xpl	Half-open connections
-K	traffic_pureacks.xpl	Pure ACKs per second
-L	traffic_loss.xpl	Losses per second
-O	traffic_open.xpl	Open connections
-I	traffic_I_open.xpl	Instantaneous open connections
-P	traffic_packets.xpl	Packets per second
-Q	traffic_idle.xpl	Idle connections
-R	traffic_rtt.xpl	Round-trip time
-T	traffic_data.xpl	Total data sent
-D	traffic_long.xpl	Long-duration connections
-G		Produce all graphs

Most of the traffic module graphs separate out information based on TCP port number; thus, each graph will show multiple lines, one for each port present in the session. Like standard graphs, the traffic module graphs show individual data points, along with separate lines to show averages.

Summary

The tcptrace application is an excellent way to decode network captures performed using the tcpdump (or a similar) package. Instead of having to pore over line after line of trace information, you can look at the perfectly formatted tcptrace information.

tcptrace can produce information in two separate formats. The first format is as text output, showing each detected TCP session, along with pertinent TCP information for the session. This allows you to see which sessions are using the most bandwidth on the network, and which sessions are experiencing network problems, such as retransmitted packets.

The second tcptrace output format is a graphical mode. Graph files are produced of the TCP session information found in the dump file. You must use the xplot or jPlot graphing programs to analyze the graphing data. Often, being able to see the data graphed out allows trends and abnormalities to be seen more easily.

The next chapter describes another application that analyzes existing network data. The ntop application produces graphical results of real-time network data as seen from the monitoring device. This allows you to monitor actual data to look for network problems as they occur, as well as see cumulative network information, such as protocol distribution. With this feature, you can easily see what types of traffic are present on your network, and the percentage of bandwidth they are consuming.

ntop

The ntop application demonstrates still another type of network performance tool. ntop monitors network traffic that traverses the host network connection. By analyzing packet headers, ntop can watch for trends in the network traffic, and display charts and graphs showing network application trends. This can be extremely helpful when you don't know what types of packets are present on busy networks, or which hosts generate or receive the bulk of the network traffic. This chapter describes how to install and configure ntop to monitor network traffic on your network, and shows you how to use its information to watch your network performance.

The ntop application was developed at the University of Pisa in Italy to help network administrators determine which devices are consuming the most resources on a network. Like the Unix top program, which shows what programs consume the most system resources, ntop shows network usage based on which hosts and protocols are consuming the most network resources. Identifying applications and hosts that are the most active on the network often allows you to rearrange existing network resources to accommodate the traffic patterns.

What Is ntop?

The ntop application consists of a single program (ntop) that provides the following functions:

- Monitors network packets on a host network interface
- Stores packet header information in a local database
- Provides a Web interface for users to display network information using charts and graphs

The ntop application uses the libpcap Unix packet capture library for all of its packet capturing (see Chapter 2, "Watching Network Traffic," for more information on the libpcap library). Once the packet is captured, ntop places the header information into a database (either a proprietary ntop database or a standard SQL database, such as mySQL). ntop is not concerned about the data contents of the packets. Instead, it only reads the pertinent IP, TCP, or UDP header information to determine the who, what, where, and when of the network traffic. This information is stored in the database, and can be retrieved using a standard Web browser from any network client.

There are two classes of information that can be retrieved from the ntop database:

- Network traffic measurements
- Network traffic monitoring

The following sections describe how ntop is used to record and observe these two classes of traffic information.

Traffic Measuring

The ntop application can be used to determine the network bandwidth utilization on a local network. Both the total network bandwidth utilization and individual host bandwidth utilization are tracked by analyzing the packets on the network. Here are some of the bandwidth elements that are tracked by ntop.

Data Received

The ntop application tracks how much data is received by each host identified on the network (the destination host in the IP header). The data is displayed in five different categories, shown in Table 11.1.

Table 11.1   Data Received Categories

CATEGORY	DESCRIPTION
Protocol	Displays data received by protocol (such as IP, IPX, Decnet, and Appletalk)
TCP/UDP	Displays data received by TCP/UDP application port (such as FTP, Telnet, SMTP, and DNS)
Throughput	Displays bits per second of received data (shown as actual, average, and peak throughput)
Host Activity	Displays the time of day each host was actively receiving data
NetFlows	Shows NetFlow activity

Each of these categories displays the received data information in chart format. The chart is sorted based on the received data rate. This feature allows you to see which hosts are receiving the most data on the network. It can be used to identify busy servers that could be segmented to another place on the network to increase performance.

Data Sent

The ntop application also tracks the sending hosts, and the type of data sent by each host. As with the data received, the data sent is displayed in five different categories (the same categories as for the received data). Each of these categories displays the sent data information in chart format. The chart is sorted based on the sent data rate. This feature allows you to see which hosts are sending the most data on the network. Often, busy clients can be moved to switched environments to help distribute the network load.

Network Throughput

The network throughput is displayed using graphs, showing the average network load at different points of time. The first graph shows the network throughput for the last 60 minutes. If ntop has been running longer than one hour, a second graph is generated, showing a 24-hour graph of network throughput. If ntop has been running longer than one day, a third graph is generated, showing a 30-day graph of network throughput. These additional graphs can be used to see trends in network throughput, or to determine if any one day of the week or time of day demonstrates a higher network throughput than any other.

Traffic Monitoring

Besides seeing how much data is traversing the network, ntop also provides information on the type of traffic that is present. This information can help you determine what applications are consuming bandwidth on the network, and take appropriate actions. This section describes the different types of data ntop monitors.

Statistics

The ntop application maintains statistics for different packet features. These statistics show how much traffic of a specific type has been seen by ntop, as well as indicating which hosts have produced the different types of network traffic.

Multicast

The Multicast statistic display shows a chart containing information about each host that has either sent or received multicast packets on the network. The *multicast packets received* category indicates the type of multicast packets, using the standard multicast network addresses. You can track multicast applications by the network address used in the multicast.

Traffic

The Traffic statistic displays information about all the packets captured by ntop. It produces five separate pie charts, showing:

- Packet destination type (multicast, broadcast, or unicast)
- Packet size
- Packet protocol (IP, fragmented IP, or non-IP)
- IP TTL values
- Remote host distance (hop counts)

This basic information about the packets traversing the network can be used as an overall barometer to determine the health of the network. You can often tell if the network is experiencing problems by comparing these values against values recorded during normal network activity.

Hosts

The Hosts statistic chart shows network throughput for each host seen on the network, sorted by the most active. This display shows the hostname (if found), the IP address and MAC address of the host, and a bar graph showing the relative bandwidth consumption of the host. This chart makes it easy to find busy hosts on the network.

Domains

The Domains statistic chart shows all of the network domains found in host-names listed as either the source or destination of captured packets. Each domain name is listed with its bytes sent and received statistics, and a percentage of the total network traffic that the domain data represents.

IP Traffic

The ntop application monitors all IP traffic seen on the network interface and divides it into three categories, based on the location of both hosts in an IP session. The statistics for each category are displayed in separate data charts.

Remote to Local

This chart displays network traffic sent by remotely located hosts destined for hosts on the local network. The hostname and IP address, along with the total bytes sent and received for each remote host, are displayed in the chart. At the bottom of the chart, the total bandwidth consumption from this traffic is shown. These statistics show how much network traffic is generated from remote hosts sending data to local hosts.

Local to Remote

This chart displays network traffic sent by hosts on the local network destined for hosts on remote networks. Again, the hostname and IP address, along with the total bytes sent and received, are displayed in the chart.

Local to Local

The local to local chart displays network traffic sent by hosts on the local network destined for other hosts on the local network. As with the other categories, the hostname and IP address for each local host is shown, along with the total bytes sent and received.

IP Protocols

Besides separating the network traffic by host, ntop also keeps statistics for each protocol within the IP packets, such as TCP and UDP. Each IP application is tracked to determine which hosts are using it (local or remote hosts), and how much traffic it has generated. This information allows you to monitor which network applications are consuming the most network bandwidth.

Distribution

The Distribution statistics appear in both a pie chart and a text chart, showing how the IP applications are distributed between local and remote hosts. Each category is shown within the pie chart, allowing you to see which hosts are contributing the most to the network bandwidth.

Besides the pie chart, each category of traffic is shown in a separate data chart, showing exactly which IP application (shown by TCP or UDP service name) is producing traffic on the network. The traffic is displayed using both raw numbers of bytes seen and a bar graph showing the percentage of the overall network traffic contributed by the application.

Usage

The Usage statistics chart shows each individual IP service detected in the network traffic. Both the service name (such as Telnet or FTP) and the TCP or UDP port number assigned to the service are displayed. After the service information, the clients and servers that were seen using the service are displayed.

This information can be used to detect which IP applications are being used on the network, along with the clients and servers that are using the applications.

Sessions

The Sessions statistics chart shows all active IP sessions detected on the network. Each session is displayed in a separate chart, showing the hosts involved in the session, the session start and end times, and how long the session has been active. The amount of data sent and received in the session is also displayed in the chart.

Routers

If any routers are detected on the network, ntop shows the Router statistics chart, which displays each detected router and the hosts that have forwarded packets through the router.

It is usually common knowledge what routers are connected to a network. However, it is also possible for ordinary hosts to unwittingly act as routers, if they have multiple network cards connected to separate networks. The ntop application can detect and display these hosts and the hosts that have been forwarding packets through them. This can help you detect back doors to the network and block them.

Before Installing ntop

There are a few things that you must do on the host system before installing and running ntop. This section describes these functions, and explains how to prepare the system for ntop.

Creating the ntop User ID

Although the ntop application must be started by the root user (so it can access the promiscuous mode on the network card), after it starts it can switch to using a normal user account on the sytstem. This feature should be used if at all possible, because it can help prevent hackers from having control of the host if they happen to break into the ntop program.

The user ID created for ntop should have extremely limited privileges on the host system. Ideally, it should not have write permission on any system area of the file system (such as /usr/sbin or /etc), limiting the damage that can be done if ntop is compromised.

Different Unix systems have different ways to create new user accounts. Most Linux systems use the adduser program. There are lots of fancy options, depending on your Linux environment and how you create new users. The default method:

```
# adduser ntop
```

(1) creates the user ntop, using the next available user ID number, (2) creates a group called ntop, using the next available group ID number, and (3) creates a home directory ntop in the default home directory location (usually /home). By default, the ntop user will have full permissions for its home directory, and limited access to system areas (read only). You can take advantage of the ntop home directory to place all ntop-related database and log files there. This ensures that the ntop user will have access to the necessary files, and that other users on the system will not be able to modify them.

NOTE If you do not want to automatically create a home directory for ntop, use the -M command-line option for adduser.

Loading Support Software

There are plenty of support packages that must be present on the host system for ntop to compile and run properly. Besides the normal C compiler programs and libraries, ntop also requires:

- The autoconf and automake programs
- The gawk program
- The gdbm packages (including development files)
- The libpcap library

- The OpenSSL package (if you want to use secure HTTP connections)

- The mySQL package (if you want to use a mySQL database to store information)

The autoconf and automake packages are installed by default on most Linux distributions. If you are using another type of Unix platform, you may have to download these packages and install them yourself. Both of these packages can be found at the GNU Foundation Web site (http://www.gnu.org).

WARNING At the time of this writing, the current stable version of ntop, 2.1.3, could work with most of the recent versions of autoconf. Unfortunately, the current development version of ntop, 2.1.51, requires the latest version of autoconf, 2.50, or higher. I assume that this will be the case when this development version becomes the latest stable version. In this case, you may have to upgrade the autoconf program on your Unix distribution to compile ntop.

Downloading and Installing ntop

The main Web site for ntop is located at http://www.ntop.org. From this main page, there is a download link, which points to the ntop area on the Source-Forge download server.

The main SourceForge Web page shows the current development release source code available for download (currently 2.1.50). To see the latest stable ntop release, click the *View ALL Project Files* link. This page shows all of the available ntop distribution downloads.

The stable release represents the ntop distribution that is known to work in most Unix environments. You can download the stable source code distribution, or the RPM binary distribution, from the SourceForge download Web site. At the time of this writing, the current stable source code distribution of ntop can be downloaded from the URL:

```
http://prdownloads/sourceforge.net/ntop/ntop-2.1.3.tar.gz?download
```

This link takes you to a download area, which allows you to select the server from which to download the distribution file. The source code distribution file is a standard .tar.gz file, which needs to be uncompressed and expanded into a working directory, using the tar command.

NOTE Alternately, you can download the binary RPM distribution, and use the RPM installation program to install it. The RPM package will check the system for software dependencies, and inform you if any additional software packages are required.

Compiling and Installing gdchart

To create all of the fancy graphs used on the Web pages, ntop uses the gdchart application. gdchart is an open source application that provides libraries for easily drawing graphs and pie charts. Before you can begin the ntop compile, you must first compile and install the gdchart library. Fortunately, this package is included with the ntop source code distribution. The gdchart distribution is located under the ntop-2.1.3 directory in the gdchart0.94c subdirectory. This contains the source code for gdchart and its required libraries. You must create the library files for each of the required packages before compiling gdchart, and subsequently, ntop.

To start off, change to the gdchart0.94c directory, and run the configure program. This creates the makefile for the gdchart libraries. However, before you can build the gdchart libraries, you must create the libraries that it requires (the gd and zlib libraries). The gd libraries are used to create PNG and JPEG images, which are used to display the fancy graphs on the ntop Web page. The zlib library is used for data compression of the graphs.

First, you must create the zlib library. This is located in the directory zlib-1.1.4, under the gdchart0.94c directory. After changing to this directory, run the standard configure and make programs to create the zlib library files.

Next, you must create the libpng library. Change to the gd-1.8.3/libpng-1.2.1 directory (in case you are getting lost in directories, you should now be in the ntop-2.1.3/gdchart0.94c/gd-1.8.3/libpng-1.2.1 directory). Instead of using the configure program, the libpng application contains sample makefiles for different Unix platforms in the scripts directory. Each platform makefile is named makefile.*platform*, where *platform* represents your Unix distribution name (such as hpux, linux, macosx, and so on).

> ■■■■**WARNING** While the makefile samples are created for different Unix platforms, there is one exception to this rule. If your Unix distribution is using the GNU C compiler (gcc), you should use the makefile.gcc sample file, no matter what your Unix distribution is.

Copy the appropriate makefile for your particular Unix distribution to the libpng-1.2.1 directory (make sure you rename it Makefile):

```
[rich@shadrach libpng-1.2.1]$ cp scripts/makefile.gcc Makefile
```

Now that there is a makefile, you can run the standard make command to build the proper libpng libraries.

Now that you've created all of the necessary libraries, you can finally compile the gdchart library. Go to the gdchart0.94c directory, and run the make program. If all went well, you should get a clean compile, which creates the library file libgdchart.a.

NOTE If you are using the GNU C compiler to build ntop, you can run the
buildAll.sh script in the gdchart0.94c directory to perform all of the above
steps automatically.

As a last step before compiling ntop, it is a good idea to install the gdchart
and zlib libraries on the host system. While some systems do not require this
step to compile ntop, many do. To install the libraries, change to the appropriate directories, and run the make program with the install option (make
install) as the root user.

NOTE The libpng library does not include an install option in the makefile.
ntop will need to find this library to compile properly. You must copy the
libpng.a file to a common library directory on your system (such as /usr/lib),
or to the ntop distribution working directory.

Compiling ntop

Now that all of the pieces are ready, you can begin the ntop compile process.
You may notice that ntop does not have a configure script in the working
directory. The ntop distribution uses a different script file to create the configure program script: autogen.sh.

The autogen.sh script is located in the ntop-2.1.3/ntop directory. When you
run the autogen.sh script, it will automatically build the configure script, and
run it. You will see the standard configure script output, looking for packages
and files within the system. After the autogen.sh script finishes, it displays a
message showing the ntop configuration that will be created by the compiler.

If you are satisfied with the compiler options, you can run the make program to create the ntop executable file. After creating the executable file, you
can install it to the installation directory by running the make program with
the install option (again as root user).

Running ntop

The ntop program is an extremely versatile application, which allows you to
specify many options for how it runs. Unfortunately, with versatility comes
complexity. There are lots of command-line options that must be set for ntop to
work properly. This section describes how to get started using ntop for your
network environment.

Starting ntop for the First Time

The first time you run ntop, it must create the databases that it needs to track network information, as well as set the password used by the administrator account (called admin). This requires a special session to be started, separate from a normal ntop session.

Since ntop attempts to place the network interface cards in promiscuous mode, you must be the root user to start ntop. The -A command-line option is used to tell ntop to prompt for the admin password, and to stop ntop. You will also want to use the -P option, which allows you to specify where the ntop database files will be located. The easiest place to put them is in the newly created home directory for ntop, /home/ntop. You will also probably want to use the -u option, which allows you to specify ntop to run as the ntop user ID.

A sample ntop first session should look like this:

```
# /usr/local/bin/ntop -P /home/ntop -u ntop -A
04/Dec/2002 19:34:39 Initializing GDBM...
04/Dec/2002 19:34:39 Started thread (1026) for network packet analyser.
04/Dec/2002 19:34:39 Started thread (2051) for idle hosts detection.
04/Dec/2002 19:34:39 Started thread (3076) for DNS address resolution.
04/Dec/2002 19:34:39 Started thread (4101) for address purge.

Please enter the password for the admin user:
Please enter the password again:
04/Dec/2002 19:34:46 Admin user password has been set.
#
```

The admin user password is used for changing settings and permissions from the ntop Web interface. Be sure to set the password to something that will not easily be determined (but, of course, don't forget what you set it to).

After the admin password is set, ntop will exit back to the command prompt. You can see what files were created by looking in the /home/ntop directory (or whatever directory you specified as the default directory):

```
# ls -l /home/ntop
total 160
-rw-rw-r--   1 root     root        12288 Dec  4 13:36 LsWatch.db
-rw-r--r--   1 root     root        12348 Dec  4 14:12 addressCache.db
-rw-r--r--   1 root     root        19184 Dec  4 14:12 dnsCache.db
-rw-r--r--   1 root     root        12288 Dec  4 13:34 hostsInfo.db
-rw-r--r--   1 root     root        12437 Dec  4 13:36 ntop_pw.db
-rw-r--r--   1 root     root        12517 Dec  4 13:36 prefsCache.db
#
```

These files are the database files (in gdbm format) used to contain all of the network information retrieved from the network monitoring. The ntop Web interface can be used to extract the information from these databases.

ntop Command-Line Parameters

After the first run of ntop to create the database files and the admin password, you are ready to start ntop for real. There are lots of command-line parameters that can be used when starting ntop. Table 11.2 shows some of the more common command-line parameters, and what they are used for.

Table 11.2 ntop Command-Line Parameters

PARAMETER	DESCRIPTION
-a	Specifies the location of the Web server access log
-c	Specifies that idle hosts are not purged from the database
-d	Runs ntop as a daemon process
-f	Specifies a traffic dump file
-i	Specifies interface name (or names) to monitor
-l	Specifies a file to dump captured packets to
-p	Specifies the TCP/UDP protocols to monitor
-q	Creates a file in which to place suspicious-looking packets found on the network
-u	Specifies the username or ID of a user ntop should run as after initializing
-w	Specifies the HTTP server port number (the default is 3000)
-A	Prompt to set the admin password
-B	Specifies a tcpdump expression for filtering monitored packets
-L	Sends all ntop output to the syslog instead of standard output
-M	Merges data from all network interfaces instead of keeping them separate
-O	Specifies a directory in which to place captured packets (if enabled)
-P	Specifies a directory in which to place ntop database files
-S	Saves traffic information on shutdown (default is start fresh on each startup)
-W	Specifies for ntop to run in secure web mode, and sets the port number (default is 3001)

Using ntop Command-Line Parameters

With a plethora of different command-line options, you can fine-tune ntop to perform many different monitoring functions. The amount and type of traffic that ntop monitors greatly depend on where it is plugged into the network. This section describes some different scenarios for using ntop, and explains how to configure ntop to produce meaningful information for the scenario.

Monitoring Network Traffic

The most basic use for ntop is to allow an existing network device to monitor network traffic. When using an existing host, you will most likely want to place the ntop log and database files in a separate directory apart from the normal system files, allowing only the ntop user ID access to them. You will also want to run ntop as a background process, and redirect any messages generated by ntop to the standard system log.

The following command shows ntop running as a daemon process, using the /home/ntop directory for the database files and for the HTTP access log. Any standard ntop messages will be logged in the normal system log file, using syslog:

```
# /usr/local/bin/ntop -d -P /home/ntop -u ntop -a /home/ntop/access.log
-L
Wait please: ntop is coming up...
#
```

That's it—no other information is displayed on the terminal. All of the ntop information is sent to the standard log file for your Unix system. On my Linux distribution, it is placed in the /var/log/messages file.

Note that there are several separate threads started for various ntop functions. If you look at the running processes, you should see each of the ntop threads running:

```
# ps ax | grep ntop
1878 ?    S    0:00 /usr/local/bin/ntop -d -P /home/ntop -u ntop -L -a /h
1879 ?    S    0:00 /usr/local/bin/ntop -d -P /home/ntop -u ntop -L -a /h
1880 ?    S    0:00 /usr/local/bin/ntop -d -P /home/ntop -u ntop -L -a /h
1881 ?    S    0:00 /usr/local/bin/ntop -d -P /home/ntop -u ntop -L -a /h
1882 ?    S    0:00 /usr/local/bin/ntop -d -P /home/ntop -u ntop -L -a /h
1883 ?    S    0:00 /usr/local/bin/ntop -d -P /home/ntop -u ntop -L -a /h
1884 ?    S    0:00 /usr/local/bin/ntop -d -P /home/ntop -u ntop -L -a /h
1885 ?    S    0:00 /usr/local/bin/ntop -d -P /home/ntop -u ntop -L -a /h
#
```

In this instance, there are eight total ntop processes running on the system after ntop is started.

Analyzing a tcpdump Dump File

The ntop application can also be used to analyze sessions contained in a tcp-dump file. The -f option tells ntop to take its network data from a stored tcp-dump file instead of from a network interface. This feature can be invaluable in analyzing captured network traffic.

Remember that once the dump file has been read by ntop, all of the data will be available on the ntop Web page interface. No additional data will be captured from the network interface(s). Depending on the data present in the dump file, it is possible that not all of the ntop statistics pages will have useful information. Figure 11.1 shows a sample statistics page from a sample FTP session captured by tcpdump.

The ntop chart shows both hosts involved in the FTP transfer. You can click on either host IP address to display detailed statistics about the host, and the data that was transferred.

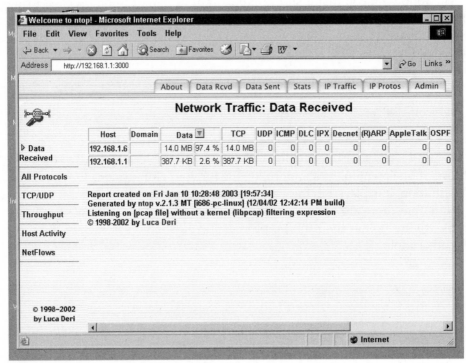

Figure 11.1 ntop data received window.

ntop Access Log File

Each time the ntop Web server is accessed, it logs the access into a log file as an entry. By default, the log file is ntop.access.log, and is located in the directory from which ntop was started (assuming that the user ID that ntop is running under has write permissions to the directory). You can use the -a option to specify an alternate location for the access log file (as shown in the previous command-line example).

Each item retrieved from the ntop Web server is logged in the database, creating quite a lot of entries for a single access. A few sample entries look like:

```
192.168.1.6 - - [04/Dec/2002:18:23:39 -0500] - "GET / HTTP/1.1" 200 1484 4
192.168.1.6 - - [04/Dec/2002:18:23:39 -0500] - "GET /index_top.html
HTTP/1.1"  200 2301 5
192.168.1.6 - - [04/Dec/2002:18:23:39 -0500] - "GET /index_inner.html
HTTP/1.1" 200 1443 4
192.168.1.6 - - [04/Dec/2002:18:23:39 -0500] - "GET /home.html HTTP/1.1"
200 1056/3046 22
192.168.1.6 - - [04/Dec/2002:18:23:39 -0500] - "GET /functions.js
HTTP/1.1" 404 675 0
192.168.1.6 - - [04/Dec/2002:18:23:39 -0500] - "GET /functions.js
HTTP/1.1" 200 624/1740 8
```

The entries are recorded using the standard Apache Web server log format. The remote host IP address, the time the access occurred, the file downloaded, and information about the bytes transferred are displayed.

Viewing ntop Data

Using the ntop Web interface puts lots of network data at your disposal. Most of the data charts and graphs are fairly self-explanatory. This section guides you through some of the data, explaining which pieces to watch to gain information about your network.

Connecting to ntop

The ntop application contains a built-in Web server, so connecting to ntop is a snap. By default, the ntop Web server listens to TCP port 3000, so it should not interfere with any other Web servers running on the host (unless, of course, they too are using port 3000). You can always change the Web server port, using the -w command-line parameter. After connecting to the ntop host, you should see the main ntop Web page.

There are five network information categories to choose from, along with one administration category. To access the individual categories from this page, you must click on one of the tabs at the top of the page:

- Data Rcvd contains information about received data.

- Data Sent contains information about sent data.

- Stats contains information about packets (packet size, packet type, and network load).

- IP Traffic contains information about IP packet trends (senders and receivers).

- IP Protos contains information about IP application distribution.

- Admin allows you to reset statistics, shut down the server, and create and modify ntop users.

When you click on each of the general tabs, a new frame appears on the left side of the window, providing additional menu items to select. Each menu contains links to additional Web pages that contain the individual charts and graphs used to display the data.

Watching Hosts

The information about each host captured by ntop is stored in the ntop database. You can easily find information about individual hosts in the Data Rcvd and Data Sent sections. The main charts for these categories show the protocols, activity times, and throughputs for each host detected on the network. Figure 11.2 shows a sample throughput chart for the Data Rcvd category.

This chart displays the actual, average, and peak throughput for each host detected, in both bits per second and packets per second. This information can be used to detect busy hosts on the network.

By clicking on a single host entry, you can see the overall information about that host. Figure 11.3 shows an individual host information Web page.

Lots of useful information is available on the host information page. The Total Data Sent entry shows not only the total amount of data sent, but also if there was any data sent in retransmitted packets. A high percentage value here could indicate a network problem.

You can also compare the Sent vs. Recvd packets and data lines. In this example, the packets sent and received are close, but the data is vastly different. This indicates that most of the data was sent from the host to the remote device, although the packet counts were similar. Most likely, an acknowledgment packet was sent for almost every data packet. This could be indicative of a small TCP window size on the host or the client.

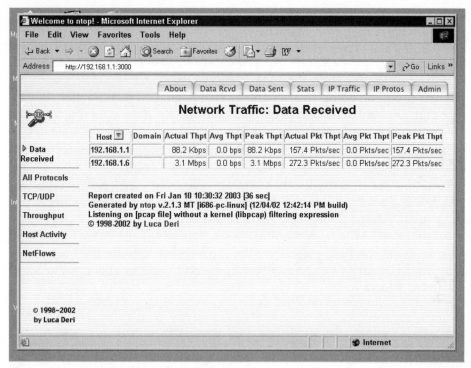

Figure 11.2   Data Rcvd host throughput chart.

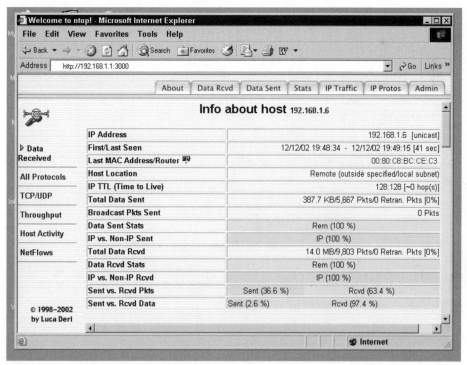

Figure 11.3   ntop host information page.

Watching Network Traffic

The ntop application also provides charts and graphs allowing you to monitor the overall network performance. The most obvious graph is the Network Load page, available under the Stats category tab.

By watching the graph(s) available on that page, you can monitor the network segment load at each time of the day or week. Often, data trends can be detected, such as high data volumes that are present at the same time of day (or day of the week). Remote host backups and regular file transfers often cause this. Figure 11.4 shows a sample network load graph.

When ntop is first started, only a single graph is displayed, showing the network load values for the last 60 minutes. After ntop has been running for an hour, a second graph is displayed on the same page, showing the network load for the previous 24 hours. After ntop has been running for a day, a third graph is displayed on the same page, showing the network load for the previous 30 days. This information can be used to help detect trends, or allow you to detect odd network loads.

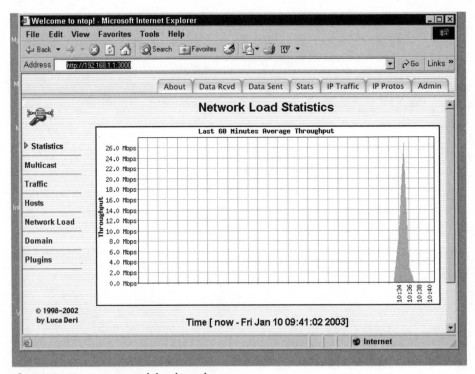

Figure 11.4 ntop network load graph.

Summary

The ntop application monitors network activity, and stores statistical information about the traffic. You can access the statistical information using the ntop Web page, which provides an easy, graphical way to analyze the network information.

The ntop application provides information about the type of traffic seen on the network. This includes protocols, applications, hosts, and network bandwidth. Using this information, you can easily monitor and analyze what is happening on the network. You can use the protocol distribution information to determine what protocols are prevalent on the network. The application information shows which applications (such as Telnet, FTP, or HTTP) are producing the most network traffic, and what hosts are participating in the applications.

Since the ntop data can be accessed via any Web browser, you do not even need to be located on the same network as the ntop host. You can access the ntop network information from any location that can access the host via HTTP. If the host is accessible from the Internet, you can access your network information from anywhere.

The next chapter rounds off the network performance tools section by showing a few network scenarios, and explaining which tools could be used to determine network performance. When you know what tools to use when, you can quickly and easily determine network performance, and possibly determine solutions to network problems.

## CHAPTER 12

Comparing Network Performance Tools

Now that you have a toolkit full of tools to use for network performance testing, its time to learn when to use each one while troubleshooting your network. This chapter first presents a simple wrap-up of each tool, describing what each is best at. This should provide you with a handy one-stop-shopping reference guide to the tools. Next, different scenarios are presented, showing how different tools can be used both to test networks and to gather different types of network information.

Each of the network performance testing tools presented in this book has unique characteristics. By knowing when to use each tool, you can make the most of your network-testing time, and find network problems more quickly. To recap, the network performance tools are:

- netperf
- dbs
- Iperf
- Pathrate
- Nettest
- NetLogger
- tcptrace
- ntop

Tools for Testing the Network

The first class of tools is those that send test data across the network to determine network characteristics. These tools provide a way for you to determine the overall throughput of the network, along with some basic characteristics, such as network speed and dropped packets.

One of the biggest complaints of network customers is network response times. The network administrator must always be aware of the network performance, and how it affects application response times for customers. Having tools available to help detect when network response times are slowing down can be an advantage for all network administrators.

The main feature of many of the network performance tools is the ability to test network bandwidth and response times. Since there are many different ways to transmit data across the network, there are also many different tests that can be performed on the network to measure response times. The two most common methods of transferring data across the network are:

- Bulk data transfers, such as network copies and FTP sessions
- Request/response pairs, such as HTTP sessions between Web browsers and servers

This section shows how to use the proper network tool to help troubleshoot problems with the different types of network traffic.

Bulk Data Transfers

Bulk data transfers, such as FTP sessions and file copies, are often difficult to diagnose when customers begin having response time problems. Often, performing a simple ping of the remote host proves nothing, as the simple ping packet has no problem reaching the host, and can possibly even reach the host in normal time. The problem is often due to dropped packets, causing packet retransmissions.

However, that is not the only cause of poor response time in bulk data transfers. Bulk data transfers are dependent on many different variables:

- How quickly the sending host can read the data from its disk
- How quickly the receiving host can write data to its disk
- How much data the receiving host can accept at a time (TCP window size)
- The network bottleneck speed between the two hosts
- The network utilization at the time of the data transfer

Often, before anyone even looks at the server variables, it is the network administrator's responsibility to prove that the network is not the cause of the poor response times. You must devise a strategy for quickly determining if the network is the source of the poor response time.

A strategy to use for testing bulk data transfer problems is to examine the network path between the two endpoints. You must determine both the maximum network speed between the two endpoints and the actual network bandwidth available for the application during normal production hours. The following sections describe how to use the different tools to accomplish this.

Using Pathrate to Find the Network Bottleneck

The first step is to determine the maximum network speed available between the two hosts. This value will greatly affect the overall performance of the data transfer. As discussed in Chapter 1, "Defining Network Performance," even though the hosts may be connected to the network at high speeds, there could always be a limiting link between the host connections. Your job is to find the limiting link.

The Pathrate application attempts to determine the overall throughput between two endpoints on the network. This will give you an idea of the network connectivity between the hosts having the data transfer problems.

Ideally, you should place the two Pathrate hosts on the same segments as the data transfer hosts (or even use the same hosts, if they are Unix devices). This will provide the best information about the network links.

> **NOTE** If you are using separate hosts for the Pathrate test, make sure that they connect to the network at the same speeds as the actual hosts.

The Pathrate application uses two programs: (1) pathrate_snd, to wait for client connections, and (2) pathrate_rcv, to connect to the remote host running pathrate_snd. Performing the Pathrate test on two hosts produces the following result:

```
$ ./pathrate_rcv 192.168.1.6
pathrate run from 192.168.1.1 to 192.168.1.6 on Wed Dec 11 19:20:11 2002

--> Minimum acceptable packet pair dispersion: 42 usec
-- Maximum train length discovery --
        Train length: 2 ->        9.7 Mbps
        Train length: 3 ->        9.7 Mbps
        Train length: 4 ->        9.7 Mbps
        Train length: 5 ->        9.7 Mbps
        Train length: 6 ->        9.7 Mbps
        Train length: 8 ->        9.7 Mbps
        Train length: 10 ->       9.7 Mbps
```

```
        Train length: 12 ->        9.7 Mbps
        Train length: 16 ->        9.7 Mbps
        Train length: 20 ->        9.7 Mbps
        Train length: 24 ->        9.6 Mbps
        Train length: 28 ->        9.7 Mbps
        Train length: 32 ->        9.7 Mbps
        Train length: 36 ->        9.6 Mbps
        Train length: 40 ->        9.7 Mbps
        Train length: 44 ->        9.7 Mbps
        Train length: 48 ->        9.7 Mbps
        --> Maximum train length: 48 packets


-- Preliminary measurements with increasing packet train lengths --
Train length:2 -> 9.7Mbps 9.6Mbps 9.7Mbps 9.7Mbps 9.7Mbps 9.7Mbps
9.7Mbps
Train length:3 -> 9.7Mbps 9.7Mbps 9.7Mbps 9.7Mbps 9.7Mbps 9.7Mbps
9.7Mbps
Train length:4 -> 9.8Mbps 9.7Mbps 9.8Mbps 9.8Mbps 9.7Mbps 9.8Mbps
9.7Mbps
Train length:5 -> 9.7Mbps 9.7Mbps 9.7Mbps 9.7Mbps 9.7Mbps 9.7Mbps
9.8Mbps
Train length:6 -> 9.7Mbps 9.7Mbps 9.7Mbps 9.7Mbps 9.7Mbps 9.7Mbps
9.7Mbps
Train length:7 -> 9.7Mbps 9.7Mbps 9.7Mbps 9.7Mbps 9.7Mbps 9.7Mbps
9.8Mbps
Train length:8 -> 9.7Mbps 9.7Mbps 9.7Mbps 9.7Mbps 9.7Mbps 9.7Mbps
9.7Mbps
Train length:9 -> 9.7Mbps 9.7Mbps 9.7Mbps 9.7Mbps 9.7Mbps 9.7Mbps
9.7Mbps
Train length:10-> 9.7Mbps 9.7Mbps 9.7Mbps 9.7Mbps 9.7Mbps 9.7Mbps
9.7Mbps
        --> Resolution:  2 kbps


--> Coefficient of variation: 0.000
    Sufficiently low measurement noise - `Quick-termination'
------------------------------------------------
Final capacity estimate :  9.7 Mbps  to  9.7 Mbps
------------------------------------------------


$
```

As can be seen from the Pathrate output, the estimated network bottleneck speed between the two devices is 9.7 Mbps. This would be consistent with a 10-Mb network connection. This shows that somewhere along the network path, a 10-Mb connection is the limiting link.

The fact that a 10-Mb connection is the limiting link doesn't mean that it is the cause of the poor response times. If this network configuration has always been there, the customers should not have noticed any difference in performance. The next step is to determine if something has happened to cause the link to become saturated.

Using netperf to See Actual Network Bandwidth

Now that you know there is a 10-Mb connection between the two endpoints, you can start looking at the traffic that is traversing that link. The netperf application allows you to perform multiple bulk data transfer tests to see the available bandwidth in the network link.

Since the problem has been noticed on bulk data transfers, you can use the stream mode of netperf to send a constant stream of data between the test hosts. This test will help determine the speed at which the bulk data transfer will occur.

The first netperf test uses the default TCP stream test. The default test time of 10 seconds is probably not a good representation of an actual data transfer. You might want to select a longer test time, such as two or more minutes:

```
$ ./netperf -H 192.168.1.6 -l 300
TCP STREAM TEST to 192.168.1.6 : histogram : interval : dirty data
Recv    Send    Send
Socket  Socket  Message  Elapsed
Size    Size    Size     Time     Throughput
bytes   bytes   bytes    secs.    10^6bits/sec

 32768  16384   16384    300.04      6.90
$
```

This example of the network bandwidth test shows a fairly low throughput level for the link, slightly less than 7 Mbps. This value shows that the transfer has a fairly good throughput value. The next step is to find out if this is the limiting factor in the bulk data transfer.

You can use the tcp_stream_script script file in netperf to perform multiple TCP stream tests, each using a different message size. This test can help determine if there could be a router problem between the two network endpoints. Routers (and sometimes switches) use different buffer pools for different sizes of network packets. Sometimes a router buffer pool for one size of packet will overflow, causing the router to randomly drop packets of that size, while the other buffer pools are just fine. By using different message sizes, you can see if the throughput is similar for each test. A sampling of the total output looks like this:

```
$ ./tcp_stream_script 192.168.1.6


------------------------------------

./netperf -l 60 -H 192.168.1.6 -t TCP_STREAM -i 10,2 -I 99,5 -- -m 4096
-s 57344 -S 57344

TCP STREAM TEST to 192.168.1.6 : +/-2.5% @ 99% conf. : histogram :
interval : dirty data
```

```
Recv   Send    Send
Socket Socket  Message Elapsed
Size   Size    Size    Time     Throughput
bytes  bytes   bytes   secs.    10^6bits/sec

 57344 131070  4096    60.06       6.89


------------------------------------

./netperf -l 60 -H 192.168.1.6 -t TCP_STREAM -i 10,2 -I 99,5 -- -m 8192
-s 57344 -S 57344

TCP STREAM TEST to 192.168.1.6 : +/-2.5% @ 99% conf. : histogram :
interval : dirty data
Recv   Send    Send
Socket Socket  Message Elapsed
Size   Size    Size    Time     Throughput
bytes  bytes   bytes   secs.    10^6bits/sec

 57344 131070  8192    60.07       6.86


------------------------------------


    .

    .

------------------------------------

./netperf -l 60 -H 192.168.1.6 -t TCP_STREAM -i 10,2 -I 99,5 -- -m 32768
-s 8192 -S 8192

TCP STREAM TEST to 192.168.1.6 : +/-2.5% @ 99% conf. : histogram :
interval : dirty data
Recv   Send    Send
Socket Socket  Message Elapsed
Size   Size    Size    Time     Throughput
bytes  bytes   bytes   secs.    10^6bits/sec

  8192  65536  32768   60.01       8.48
If you wish to submit these results to the netperf database at
http://www.cup.hp.com/netperf/NetperfPage.html, please submit each
datapoint individually. Individual datapoints are separated by
lines of dashes.
$
```

Although the larger packets in the TCP stream test had a faster throughput, it is not significantly faster, so it does not indicate a router buffer problem. It appears that something has overloaded the network link. The next step is to try to determine what is overloading the network.

Using ntop to Analyze Network Traffic

Determining what traffic is present on a network path is often a tricky thing to do. The hardest part is determining the point in the path where you should take your samples. Depending on where the bulk data transfer is traversing the network, you may have to sample several points on the network to determine where the network bottleneck is located.

Since the goal is to see what network traffic is clogging the bulk data transfers, ideally you want to find the bottleneck point in the network, and determine what traffic is passing through it. Mapping out the network path between the two endpoints is helpful in getting a handle on where the bottleneck can be. Once the bottleneck is found, try to place the network monitor on it and capture packets for a while.

NOTE Many switches have the ability to set a port in monitor mode, where it can snoop on the traffic present on another port on the switch. You can use this feature to capture packets for ntop.

After letting ntop collect network data for a while, you can connect to the ntop host, using your Web browser, and watch the data statistics. First, you should check out the Stats category of data, starting with the Traffic menu item. This will give you a quick overview of the traffic seen on the network segment. Figure 12.1 shows the traffic distribution based on destination type.

The traffic distribution shows that the majority of the packets were unicast packets—that is, they were destined for a single host. If the majority of the traffic on a segment is broadcast packets, then you may have a broadcast storm on your hands.

The next thing to check is the protocol that is the most prevalent in the captured packets. Figure 12.2 shows the protocol distribution section of the Traffic menu item graph.

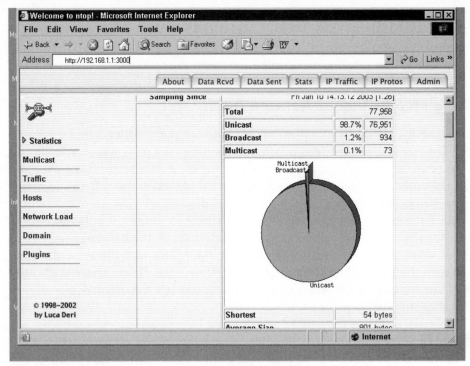

Figure 12.1   Network packet destination distribution.

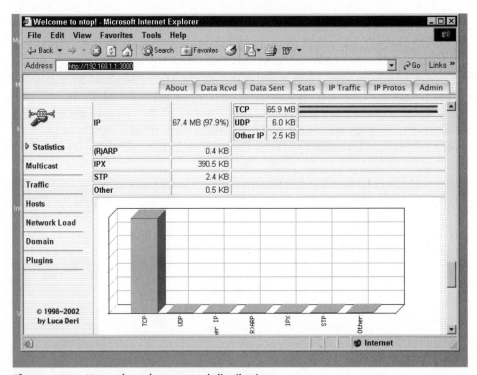

Figure 12.2   Network packet protocol distribution.

From the graph and data shown in Figure 12.2, it is obvious that the majority of the network traffic is TCP applications. The next step is to find out what applications are causing the traffic. Figure 12.3 shows the TCP/UDP application distribution found in the captured network packets.

By observing the graph in Figure 12.3, you can see that the majority of the network traffic seen on the segment is FTP-related. This shows that the bulk data transfer is consuming most of the available network bandwidth already. No additional network traffic appears to be hampering the network response times.

Using NetLogger to Analyze Host Functions

With the network showing no signs of problems, the next step is to try to determine if either of the hosts is the problem. This is right up NetLogger's alley.

You can either add NetLogger API calls to existing network applications, or, if you do not have access to the network application source code, you can create your own test application that logs the read, write, and network times for a data transfer across the network. To observe the complete process in a single NetLogger graph, you should log both host entries to a single log file. This can be accomplished by two different methods. You can create two separate log files, one on the client and another one on the server, and merge them together (remember to synchronize the system clocks). Alternately, you can use the netarchd program on a single host to accept log entries from both hosts into a single log file.

After the test log file is created, you can view it using the nlv_view program. Figure 12.4 shows a sample log file graph from two simple network tests on the same graph.

The test graph shows that the time it took the receiving host to write the data to disk was longer than the network transfer process. This indicates that the response time problem could most likely be related to the disk access speed on the receiving host.

Request/Response Traffic

Thanks to the popularity of Web servers, another common type of network traffic is the request/response packet pair. This traffic results in a client Web browser sending a short Web request packet for a Web page, and the Web server responding with a larger Web response packet. The problem with this short exchange is that it is encapsulated within a TCP session, which means that plenty of TCP overhead packets are required to establish the session, pass the data, and close the session.

While an individual Web session may not be a problem for the network, having hundreds (or even thousands) of sessions traversing across a network link can cause a problem. This section shows how to simulate and track Web traffic on the network, to watch the performance characteristics of the network links.

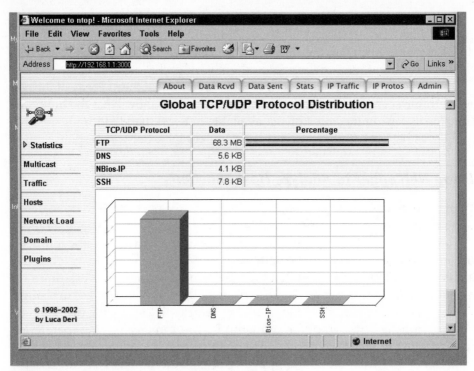

Figure 12.3 Network packet application distribution.

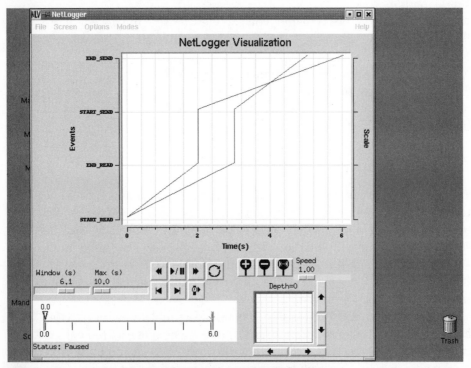

Figure 12.4 Graph of data read, network transfer, and write.

Using netperf to Simulate HTTP Traffic

The netperf application can also be used to simulate HTTP traffic on a local network. The TCP_CRR test can be used to perform simple multiconnection request/response sessions, which simulates normal HTTP trafic.

By default, the TCP_CRR test uses small packet sizes for both the request and the response. In reality, while the request packet is often small (just the URL of the Web site), the response packet returned by the Web server may be quite large. To make the test more realistic, you should specify a larger response packet size. It is also a good idea to take samples at varying test duration lengths. A sample set of tests looks like this:

```
$ ./netperf -t TCP_CRR -H 192.168.1.1 -- -r 32,1034
TCP Connect/Request/Response TEST to 192.168.1.1 : interval : dirty data
Local /Remote
Socket Size   Request  Resp.   Elapsed  Trans.
Send   Recv   Size     Size    Time     Rate
bytes  bytes  bytes    bytes   secs.    per sec

32768  32768  32       1034    10.00    339.56
16384  87380
$ ./netperf -H 192.168.1.1 -t TCP_CRR -l 60 -- -r 32,1034
TCP Connect/Request/Response TEST to 192.168.1.1 : interval : dirty data
Local /Remote
Socket Size   Request  Resp.   Elapsed  Trans.
Send   Recv   Size     Size    Time     Rate
bytes  bytes  bytes    bytes   secs.    per sec

32768  32768  32       1034    60.01    342.79
16384  87380
$./netperf -t TCP_CRR -H 192.168.1.1 -l 300 -- -r 32,1034
TCP Connect/Request/Response TEST to 192.168.1.1 : interval : dirty data
Local /Remote
Socket Size   Request  Resp.   Elapsed  Trans.
Send   Recv   Size     Size    Time     Rate
bytes  bytes  bytes    bytes   secs.    per sec

32768  32768  32       1034    300.02   340.31
16384  87380
$
```

This test shows the use of three different test lengths: 10 seconds, 60 seconds, and 300 seconds. Some servers can sustain short bursts of sessions, but have problems when the bursts become longer. By selecting three different test lengths, you can observe if there is any decrease in the transaction rate.

This test shows that the network link (and host hardware) can support about 340 transactions per second. Of course, this test doesn't take into account any database requirements on the server side.

Using tcptrace to Watch HTTP Sessions

If you want more information about how each individual HTTP session behaves, you can use tcpdump to trace the netperf test session, and then analyze the captured data using tcptrace.

> **WARNING** You won't want to capture a netperf session that's too long. As seen in the statistics above, there are over 300 sessions per second. A 10-second netperf test will generate 3,000 TCP sessions! You would not want to trudge through any more than that.

On the same host that you are using for the netperf test (either the client or the server), start the tcpdump monitor, using the command:

```
tcpdump ip host hostname -w test.dmp
```

This monitors all traffic from the specified host *hostname*. You should use the hostname of the remote device from the host performing the capture. All of the captured packets will be stored in the test.dmp file.

When the netperf test is complete, you can analyze the sessions in the test.dmp file with the tcptrace program. You will see lots of sessions, all of which are similar, with the exception of the control sessions at the start and end of the test. You can zero in on a single session using the -o command option, and display the statistics from the session using the -l option:

```
$ tcptrace -l -o6 test2
1 arg remaining, starting with 'test2'
Ostermann's tcptrace -- version 6.2.0 -- Fri Jul 26, 2002

33973 packets seen, 33973 TCP packets traced
elapsed wallclock time: 0:00:00.604255, 56222 pkts/sec analyzed
trace file elapsed time: 0:00:14.006799
TCP connection info:
3397 TCP connections traced:
=================================
TCP connection 6:
        host k:        192.168.1.1:5140
        host l:        192.168.1.6:1898
        complete conn: yes
        first packet:  Thu Dec 12 18:36:35.928762 2002
        last packet:   Thu Dec 12 18:36:35.931551 2002
        elapsed time:  0:00:00.002789
        total packets: 10
        filename:      test2
    k->l:                              l->k:
        total packets:         5           total packets:         5
        ack pkts sent:         4           ack pkts sent:         5
        pure acks sent:        2           pure acks sent:        2
```

```
    sack pkts sent:              0            sack pkts sent:              0
    max sack blks/ack:           0            max sack blks/ack:           0
    unique bytes sent:          32            unique bytes sent:        1034
    actual data pkts:            1            actual data pkts:            1
    actual data bytes:          32            actual data bytes:        1034
    rexmt data pkts:             0            rexmt data pkts:             0
    rexmt data bytes:            0            rexmt data bytes:            0
    zwnd probe pkts:             0            zwnd probe pkts:             0
    zwnd probe bytes:            0            zwnd probe bytes:            0
    outoforder pkts:             0            outoforder pkts:             0
    pushed data pkts:            1            pushed data pkts:            1
    SYN/FIN pkts sent:         1/1            SYN/FIN pkts sent:         1/1
    urgent data pkts:        0 pkts           urgent data pkts:        0 pkts
    urgent data bytes:       0 bytes          urgent data bytes:       0 bytes
    mss requested:        1460 bytes          mss requested:        1460 bytes
    max segm size:          32 bytes          max segm size:        1034 bytes
    min segm size:          32 bytes          min segm size:        1034 bytes
    avg segm size:          31 bytes          avg segm size:        1032 bytes
    max win adv:         33580 bytes          max win adv:          5840 bytes
    min win adv:         32546 bytes          min win adv:          5840 bytes
    zero win adv:            0 times          zero win adv:            0 times
    avg win adv:         33210 bytes          avg win adv:          5840 bytes
    initial window:         32 bytes          initial window:       1034 bytes
    initial window:          1 pkts           initial window:          1 pkts
    ttl stream length:      32 bytes          ttl stream length:1034 bytes
    missed data:             0 bytes          missed data:             0 bytes
    truncated data:          0 bytes          truncated data:        992 bytes
    truncated packets:       0 pkts           truncated packets:       1 pkts
    data xmit time:      0.000 secs           data xmit time:      0.000 secs
    idletime max:            1.9 ms           idletime max:            2.0 ms
    throughput:          11474 Bps            throughput:         370742 Bps
$
```

By looking at the long view of an individual session, you can see what is happening on the network and the server. In this sample session, you can see that there were no retransmitted packets and no zero window size packets. Everything appears to be working just fine.

You can also use the tcptrace -S option to produce a graph showing the time sequence of the request/response test. By observing the time sequence graph of the packets, you can see any retransmitted packets or duplicate ACKS, both of which can affect the response time of the session.

Analyzing Production Traffic

Although performing network tests using canned test packages is a good way to observe the network's behavior, there is still no substitute for real production data on the network. The tcptrace and ntop applications can be used to watch for potential problems in existing network traffic.

It is good to see actual network sessions of different types, so as to know when you see something that is not normal. This section shows how to use the tcptrace and ntop applications to watch different types of common IP sessions.

Analyzing an FTP Session

When watching FTP sessions, it is important to watch the packet retransmissions. Retransmitted packets can greatly increase the time that it takes to transfer the file across the network. Packet retransmissions often indicate a network problem somewhere in the network path between the two endpoints, either an overloaded segment or a bad network device.

The tcpdump application can be used to capture the FTP session data. This can be done by placing the capture host along the network path of the two test endpoints, or even by capturing packets directly on one of the two test endpoint hosts. The tcpdump command to capture all FTP data is:

```
tcpdump tcp port 20 or tcp port 21 -w test.dmp
```

This command monitors the network for traffic destined to (or originating from) TCP ports 20 (FTP data) and 21 (FTP control). This ensures that the entire FTP session will be captured. The -w parameter is also used to store the captured packets into a dump file, called test.dmp in this example. Once the FTP session has been captured, you can use the tcptrace and ntop applications to analyze it.

Using tcptrace

The first step is to see what TCP sessions are found in the FTP trace. This can be done using the default settings for tcptrace:

```
$ tcptrace test.dmp
1 arg remaining, starting with 'test.dmp'
'Ostermann's tcptrace -- version 6.2.0 -- Fri Jul 26, 2002

15470 packets seen, 15470 TCP packets traced
elapsed wallclock time: 0:00:00.316019, 48952 pkts/sec analyzed
trace file elapsed time: 0:00:40.241734
TCP connection info:
*** 32 packets were too short to process at some point
        (use -w option to show details)
  1: 192.168.1.6:1057 - 192.168.1.1:21 (a2b)      84>    67<  (complete)
  2: 192.168.1.1:20 - 192.168.1.6:1059 (c2d)       5>     3<  (complete)
  3: 192.168.1.1:20 - 192.168.1.6:1060 (e2f)     747>   438<  (complete)
  4: 192.168.1.1:20 - 192.168.1.6:1061 (g2h)    1528>   895<  (complete)
  5: 192.168.1.1:20 - 192.168.1.6:1062 (i2j)     157>    90<  (complete)
```

```
 6: 192.168.1.1:20 - 192.168.1.6:1063 (k2l)      5>    3< (complete)
 7: 192.168.1.1:20 - 192.168.1.6:1064 (m2n)    749>  445< (complete)
 8: 192.168.1.1:20 - 192.168.1.6:1065 (o2p)   1525>  871< (complete)
 9: 192.168.1.1:20 - 192.168.1.6:1066 (q2r)    156>   90< (complete)
10: 192.168.1.1:20 - 192.168.1.6:1067 (s2t)      5>    3< (complete)
11: 192.168.1.1:20 - 192.168.1.6:1068 (u2v)    746>  434< (complete)
12: 192.168.1.1:20 - 192.168.1.6:1069 (w2x)   1525>  860< (complete)
13: 192.168.1.1:20 - 192.168.1.6:1070 (y2z)    156>   91< (complete)
14: 192.168.1.1:20 - 192.168.1.6:1071 (aa2ab)    5>    3< (complete)
15: 192.168.1.1:20 - 192.168.1.6:1072 (ac2ad)  746>  430< (complete)
16: 192.168.1.1:20 - 192.168.1.6:1073 (ae2af) 1525>  838< (complete)
17: 192.168.1.1:20 - 192.168.1.6:1074 (ag2ah)  156>   89< (complete)
$
```

For a single FTP session, there were 17 different TCP sessions generated. You may be wondering how this can be. For the FTP session, a single FTP control session is established. This should be seen in session 1 of the trace. A partial long display of the session looks like:

```
$ tcptrace -l -ol test.dmp
1 arg remaining, starting with 'test.dmp'
Ostermann's tcptrace -- version 6.2.0 -- Fri Jul 26, 2002

15470 packets seen, 15470 TCP packets traced
elapsed wallclock time: 0:00:00.178000, 86910 pkts/sec analyzed
trace file elapsed time: 0:00:40.241734
TCP connection info:
17 TCP connections traced:
TCP connection 1:
        host a:        192.168.1.6:1057
        host b:        192.168.1.1:21
        complete conn: yes
        first packet:  Thu Dec 12 19:48:34.815585 2002
        last packet:   Thu Dec 12 19:49:15.057319 2002
        elapsed time:  0:00:40.241734
        total packets: 151
        filename:      test.dmp
```

Sure enough, this session shows host b as using TCP port 21, the FTP control port. The FTP control session is what the client uses to send the FTP commands to the server, and the server uses it to send the response back.

For each file transferred via FTP, a separate FTP data session is used. This results in a new TCP session for each file transferred. This is why there can be so many TCP sessions in a single FTP session.

NOTE As a side note, each time you perform a **dir** command in an FTP session, an FTP data session is opened to receive the directory listing information, resulting in yet another TCP session to add to the list.

You can use the tcptrace -o option to analyze an individual TCP session within the trace, such as using the -l option to produce a long listing of an actual file transfer. You can also use the -S and -o options to produce a time sequence graph of a particular transfer:

```
tcptrace -S -o4 test.dmp
```

For this example, the files g2h_tsg.xpl and h2g_tsg.xpl are created. You can view these with xplot or jPlot to see the time sequence trends for the file transfer. Figure 12.5 shows the sample g2h_tsg.xpl file graphed.

Note that the time sequence graph shows a perfect stairstep sequence. This indicates a good session, as one host is acknowledging data packets in the proper order in which they were sent, and no duplicate packets (retransmissions) are sent. You can zoom in on the graph to observe individual packets, to see if any duplicate ACKS or TCP window sizes are present.

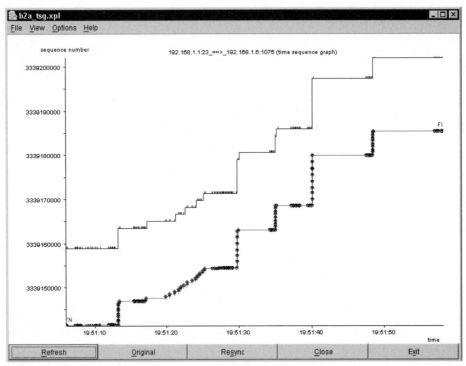

Figure 12.5   Sample FTP data session time sequence graph.

Using ntop

You can use the ntop application to analyze the tcpdump dump file for packet and protocol characteristics. To use ntop on a file instead of actual network traffic, you must use the -f option:

```
# ntop -d -u ntop -P /home/ntop -a /home/ntop/ -L -f /home/ntop/test.dmp
```

This command starts ntop as a background daemon, uses the ntop data-bases in the /home/ntop directory, and logs any messages in the standard system log files. After the ntop application starts, you can access it using any Web browser, at the host IP address and port 3000.

The Data Rcvd and Data Sent categories show information about the hosts involved in the FTP session, along with the statistics of the data transfers. Figure 12.6 shows a sample Data Rcvd category window with the Throughput menu option.

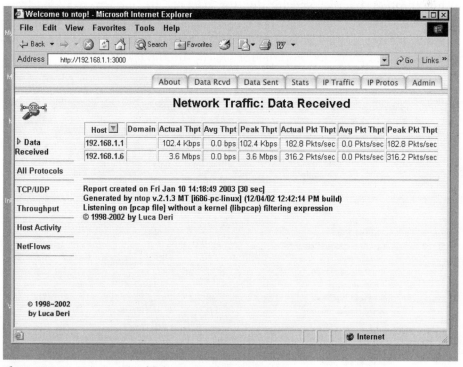

Figure 12.6   Data Received information for FTP session.

You can see detailed information about each host by clicking on the host address link in the chart. Figure 12.7 shows this display.

The detailed host information shows how much data was sent by each host, and how much of the data sent was due to retransmitted packets.

Analyzing a Telnet Session

Telnet sessions are unique in that they are very sensitive to network delays. Every time a Telnet user types a character on the display screen, it must immediately be sent to the remote host, and the echo must then be returned to the client, before the character appears on the screen. This process magnifies even the slightest network delay.

As with the FTP trace, you can use the filtering capabilities of tcpdump to watch individual Telnet sessions on the network:

```
tcpdump ip host 192.168.1.1 and tcp port 23 -w test2.dmp
```

This command looks specifically for packets to and from IP address 192.168.1.1 using the Telnet TCP port (23). Depending on where and what you are monitoring, you may have to change the actual command. Again, the -w option is used to create a dump file for the captured packets.

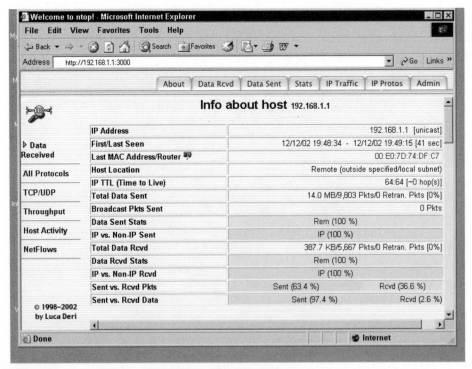

Figure 12.7   Detailed host information for FTP session.

Using tcptrace

Unlike the FTP session, a single Telnet session produces only one TCP session. This makes analyzing the tcptrace files much easier. The output from the long view display of tcptrace for the session looks like:

```
$ tcptrace -l test2.dmp
1 arg remaining, starting with 'test2.dmp'
Ostermann's tcptrace -- version 6.2.0 -- Fri Jul 26, 2002


349 packets seen, 349 TCP packets traced
elapsed wallclock time: 0:00:00.047788, 7303 pkts/sec analyzed
trace file elapsed time: 0:00:52.136647
TCP connection info:
1 TCP connection traced:
TCP connection 1:
        host a:        192.168.1.6:1076
        host b:        192.168.1.1:23
        complete conn: yes
        first packet:  Thu Dec 12 19:51:05.875319 2002
        last packet:   Thu Dec 12 19:51:58.011966 2002
        elapsed time:  0:00:52.136647
        total packets: 349
        filename:      test2.dmp
    a->b:                                b->a:
        total packets:         191           total packets:         158
        ack pkts sent:         190           ack pkts sent:         158
        pure acks sent:         87           pure acks sent:         13
        sack pkts sent:          0           sack pkts sent:          0
        max sack blks/ack:       0           max sack blks/ack:       0
        unique bytes sent:     151           unique bytes sent:   44062
        actual data pkts:      102           actual data pkts:      144
        actual data bytes:     151           actual data bytes:   44062
        rexmt data pkts:         0           rexmt data pkts:         0
        rexmt data bytes:        0           rexmt data bytes:        0
        zwnd probe pkts:         0           zwnd probe pkts:         0
        zwnd probe bytes:        0           zwnd probe bytes:        0
        outoforder pkts:         0           outoforder pkts:         0
        pushed data pkts:      102           pushed data pkts:      144
        SYN/FIN pkts sent:     1/1           SYN/FIN pkts sent:     1/1
        req sack:                Y           req sack:                Y
        sacks sent:              0           sacks sent:              0
        urgent data pkts:        0 pkts      urgent data pkts:        0 pkts
        urgent data bytes:       0 bytes     urgent data bytes:       0 bytes
        mss requested:        1460 bytes     mss requested:        1460 bytes
        max segm size:          10 bytes     max segm size:        1460 bytes
        min segm size:           1 bytes     min segm size:           1 bytes
        avg segm size:           1 bytes     avg segm size:         305 bytes
        max win adv:         17520 bytes     max win adv:         32120 bytes
        min win adv:         16130 bytes     min win adv:         32120 bytes
        zero win adv:            0 times     zero win adv:            0 times
```

```
avg win adv:        17130 bytes        avg win adv:        32120 bytes
initial window:         6 bytes        initial window:        12 bytes
initial window:         1 pkts         initial window:         1 pkts
ttl stream length: 151 bytes      ttl stream length:   44062 bytes
missed data:            0 bytes        missed data:            0 bytes
truncated data:         0 bytes        truncated data:     43013 bytes
truncated packets:      0 pkts         truncated packets:     64 pkts
data xmit time:    52.003 secs         data xmit time:    52.085 secs
idletime max:       8182.4 ms          idletime max:        8382.0 ms
throughput:             3 Bps          throughput:           845 Bps
$
```

Since the Telnet session is only one TCP session, you can see all of the information from the session in the single listing. Similarly, when you plot the session information in a time sequence graph, you will see all of the packets for the session. Figure 12.8 shows the time sequence graph for the sample Telnet session.

Unlike the FTP data session, the Telnet session does not produce a nice stairstep graph. Since the data transfer in a Telnet session is not consistent, you will see long periods of time (relative to the packet transmission times) of no activity in the session. You will have to zoom in on specific sections of the session to see any useful information.

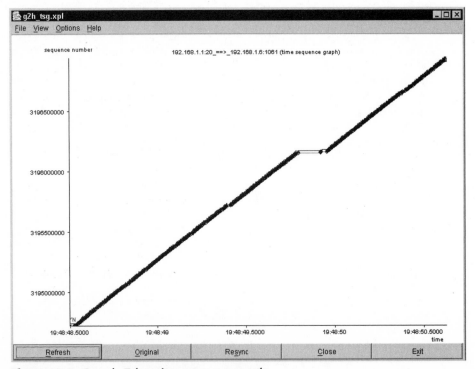

Figure 12.8 Sample Telnet time sequence graph.

Using ntop

Again, as with the FTP session, you can use the ntop application to analyze the captured Telnet session using the -f ntop command-line option. After ntop starts, you can use your Web browser to see the session information displayed from ntop.

Summary

This chapter discussed all of the network performance tools presented in Part II, showing how each one can be used in a testing environment to produce useful information. Different tools have different strong points, and knowing when to use which tool can simplify the task of network monitoring.

The first set of tools represents tools that can be used to produce test traffic on the network, and measure the bandwidth, round-trip times, and other packet parameters. These tools are invaluable when you are trying to identify network bottlenecks and high-utilization points. By producing your own traffic, you can observe the behavior of the network for specific types of applications. The netperf, dbs, Iperf, Pathrate, and Nettest applications provide functions for generating network traffic and observing the results.

The second set of tools represents tools that can be used to analyze captured network data. This allows you to use normal network traffic and analyze how it behaves on the network. Watching busy hosts, protocols, and network segments can show you how to reallocate network resources to accommodate your production data. The tcptrace and ntop applications are useful in performing these tasks.

This chapter concludes the section on network performance tools. The next chapter begins Part III of the book, "Application Performance Tools," which discusses ways to test network applications before they hit your network. When you understand how an application works in a network environment, you can more easily modify your network (or the application) to make it work peacefully with other network applications.

Application
Performance Tools

## CHAPTER 13

Measuring Application Performance

Part III of this book approaches network performance from a different perspective. Not only is it crucial to have the network configured for maximum performance, it also helps to have network applications that are configured to operate efficiently across the network. This part of the book describes some methods and tools that can be used to help determine how an application will behave within your network environment. By modeling the network, you can observe how network applications behave within the model environment, and extrapolate from the results an idea of how the application would behave in the production network environment. This chapter provides an overview of the methods used for modeling production networks and using those models to test network applications.

Trying to determine how an application will perform on a network is often a task that falls to the network administrator. While programmers work to make network applications functional for their customers, they sometimes forget to consider how the application will affect the existing production network, or conversely, how the existing production network will affect the application's performance. Often, customers, programmers, and network administrators do not find out that a new network application is the cause of network performance issues (or again, that the network is responsible for network application performance issues) until it is too late.

This chapter begins by introducing the concept of network modeling, by showing the different methods used for testing network applications. All of the network models described are ways that programmers and network administrators have used to determine how a network application might perform within the production network environment.

Methods of Testing Network Applications

The point of testing network applications is to observe how an application will perform when run on a network. In today's world of "do everything on the network," each network application is competing for network resources with lots of other applications, from bulk file transfers to Web browsing. The key to good network application performance is to determine how an individual application will behave in your particular network environment.

There are four basic methods that can be used for testing network applications:

- Using a test network
- Using the production network
- Using a network emulator
- Using a network simulator

Each of these testing environments has a unique set of benefits and challenges for programmers and network administrators. This section walks through each of the test environments, and describes the pros and cons of each.

The Test Network

Creating a test network is the most common method used in programming shops. It is usually the quickest and easiest solution for testing network applications. Unfortunately, it can also produce the least useful results. It is not uncommon for a network application to perform flawlessly within the test network, but fail miserably when placed in the production network environment. Most test networks fail to take into consideration the problems associated with the actual production network.

Usually, the test network is nothing more than a group of workstations connected together on a standalone network where no other applications are running. This can create a false sense of security for the application developers, as real network problems are not addressed in the application. To create a useful test network, the testers should attempt to mimic the network problems of the production network (discussed later in the *Modeling Network Problems* section).

Production Network

The most accurate method to use for testing network applications is to run the application in the production network environment. This ensures that all of the network factors present in the production network will affect the application, as in real life, which makes it the best method of determining if the network will affect application performance, or if the application will affect network performance. Of course, there are downsides to testing on the production network.

Often it is not feasible for the application to be developed on the production network. Often, application developers are not located in the same area where the application will be run, making it impossible for them to use the production network for testing. This is the case for almost all commercial network applications used. However, even with in-house programming, the programmers often do not have access to the application area where the program will be run.

Even when the application developers do have access to the production network, it is not always a good idea to test the application on the network. There have been incidents of runaway applications that consumed the entire bandwidth of a production network, effectively crashing the network for other production data. In environments where high availability is a necessity, this could cause catastrophic results.

Network Emulation

The compromise between the test and production network is the *network emulation*. A network emulation is a canned environment, where all of the problems and issues found in the production network are duplicated within a test network environment. Creating a standard test network, but including one or more devices that are capable of emulating the behavior and characteristics of the production network, will accomplish this.

The key to network emulation is to have devices that can introduce network problems into the test network environment. There are two common methods that are used for this purpose:

- Have network devices that produce network traffic, emulating production traffic on the test network.
- Have network devices that can accept packets, and delay, drop, or misorder them, as in the production environment.

The following sections describe how these two methods are used.

Network Traffic Generator

The first method consists of network devices that can produce network traffic that mimics the traffic found in the production network. Just as the netperf network performance tool was capable of sending test data streams similar to application traffic, a network traffic generator can send traffic emulating anything from FTP data transfers and interactive Telnet sessions to database access and Web browsing. Many advanced network emulation devices also include options to combine different types and amounts of traffic generated, such as emulating 10 FTP users and 100 Web browser users simultaneously.

By adding one or more network traffic generators to a simple test network, you can more accurately observe how the network application will perform given other network traffic. While this is still not a complete emulation of the production environment, it gets the tester closer to the desired results.

Not only can network traffic generators be used to test network applications, they are also used to test the performance of network devices. Many network administrators use network traffic generators to simulate normal network traffic for switches, routers, and WAN links. By simulating the actual traffic that could be present during normal production times, you can observe the behavior of the network devices before customers complain.

Network Emulation Device

Instead of generating network traffic for the test network, the second type of network emulation device provides a way to model an entire production network within one or more devices. As packets enter the network emulator, they are processed to simulate network problems that could be present on the production network. The network emulation device plugs in between the client and server devices testing the network application.

For packets to pass from the client to the server, they must pass through the network emulator. The emulator is configured to process each packet in some manner, depending on the type of network emulated, before it is passed to the server. The idea is to inflict the same network problems on each packet sent as would be seen on the production network.

To accomplish this, most network emulators create one or more pipelines between the device input and output. As packets are received on the input, they are fed through the pipelines on their way to the output. Within each pipeline, the packets are subjected to different delays, errors, and even drops before they are sent to the device output. This is demonstrated in Figure 13.1.

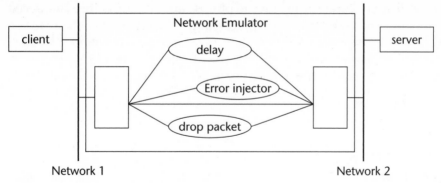

Figure 13.1 Network emulation within the pipeline.

The network emulator sends packets between the different pipelines randomly, so each of the network effects is distributed among the incoming packets. The pipeline can perform the network emulation using either hardware or software solutions. Often the pipelines are implemented internal network functions within the emulation device, such as interprocess communication (IPC) on Unix systems.

Network Simulation

Network simulators perform network-modeling functions completely within a software environment. Mathematical algorithms are used to model the behavior of each network link and device, and also represent the data produced and consumed by the network application. The way the mathematical algorithms work on the input data is similar to the way the actual production network would affect the data, using delays, drops, and out-of-order packets. Each device within the network path is modeled, with the individual models connected together within the simulation.

The network model connects the hubs, links, and router models together to produce a single network model. The output from one device model is fed into the input of another device model, representing the various aspects of the network connections. Using this technique, any type of network can be modeled in the network simulation environment.

Modeling application data can be tricky. Just like the network traffic generators, network simulators must simulate different types of network traffic. The only difference is that the simulators do it mathematically, without using real packets. By sending data streams that represent real traffic, the network simulation can produce results showing how the output of each network device would look.

A network simulator does not have to process information at the same speed as the modeled network (real-time processing). The purpose of the network simulator is not to simulate real-time data, but to produce results that indicate what the overall performance of the network application would be, given the modeled network. There are basically two types of network simulators:

- Discrete event
- Analytical

Discrete Event

Discrete event simulators perform calculations on individually simulated packets, just as a network would see each packet of a data stream and process it. Each network device and each data packet in the data stream is simulated. This produces the most realistic information, modeling the behavior of the network as data streams are handled.

Unfortunately, this simulation method is computationally intensive, requiring lots of calculations for each packet within the data stream and each network device handling the packet along the network path. To simulate large quantities of network traffic within large networks, discrete event simulators often have to perform calculations for hours, and even days, before producing results.

Analytical

Analytical simulators attempt to decrease the calculation times by using mathematical equations to estimate the behavior of different network devices and the way they would handle particular types of traffic. Each network device is simulated using a simple mathematical equation, and each data stream is represented as information passes through the equations.

Instead of having to process each packet through each device, the analytical simulator just needs to process a group of calculations on input data. This results in extremely fast simulation results, although they are not as accurate as the discrete event results.

Modeling Network Problems

No matter which network-testing method you use, to fully test a network application, you must be able to simulate the way the application behaves within the normal network environment. This means that the method must be robust enough to simulate all of the problems associated with busy networks.

Each of these problems must be duplicated within the network model used to predict the performance of the network. There are several problems that must be taken into consideration:

- Network bandwidth constraints
- Packet errors
- Lost packets
- Out-of-order packets
- Delayed packets

This section explains each of these problems, how they can affect a network application running on a production network, and how the network model must take them into consideration when producing test results.

Bandwidth Constraints

A network application should never assume unrestrained communication between network devices. One of the primary factors in determining network application performance is how often the application sends data across the network. The network can make or break the network application's performance.

Network applications that send lots of packets between devices are dependent on the efficiency of the network. Any delays between packets introduced by busy networks can be catastrophic for the application. It should be a fundamental design goal of all network application programmers to minimize the data traffic that must traverse the network.

There are many applications that violate this principle. Database applications are usually the biggest culprits. There are two basic ways to perform client/server database functions across the network.

In the first method, the database engine is located on the client device, while the database data is located on the server. For a simple data query, the database engine must select each record within the database index to look for the query result. This requires each index record to be passed across the network to the client, causing lots of network traffic.

In the second method, the database engine is located on the server device, along with the database data. The client contains simple code that sends the query to the database engine, which then does all of the database index lookups internally, and sends a single response with the result. This method produces minimal network traffic, and is more network-friendly, especially for slower networks.

In both scenarios it is crucial to model how much network bandwidth is being consumed by the network application. The key is knowing the characteristics of the network application, and being able to quantify those characteristics. Network traffic generator applications can be used to simulate the network traffic generated by each type of database application—either in real life, by sending dummy database packets across the network, or in simulation, by performing the calculations necessary to simulate the traffic.

Packet Errors

The network application should also be prepared to deal with faulty data received in packets. Most network applications that use the TCP or UDP protocols do not have to worry about this, as it is taken care of at the network level. However, applications that use their own protocols must be prepared to handle errors.

The most common method used in network applications to handle packet errors is the checksum method. Most standard protocols provide a system for calculating a checksum of the data contained in the packet, and including the value within the packet (the checksum part of the packet is set to zero for the calculation). The receiving device must extract the checksum value, perform its own checksum calculation, and compare the two values. If the values match, the packet is assumed to be error-free.

NOTE There are lots of methods for calculating checksums. The most common method used for network packets uses 16-bit arithmetic to break the packet into 16-bit chunks, add them, and take the complement of the result.

Network models simulate network errors by injecting errors within a certain percentage of packets received in the model. Network emulation devices do this by purposely altering the packet before it is forwarded to the output. Network simulators perform this task mathematically.

Lost Packets

Besides error packets, the network application should also be prepared to deal with missing packets. While applications that use TCP don't have to worry about this, it is a big concern for applications that use UDP for communications.

For applications in which lost packets are devastating, a trustworthy protocol, such as TCP, is recommended. Barring a total network failure, this will cause the underlying network devices to ensure that the remote host receives each packet sent. This often requires retransmission of packets that are not acknowledged as being received. While it is perfectly normal to have some retransmitted packets on the network, too many may be an indication of a network problem, such as an overloaded switch or router that is dropping packets.

For some applications, however, lost packets are not a problem. Applications that transmit information at regular intervals can just send another data sample with either updated information or duplicated information, and go about their business. UDP does not provide a method for tracking packets. The receiving device does not recognize any packets lost in the network. Network game applications often use UDP for its quick turnaround times (no connection establishment phase is required). Most multiplayer network games send out user information (such as location, health status, and so on) at preset intervals to each of the players. If a status packet is lost, the next one updates the player information on the clients.

Simulating lost packets is not too difficult for network models. Network emulators can be set to drop packets as either a percentage of the overall data stream or as a random event occurring over a set amount of time. Network simulators represent dropped packets as retransmissions (as the sender must retransmit the dropped packets). Retransmitted packets appear as additional packets within the data stream, increasing the bandwidth required for the data stream.

Similarly, many network emulators and simulators also model *decimated* packets. Decimated packets occur when a network device drops a fixed amount of traffic—for example, when a router or switch runs out of buffer space and drops entire data streams (as described in the *Modeling Network Devices* section, presented later in this chapter). Instead of dropping a percentage of packets, the model drops a set number of packets within the same data stream, for example, losing 10 packets in a row within the stream. The results of this can be significantly different from the results of dropping just a single packet within the data stream. Sometimes, network applications that can recover from dropped packets will crash and burn as a result of decimated packets.

Out-of-Order Packets

Another UDP problem is out-of-order packets. This problem is most often seen in WAN environments, where multiple network paths can be taken between two endpoints. If any network routers are performing dynamic routing, there is no guarantee that all of the transmitted packets will take the same path to reach the same destination. With all of the different WAN connectivity options available (56 kbps, T1, ISDN, DSL, ATM), it is possible that some packets will take a slower path than others will.

This can result in packets arriving at intervals different from those at which they were sent. If the delays between paths are long enough, the packets can even arrive out of order. Figure 13.2 demonstrates this problem.

It is up to the network application to ensure that the out-of-order packets are reassembled back in the proper order. This of course will slow down application-processing time, and cause performance problems.

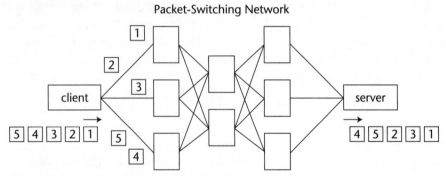

Figure 13.2 Packets arriving out of order at the client.

Network emulation devices simulate out-of-order packets by creating multiple pipelines to process incoming packets, and delaying one pipeline more than another. As a result, some packets are processed more quickly than others, causing them to be sent out ahead of time, which creates out-of-order packets. Of course, you don't want all of the packets within a data stream to be out-of-order, just a percentage of them. This requires the pipeline to use random amounts of delays within the pipeline, changing delay values over the period of the data stream.

Delayed Packets

With the increase of voice and video applications on the network, network delay has become a hot topic of discussion. Any delays introduced by the network between the two endpoints can be devastating to the quality (or even availability) of the voice or video stream.

There are plenty of opportunities for delays to be introduced in the packet flows. Any device that must handle the packet and retransmit it is suspected of injecting a delay in the process. Overloaded switches and routers are the prime suspects, as well as overambitious firewalls.

Many network device vendors implement an IP quality of service (QoS) feature, allowing voice and video packets to be marked as having high priority.

Even with QoS features on routers, however, there is no guarantee that packets will arrive at the same intervals at which they were sent from the server. As routers become congested and reach their buffer limits, processing times can become longer, and even high-priority packets will be delayed.

Creating network delays is not difficult within the network emulator or simulator; the hard part is knowing how much and how often packets should be delayed to replicate the production network environment. There are several different methods used to simulate network delays:

Fixed delay.   This method produces a fixed amount of delay between data packets.

Uniform increase delay.   Produces a variable amount of delay between data packets. The delay time increases by a fixed amount for each packet.

Exponentially increasing delay.   Produces a variable amount of delay between data packets. The delay time increases exponentially for each packet.

Gaussian distribution delay.   This is the most common method used. It provides a fixed distribution for the amounts of delay used on the network data.

Modeling Network Devices

Not only do network emulators and simulators have to model network problems, they also need to model the specific behaviors of different types of network devices. Different types of network devices require different types of models to emulate the way they handle and/or process packets. This section describes the characteristics of different types of network devices, and explains how those characteristics are modeled within network emulators and simulators.

Hubs

A network hub is used to connect multiple devices together on a shared network medium. All packets sent to the hub by any device are forwarded to every port on the hub (except the port that received the packet).

Since the network hub operates as a shared medium, its performance is directly related to how much traffic is present on all of the hub ports at any given time. The hub software sequentially handles each packet received by each port. This behavior is modeled as a single packet queue, operating in *first in, first out* (FIFO) mode.

The network speed of the hub is represented by the capacity of the FIFO queue. The faster the network hub, the larger the queue (more packets can be processed in the same amount of time). Figure 13.3 demonstrates this principle.

Each port on the hub places packets into the single packet queue. The hub removes each packet individually from the queue, and sends it to all of the ports on the hub. When the queue fills up (which represents network overload), packets are dropped, representing network problems such as collisions and error packets on an overloaded network hub.

packets coming in from ports

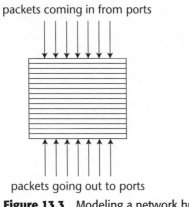

packets going out to ports

Figure 13.3   Modeling a network hub.

The idea for modeling network hubs is to determine how much traffic causes the network hub to fill. This can be the result of either a short burst of network traffic from a single device, or a sustained network load caused by lots of network traffic. In either situation, the model must account for which packets will cause errors, and how many errors.

Switches

Like the hub, the network switch also connects multiple devices together on the network. However, instead of blindly forwarding each packet out every port, the switch examines the destination of each packet, and forwards the packet only to the port where the destination is supposed to reside.

To perform this task, the switch must maintain large tables of MAC addresses, so it can tell which devices are located on which switch port by their MAC address. This greatly complicates the packet-forwarding process, and creates a much more complicated model.

Instead of a single queue, switches are usually modeled as multiple queues, two queues for each port on the switch. As a new packet is received on a port, it is placed in an input queue for the port. After the switch has examined the packet and determined which port it must be forwarded to, the packet is placed in an output queue for the appropriate port. Figure 13.4 demonstrates this process.

The network switch model must account for situations in which one or more port queues fill up with packets, and drop packets. This situation results in missing packets for the network application. The trouble with the switch model is that, although a single port queue may be full, other ports can handle network traffic just fine. Of course, when a switch's processing capabilities are overloaded due to excessive network traffic, packets are delayed (and possibly dropped) across all of the switch ports.

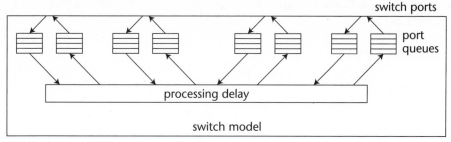

Figure 13.4   Modeling a network switch

Routers

Routers present a wide array of modeling problems. Routers perform many functions, and each function must be accurately modeled. Obviously, the basic function of routers is to forward packets between networks. To perform this process requires three functions:

- Receive a packet on a network interface
- Examine the packet and determine the destination
- Send the packet out the appropriate network interface

The receiving and sending functions are usually modeled similarly to the switch and hub interfaces, as a simple queue—two queues for each router interface (one for input and one for output). The size of the interface queues is related to the speed of the network interface. Since routers are often used to connect dissimilar networks, this can be somewhat tricky.

Since the port queues can be different sizes, it is very possible that one interface can overrun another interface, for instance if a 100-MB LAN sends lots of packets out a T1 Internet connection. Because of this probability, most routers also incorporate some type of buffering system for the interfaces, to help reduce packet loss. To complicate things even more, many routers supply different sizes of buffers for different sizes of packets. Since smaller-sized packets are more common than larger-sized packets, more buffers are allocated for them. Of course this complicates the router model.

The interesting part to model is the lookup function. The router must use tables to store information about which networks are connected to which interfaces, and which remote networks can be accessed through which interfaces. These tables must then be referenced for each packet received by the router. This is often the bottleneck function within the router.

The lookup table can be modeled using a simple packet delay function, similar to that of the switch model. Of course, the packet delay injected by the lookup table is not consistent, so the packet delay model should include a way to randomize the delays caused by the router.

Besides the basic router functions, there are some advanced functions that also require modeling:

- Quality of service (QoS)
- Weighted fair queuing (WFQ)
- Stochastic fair queuing (SFQ)
- Random early detection (RED)

The following sections describe these router features, and how they are often modeled.

Quality of Service

The quality of service function on routers allows applications to use the IP Type-of-Service (ToS) field to indicate priority packets. When the router determines that a packet is marked at a higher priority, it moves the packet ahead in the queue of packets waiting to be processed.

The job of the network model is to be able to model situations in which all traffic is at the same priority, and those in which there is a mix of high- and low-priority traffic. Obviously, in a mixed situation, when the router becomes overloaded, the first packets to be dropped should be the lower-priority packets. This results in the high-priority packets having a lower packet drop rate (close to zero) than the lower-priority packets.

Weighted Fair Queuing

Routers apply the weighted fair queuing (WFQ) method to help balance packet streams received from different sources. Instead of allowing a single network source to monopolize the network resources, the router attempts to forward packets from multiple sources in a fair and equal manner.

This may result in packets being dropped from busy sources more frequently than from sources sending fewer packets. It is assumed that the busy sources will recover from the loss of packets more quickly than the sources sending fewer packets.

Stochastic Fair Queuing

Routers also can apply the stochastic fair queuing (SFQ) method to help balance packet streams received from different sources. Instead of tracking which network devices are sending the most traffic, SFQ uses multiple queues, and distributes the received packets equally among the queues. Each queue is then processed in a round-robin fashion, assigning equal priority to each queue.

The SFQ method does not solve the problem of a single network device monopolizing the network bandwidth, but it does provide a method for attempting to equally distribute the chance of dropped packets among different network data streams.

Random Early Detection

Random early detection (RED) is a technique used by routers to drop packets fairly, when buffers are becoming overloaded. In a normal situation, a router will accept incoming packets on interfaces until the specific packet buffer assigned to the interface, or packet size, is full. When the buffer becomes full, all incoming packets are dropped until more room becomes available in the buffer.

The problem with this method of dropping packets is that a single application with a large amount of data can fill the buffer, and other smaller applications will suffer, as their packets are dropped along with the packets from the network-hogging application. This method is referred to as the tail-drop FIFO method.

RED helps make this system fair by attempting to intelligently drop packets before the buffer actually fills. The router must identify which source device is sending more packets than others, and attempt to drop more packets from that source than from others. Due to the nature of TCP, as more packets are dropped from the busy source, the source should throttle the packet transmissions, thereby reducing the bandwidth it consumes.

Modeling RED is often difficult, and not many network emulators or simulators tackle that situation. Usually RED doesn't play into router behavior until network overload conditions are present.

Firewalls

With the increase of hacking on networks connected to the Internet, firewalls have become commonplace in most corporate networks (and even many home networks). Unfortunately, firewalls add another element to the network that can affect the performance of network applications.

While firewalls protect our networks from intruders, the downside is that protection comes at a price—performance. Each packet that traverses the firewall must be checked against a database, or access control list (ACL). The ACL contains rules that define the level of protection the firewall offers. There are several different types of traffic that the firewall can be configured to block:

- Packets going to a specific IP address
- Packets coming from a specific IP address
- Packets containing a specific protocol (such as ICMP or UDP)
- Packets containing a specific application (such as FTP, Telnet, or Web)

The trick with firewalls is to configure them to be secure enough to prevent unauthorized users from accessing network resources, but not so strict that each packet must be compared against dozens of rules. The more rules contained in the ACL, the more delay introduced by the firewall.

As you would expect, the firewall's main network problem is packet delay, although it is not unheard of to see packet loss associated with a firewall. Modeling a firewall in a network requires adding additional delays to the network path, along with possible packet loss.

Wide Area Networks

While modeling LANs requires building networks of hubs and switches, modeling WANs presents another problem. There are many different methods that are used to create a WAN, each with different characteristics. The two most common techniques used to create WANS are:

- Point-to-point networks
- Packet-switching networks

The following sections describe these two methods, and explain how they are modeled in emulation and simulation software.

Modeling Point-to-Point Networks

A point-to-point network directly connects two endpoints with a single transmission link, such as a T1 or OC-3 line. Point-to-point networks incorporate three components in the model:

- The sending overhead
- The receiving overhead
- The transmission overhead

The sending and receiving overhead models are similar to the standard hub method of creating input and output queues for the incoming and outgoing packets. The transmission overhead is somewhat different.

Each network link will contain its own delay function, along with a particular amount of packet error. Both of these problems must be modeled in the emulation or simulation, to accurately duplicate the WAN environment.

Modeling Packet-Switching Networks

While point-to-point networks have dedicated links between the endpoints in the network, packet-switching networks introduce multiple paths to endpoints. Packet-switching networks consist of a series of routers interconnected to produce a grid, providing multiple paths between any two points on the network.

Each packet transmitted from one endpoint to another is handled independently from the rest of the data stream. As a router in the packet-switching network receives each packet, it determines the best path to its destination. As network links become congested, alternate routes are taken.

As packets going between the same two network endpoints can traverse different routers, there is no way to determine exactly how much delay will be injected into any packet's path. Since each packet within the same data stream can take a different route, there is also no guarantee that the packets will arrive at the destination endpoint in the same order in which they were sent.

This out-of-order problem was discussed earlier in the *Modeling Network Problems* section. The WAN model must incorporate a method to randomly mix up packets, so it is possible for them to arrive out of order at the endpoint model.

Wireless Networks

With the increased use of wireless networks, network models must provide methods to model wireless behavior. While wireless networks provide functions similar to those of LANs, they also present some unique problems to network traffic that must be accounted for in the network models.

Due to the behavior of the wireless radio transmissions, simulating errors within the wireless network can be a major task. Often, a full simulation of a wireless environment is impossible, as the vast amount of data required to simulate the radio propagation and energy consumption can be overwhelming.

To compensate for the varying quality of wireless network behavior, most wireless network models focus on the effect of the slower network speed introduced by the wireless network. In most LAN situations, the wireless network is the bottleneck within the network path, and should be considered the limiting factor within the network model.

Due to the significantly slower wireless network speed (usually less than 3 Mbps), packet overhead (such as TCP/IP headers) has a greater affect on the data stream. Packet size becomes a driving issue in wireless networks, as smaller packets result in larger overhead, and lower data throughput.

Network emulators and simulators must be capable of varying the packet sizes within the model to account for the lower bandwidth associated with wireless networks.

Summary

Determining how network applications will behave on the production network is often the job of the network administrator. Fortunately, there are lots of tools available that can be used to perform this task. This chapter describes the various methods of determining how an application will perform on the network.

There are many different ways to test network applications. The easiest method is usually to create a small standalone test network of a few workstations and servers. The downside to using a test network is that it does not accurately duplicate the production network environment. Alternately, some network testing can be done on the actual production network. This provides the best method for determining how a network application will perform for customers. Unfortunately, it is often not possible to use the production network, and sometimes it is dangerous to test new applications on the production network.

To solve the testing dilemma, many network administrators are turning to network emulation and simulation. Network emulators provide a way to feed actual network application data through a device that emulates the actual production network, and watch the results. The benefit to network emulation is that the actual network application can be used without having to use the actual production network.

Network simulators allow networks and applications to be mathematically modeled, producing a generic test environment to help determine how the application will perform. The downside to network simulators is that they do not use the actual network application, but rather an estimation of the type of data it will produce on the network. Network simulators can also require lots of processing time, for performing calculations to simulate each network device and link in the network path.

Both network emulators and simulators must be able to accurately model the devices found on the network and also the problems associated with networks. Each network device has unique characteristics that must be accurately modeled, using either mathematical equations or a combination of hardware and software. Each of the different problems found on the network, such as packet loss, delays, and errors, must also be factored into the emulation or simulation.

The next chapter begins the network application testing toolkit by describing the dummynet application, which can be used to emulate a production network environment on a single network device. When application data is fed into dummynet, the output data will look as if it has passed through the emulated network.

dummynet

This chapter introduces the first network emulation tool, dummynet. The dummynet application provides a method for network administrators to emulate network problems such as delayed packets, dropped packets, and network errors. First the chapter discusses dummynet, and how it works. Next, a discussion of the ipfw program, the main building block of dummynet, is presented. Finally, the chapter describes in detail how dummynet is installed and configured, and offers some examples of ways to configure dummynet to emulate different types of networks.

FreeBSD, another open source Unix distribution, includes the ipfw application, which is used for providing firewall functions within FreeBSD to process incoming and outgoing packets. By using the firewall features, ipfw can drop, delay, and limit the bandwidth of packets traversing the FreeBSD system. The dummynet application, created by Luigi Rizzo, exploits the features of ipfw by using them to create a network emulation system. The next section describes dummynet, and how it can be used in different network environments to emulate serious network problems.

What Is dummynet?

The dummynet application is an internal FreeBSD system facility that manipulates IP packets as the kernel handles them. The dummynet system can provide the following network emulation features:

- Bandwidth restrictions
- Multipath packet routes
- Packet delays
- Packet loss
- Finite packet queues
- Weighted fair queuing

You can combine different dummynet features within a single dummynet implementation to create a system that closely emulates the behavior of your production network.

WARNING Since dummynet uses the IP firewall features of FreeBSD, it can only be used to emulate IP network behavior. Only applications that use IP can be tested with dummynet.

dummynet Features

The dummynet system works by creating communication pipes between the input and output network facilities of the FreeBSD device. Each communication pipe can be configured separately with individual dummynet features. Figure 14.1 shows a simple dummynet configuration that includes three communication pipes.

Two pipes are used for handling packets received on the standard system network interface card, while the third pipe handles packets sent from the system out to the network interface card. Each pipe acts independently from the other, processing packets according to its own rule set.

The first two pipes are configured in a weighted fair queuing (WFQ) system, dividing incoming packets between the two pipes, based on a WFQ algorithm. Each pipe is configured with a set bandwidth limitation, allowing only a set number of packets to traverse the pipe for a given time. This can be used to emulate specifically sized network links, from slow WAN links to high-speed Ethernet links.

Also associated with the first pipe is a packet loss directive. The packet loss is defined as a percentage of the overall network traffic in the pipe. This feature emulates a consistent packet drop situation, such as a faulty network device or bad cabling.

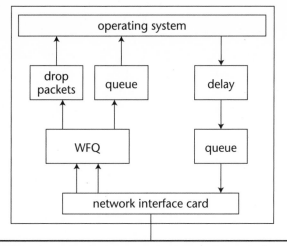

Figure 14.1 Simple dummynet configuration with three pipes.

The second pipe includes a queue limitation. When the pipe queue is full, packets will be dropped, as with a switch or router buffer overload. Since both pipes are combined in a WFQ system, there is a chance that incoming packets will be serviced by either pipe.

The third pipe handles packets sent from the system to the network. Again, it includes simple delays and queue limitations to emulate problems found on the production network.

Using the dummynet Host

There are basically three different ways to implement a dummynet host in a test network:

- As a standalone test host
- On a bridge connected between network segments
- On a router connected between networks

The first method implements dummynet directly on the application host. The dummynet configuration handles all packets received by the test host before they get to the application, and also handles all packets sent by the application before they go to the network. This is shown in Figure 14.2.

As packets are received from the network, they are fed through the dummynet system, which emulates network problems by using delays, packet loss, and bandwidth limitations. After the packets emerge from the dummynet system, they are received by the network application running on the test host, and processed normally.

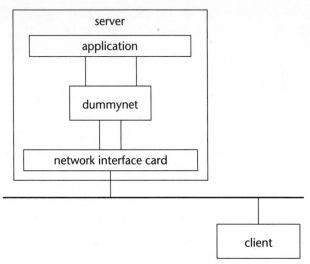

Figure 14.2 Using dummynet on a test host.

When the network application is prepared to send packets to the network, the dummynet system intercepts them, and again applies the configured network emulation rules to the packets. After they emerge from dummynet, they are placed on the network and will be received by the appropriate test host.

The second and third methods require the FreeBSD system running dummynet to have two network cards. Each network card is placed on a separate network segment, as shown in Figure 14.3.

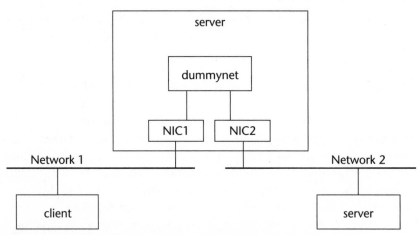

Figure 14.3 Using dummynet as a network bridge or router.

All traffic from one network to the other must pass through the FreeBSD system, and dummynet. The second method uses the FreeBSD bridging facilities, connecting two network segments on the same subnet. Network traffic that must traverse from one network segment to the other must pass through the dummynet system, which then injects the configured network problems into the network traffic.

This method provides an easy way to emulate network problems in an existing test network. Since the FreeBSD system is configured as a bridge, no network configuration is required, and test network traffic can pass with no configuration requirements on the test hosts.

The third method uses the FreeBSD routing facilities to act as a router between network subnets. As packets are passed through the router, the dummynet system intercepts them and provides the configured network problems. To use the FreeBSD routing system, you must configure the test network to work on two separate subnets.

The ipfw Application

The dummynet system uses the FreeBSD ipfw firewall application to create the pipes and network problem emulation. The ipfw application hooks directly into the FreeBSD kernel-level packet-handling facility, filtering packets as the kernel receives them.

The ipfw application is configured using one or more rule sets that define its behavior. Each rule set is numbered, and rules are processed in numerical order. Both incoming and outgoing packets are matched against the ipfw rule sets. If a packet matches a rule, the rule is performed on the packet (delaying it, dropping it, limiting its bandwidth, and so on). There can be up to 65,535 separate rule sets defined in the ipfw filter.

WARNING While it is possible to have up to 65,535 rules defined, each rule requires processing time on the system. Defining lots of rules can significantly slow down the performance of the system, also affecting the network emulation.

The default ipfw configuration always contains one rule:

```
deny all from any to any
```

This rule prevents all IP traffic from traversing the FreeBSD system (the details of the rule format will be discussed later in the *Using ipfw Rules* section). This blocks all IP traffic unless it is specified to be passed by a rule.

NOTE It is possible to alter the kernel configuration to change the default firewall behavior from blocking to accepting all packets. This will be discussed in the *Installing dummynet* section.

The next section describes the ipfw command-line options, and how they can be used to emulate different network problems.

Each ipfw rule is defined from the command-line options. This creates lots of options that can be used on the command line. There are five basic options that control ipfw, shown in Table 14.1.

After the general command-line options, each ipfw function has its own set of options used for handling the rule set. This section defines the basic ipfw commands that are used in the firewall configuration.

Creating New Rules

To add new rules to the ipfw filter, you must use the add command-line option. The format of the add ipfw command line is:

```
ipfw [-q] add [number] [prob value] action [log logamount number] proto
from src to dst [via name | ipno] [options]
```

Rule Number

The first option available is the optional *number* value. As mentioned, each rule is assigned a number, and processed in order of rule number. If no number is specified, ipfw assigns it a number 100 higher than the highest existing rule number.

Table 14.1 ipfw General Command-Line Options

OPTION	DESCRIPTION
-a	Track the number of packets matching the rule.
-f	Don't ask for confirmation when performing commands.
-q	Quiet mode. No verbose output displayed for the command.
-t	Track last match timestamp of packets matching the rule.
-N	Attempt to resolve IP addresses and service ports in output.

Rule Probability

The prob option assigns a probability, where *value* is a floating-point number from 0 to 1, representing the probability that the rule will be matched. This feature allows you to assign processes that do not necessarily happen on a regular basis, such as packet drops. The ipfw application will apply the rule to only a number of packets within the probability of the total number of packets.

Rule Action

The *action* option defines the action ipfw should take with the packet, should the packet match the rule set definition. Table 14.2 lists the different actions that can be taken.

Table 14.2 ipfw Action Options

ACTION	DESCRIPTION
allow	Allows all packets that match the rule
deny	Discards packets that match the rule
unreach *code*	Discards packets that match the rule, and sends an ICMP unreachable packet with code *code* to the source
reset	Discards packets that match the rule, and sends a TCP RST packet to the source
count	Updates the rule counters that match the rule
divert *port*	Redirects packets that match the rule to the port *port*
tee *port*	Sends a copy of packets that match the rule to the port *port*
fwd *ipaddr*	Changes the next hop for packets matching the rule to the host address or name *ipaddr*
pipe *pipenbr*	Passes the packet to a dummynet pipe
skipto *number*	Skips all subsequent rules to rule number *number*
uid *user*	Matches all TCP or UDP packets sent and received by user *user* (by name or UID)
gid *group*	Matches all TCP or UDP packets sent and received by group *group* (by group name or GID)

As seen from Table 14.2, for using ipfw with dummynet, the pipe option will be used. This redirects all packets matching the rule to the appropriate dummynet pipe. Once the packet is forwarded to the dummynet pipe, the dummynet rules are applied to the packet.

Rule Logging

The log option instructs ipfw to log matching packets to the system console if the IPFIREWALL_VERBOSE kernel option is used (this is described in the *Configuring dummynet* section). The log amount value *number* defines how many packets for the rule will be logged. After that value, no more packets will be logged to the console.

Rule Definition

This defines the rule specifics:

```
proto from src to dst
```

The *proto* value defines the protocol for the rule. The only possible values are IP, TCP, UDP, ICMP, or numeric value representing a protocol value found in the /etc/protocols file. The *src* and *dst* values represent the source and destination values within the IP packet header. These values can be specified using the following formats:

- IP address (Only a specific IP address matches the rule.)
- IP address/bits (an IP address with a subnet mask represented by the network bits)
- IP address:mask (an IP address with a specific subnet mask)
- any (All IP addresses are matched.)

When using TCP or UDP, you may also specify the port by either port number or service name. An example of an ipfw rule would be:

```
ipfw add 100 allow tcp from any to any 80
```

This rule allows any connection to the HTTP port from any device.

Listing Rules

After creating rule sets, you will want to list them. The list option is used to list either all the rule sets (the default action) or an individual rule set (when supplied an individual rule number). The format is:

```
ipfw list [number]
```

When you are listing the rules, they are displayed as they are when entered on the command line. An example of a rule set listing is:

```
# ipfw list
 00001 allow tcp from any to any 80
 00002 deny icmp from any to any
 00003 deny tcp from any to 192.168.0.6 23
 65535 allow ip from any to any
 #
```

The first three rules are configured rules added by the administrator. The first rule allows all network traffic destined for the HTTP port (80) to pass through the firewall. The second rule blocks all ICMP packets from passing through, while the third rule blocks all Telnet sessions (port 23) with the local firewall address.

The fourth rule is the default rule for the system. In this case, the default rule is set to allow all IP access from any device on the network.

To test the ICMP restriction rule, you can attempt to ping a host on the network, going through the firewall:

```
# ping 192.168.1.6
 PING 192.168.1.6 (192.168.1.6) 56 data bytes
 ping: sendto: Permission denied
 ping: sendto: Permission denied
 ping: sendto: Permission denied
 ping: sendto: Permission denied
 #
```

As can be seen from the output, the firewall software at the system kernel blocked all of the ping packets. Similarly, you can test the Telnet rule set by attempting to Telnet to the address blocked by the firewall:

```
# telnet 192.168.0.6
 Trying 192.168.1.6...
 telnet: Unable to connect to remote host: Permission denied
 #
```

As expected, the firewall rules blocked the Telnet connection attempt.

Removing Rules

Once a rule set is added to the rule list, it remains active until either the system is rebooted or the rule is manually removed. You can manually remove rules using the delete option:

```
ipfw delete number
```

The *number* parameter specifies the rule number to delete. If you want to delete all of the rule sets contained in the firewall, you can use the flush option:

```
ipfw flush
```

When this command is executed, ipfw asks if you are sure you want to remove all of the rules from the firewall. You must respond to the question with a y to delete all of the rules.

> **NOTE** If you use the -f command-line option, ipfw will not ask you to confirm your decision. Use this feature with caution, however, as all of the rules will be deleted.

After the flush command is executed, all of the rules (with the exception of the default rule) will be removed. The default rule cannot be removed from the system.

dummynet Rules

As seen in the *The ipfw Application* section, the ipfw program can create a pipe to dummynet to pass packets through for processing. Once dummynet has the packets, it uses its own command-line options to configure how the pipe handles the packets.

To build a dummynet connection, you first must have an ipfw pipe:

```
ipfw add pipe 1 ip from any to any
```

This command creates a single pipe (number 1) that matches all IP packets from any source and going to any destination. After the pipe is created, it must be configured with specific dummynet network emulation features. This is done with the config command:

```
ipfw pipe 1 config ...
```

After the config command, any dummynet command can be entered. The next section describes these commands.

dummynet Commands

After creating the dummynet pipe in ipfw, you can configure the pipe to emulate the necessary network problems. The following sections show the specific dummynet commands available.

Bandwidth

The bandwidth emulation of the pipe can be configured using the bw option. If no bandwidth value is specified, there are no bandwidth limitations placed on the pipe. However, to emulate specific network link speeds, a bandwidth value can be specified using a numeric value, along with the units of measurement:

- bit/s
- Kbit/s
- Mbit/s
- Byte/s
- Kbyte/s
- Mbyte/s

There should be no space between the numeric value and the unit designation. An example of configuring a dummynet pipe to emulate a 10-MBps LAN connection would look like:

```
ipfw pipe 1 config bw 10Mbit/s
```

There is one word of caution when using bandwidth emulation. Many network links provide full-duplex operation. If a single pipe is configured for handling traffic in both directions, the bandwidth value represents the amount of bandwidth allotted for both directions of traffic. To properly emulate a full-duplex connection, you must create two pipes, and allocate the same bandwidth for each pipe:

```
ipfw add pipe 1 ip from any to any out
ipfw add pipe 2 ip from any to any in
ipfw pipe 1 config bw 100Mbit/s
ipfw pipe 2 config bw 100Mbit/s
```

This example creates two separate pipes, one for incoming traffic and another for outgoing traffic. Each pipe is allotted a 100-Mbps bandwidth, thus emulating a full-duplex 100-MBps fast Ethernet connection.

Delay

The amount of delay introduced into the pipe stream is controlled by the delay option. The value specified should be in milliseconds. Thus, to introduce a 100-millisecond delay on a pipe, you would use the command:

```
ipfw pipe 1 config delay 100 ms
```

Again, you should use caution when configuring the delay value. Pay close attention to how the pipe is configured. If it is a two-direction pipe, the delay value will be added twice to the data stream, thus doubling the delay value.

Random Packet Loss

The percent of packets purposely dropped from the data stream can be configured using the plr option. The value specified should be a floating-point number between 0 (for no packet loss) and 1 (for 100 percent packet loss). To introduce a 5-percent packet loss on a pipe, you would use the command:

```
ipfw pipe 1 config plr 0.05
```

As with the other configuration options, you must pay attention to how the pipe is configured, as a two-directional pipe will double the packet loss value and produce results that you may not want.

There is no set method that is used to drop packets. Packets are randomly dropped from the data stream, using the specified drop percent. The packet drop is based on packet numbers, not on byte counts, so small packets have just as much chance of being dropped as large packets.

Queue Size

The pipe also contains a queue used for holding all packets for the data stream. The size of the holding queue for the pipe is controlled by the queue option. The queue size can be specified in three units:

- Number of packets held
- Bytes held
- Kbytes held

When no units are specified for the value, the value represents the number of packets held in the queue for processing. When the queue fills up, any received packets are dropped (emulating a busy switch or router buffer). When the bytes or Kbytes unit is specified, the value represents the number of bytes that the queue will hold before packets are dropped. When no queue value is specified, the default is 50 packets. If the incoming packets are being sent faster than the pipe is processing them (for example, if a delay or a bandwidth limitation is present) the queue will fill up, and packets will be dropped.

When dummynet drops packets from the queue, it is done based on the queue configuration. If the queue is handling data based on packet count, excessive packets will be dropped on a packet-by-packet basis. If the queue is configured based on the number of bytes (or kilobytes) held, then data is still dropped based on packets, although the incoming packets will be matched against the available bytes in the queue.

Configuring WFQ

To emulate WFQ in dummynet, you must use the ipfw queue option to create a queue of multiple pipes. Each pipe can be assigned a weight value to represent how much of the data flow it should receive.

To create a queue, you must assign it a unique number (from 1 to 65,535), and use the config option to assign values to it:

```
ipfw queue 1 config ...
```

Once the queue is created, it can be assigned to an existing pipe, and assigned a weight value (for WFQ) and a queue size and packet loss rate (separate from the pipe configuration). The command:

```
ipfw queue 1 config pipe 1 weight 30 plr 0.01
```

assigns queue 1 to pipe 1, gives it a weight of 30, and assigns a packet loss rate of 1 percent.

Configuring Multipath Links

The dummynet configuration also allows you to emulate networks that contain multiple paths between endpoints, as is often the case in WAN environments. For this, you use the ipfw prob option, assigning a specific probability to multiple pipes in the same path:

```
ipfw add prob 0.75 pipe 1 ip from 192.168.0.0/24 to localhost
ipfw add pipe 2 ip from 192.168.0.0/24 to localhost
ipfw pipe 1 config bw 128Kbit/s delay 100ms
ipfw pipe 2 config bw 56Kbit/s delay 200ms
```

In this example, two separate pipes are defined between the local host and the local network, representing two separate network paths. The first pipe is assigned a bandwidth of 128 Kbps, representing a fast ISDN link, along with a small amount of delay. The second link is assigned a smaller bandwidth of 56 Kbps, representing a backup 56K modem link.

The data stream is divided between the two different pipes using a probability matrix. For three-quarters of the time, the data will be matched with the first pipe, providing a fast 128-Kbps connection speed. For the remaining quarter of the time, the data stream will be assigned to the 56K pipe.

Installing dummynet

Before you can use dummynet on the FreeBSD system, you must configure the FreeBSD system to use the firewall software. This includes ensuring that the appropriate kernel hooks are in place so ipfw can intercept packets at the kernel level. If your FreeBSD installation already has firewall and dummynet support configured into the kernel, you can skip this section. Otherwise, this section describes how to configure the FreeBSD kernel to use dummynet.

Kernel Options

Since dummynet is a kernel-level facility in FreeBSD, there are several kernel options that must be configured for dummynet to operate. Besides the dummynet kernel options, you must also have the firewall kernel options installed. Table 14.3 lists the various kernel options that are used for dummynet.

Each of these kernel options must be set using the OPTION command in the kernel configuration file. The kernel configuration file is located in the /usr/src/sys/*arch*/conf directory, where *arch* represents the platform name. For IBM-compatible workstations, this is the i386 directory. A default kernel is located in the file GENERIC. This should be copied to a separate file before you work on it.

NOTE You must be the root user to work in the kernel section of the operating system.

Once the copy of the kernel configuration file is made, you can edit it and add the appropriate OPTION lines:

```
OPTION    IPFIREWALL
OPTION    DUMMYNET
```

After saving the new kernel configuration file, you must build a new kernel with the firewall and dummynet options.

Table 14.3 dummynet and Firewall Kernel Options

OPTION	DESCRIPTION
IPFIREWALL	Adds firewall support to the kernel
IPFIREWALL_VERBOSE	Enables logging of firewall events
IPFIREWALL_VERBOSE_LIMIT	Sets the limit of firewall log events
IPFIREWALL_DEFAULT_TO_ACCEPT	Sets the firewall to accept packets by default
DUMMYNET	Enables dummynet
NMBCLUSTER	Sets the number of network buffers available
HZ	Sets the system timer granularity

Building a New Kernel

WARNING Installing a new kernel is a dangerous procedure. Please make sure you have a copy of the old kernel available (preferably on a bootable floppy disk), in case anything goes wrong. If not, your system may become unbootable, and that could be bad—very bad.

With the new copy of the kernel configuration file complete, you can run the config program to create the necessary files for compiling the new kernel:

```
config DNKernel
```

After performing several steps, the config program will finish, and you are ready to compile the new kernel. The config program creates a separate directory with the files necessary for the compile operation. You must first change to that directory, and then run the make command with the depend option:

```
# cd /usr/src/sys/compile/DNKernel
# make depend
```

The name of the directory created by config will match the name of your copy of the kernel configuration file (remember that it is case sensitive). The depend option checks the files for dependencies, and creates the appropriate files for the final compile. Next, you can run the make command to compile and create the new kernel, and run make install to install the new kernel.

NOTE When the new kernel is installed, the old kernel is moved to /kernel.old. Make sure you keep this kernel, because if any problems occur with the new kernel, you will have to copy this kernel to use (assuming you remembered to make a floppy to boot from).

After the new kernel is created, you must reboot the system for it to take effect. When the new system comes back up, it should be ready to accept ipfw commands to control both the ipfw and dummynet applications.

Installing PicoBSD

If you are not adventurous enough to modify your existing FreeBSD kernel, or you do not have a FreeBSD system handy to work with, you can still experiment with dummynet. The dummynet Web site contains a link to PicoBSD, a FreeBSD implementation that fits on a single bootable floppy.

The dummynet Web site is run by Luigi Rizzo, the person who created dummynet. It is located at http://info.iet.unipi.it/~luigi/ip_dummynet/. To copy the PicoBSD floppy, you need both the binary image and a program to write it to a floppy. If you have a running FreeBSD system, you can use the dd program to copy the binary image to a blank floppy disk in the floppy drive. If you do not have a FreeBSD (or Unix) system available, you can use a DOS utility to copy the file to a floppy disk. The most common program used is rawrite.exe, which is also available on the dummynet Web site. The URLs are:

```
http://info.iet.unipi.it/~luigi/ip_dummynet/pico.000608.bin
http://info.iet.unipi.it/~luigi/ip_dummynet/rawrite.exe
```

After downloading both files, you can use dd or rawrite to copy the PicoBSD binary to a blank 1.44-MB floppy disk. When the disk is complete, you can boot any workstation with the floppy, and run the PicoBSD system. The root password is 'setup'.

The PicoBSD system includes both ipfw and dummynet, as well as drivers for ppp communication, and some network interface card support.

Controlling dummynet

After dummynet has been configured into the kernel, you can control the way both dummynet and the firewall software operate on the system, using the sysctl program.

WARNING The sysctl program is used to view and modify settings within the kernel. As with any kernel operation, be careful when modifying the kernel on a production system. Although kernel changes made with sysctl will reset after a boot, you may not want to do this on a production system.

The sysctl program accesses kernel values in a hierarchical manner, similar to the Management Information Base (MIB) structure shown in Chapter 3, "Network Device Utilization." To access individual values, you must know where they are located in the hierarchy. The values used for the firewall and dummynet are located in the net.inet.ip hierarchy.

To check to ensure that the firewall software has been properly added to the kernel, you can view the net.inet.ip.fw.enable value:

```
$ sysctl net.inet.ip.fw.enable
net.inet.ip.fw.enable: 1
$
```

The result shows that the value is set to 1, indicating that the firewall software has been enabled. Another useful value is net.inet.ip.fw.one_pass. This value controls how packets are handled by the firewall.

When the net.inet.ip.fw.one_pass value is set to 1, the firewall will drop the packet out as soon as it matches a single rule. If the value is set to 0, the packet will be reinjected back into the firewall starting at the next rule in order. By default, this value is set to 1, dropping the packet as soon as it matches a single rule in the firewall.

If you are using the dummynet host as a bridge device in the network, you must also set the bridging software to pass through the firewall. This is handled by two values:

```
net.link.ether.bridge
```

which enables bridging when set to 1, and:

```
net.link.ether.bridge_ipfw
```

which instructs the kernel to pass bridged packets through the firewall software when set to 1.

Testing dummynet

After installing ipfw and dummynet on your FreeBSD system (or loading PicoBSD from floppy), you can experiment with setting network emulation environments. This section describes a few tests you can perform to see how dummynet operates.

Setting Network Delays

First, let's set up a simple network delay emulation, and see how it behaves on a network test. This example will create a dummynet pipe for all ICMP traffic, and delay it by 100 ms.

Before starting the network emulation, let's first see the network delay associated with an unencumbered connection. This can be tested by pinging either a remote network host or the local host:

```
# ping localhost
PING localhost (127.0.0.1): 56 data bytes
64 bytes from 127.0.0.1: icmp_seq=0 ttl=255 time=0.039ms
64 bytes from 127.0.0.1: icmp_seq=1 ttl=255 time=0.015ms
64 bytes from 127.0.0.1: icmp_seq=2 ttl=255 time=0.009ms
64 bytes from 127.0.0.1: icmp_seq=3 ttl=255 time=0.018ms

--- localhost ping statistics ---
4 packets transmitted, 4 packets received, 0% packet loss
round-trip min/avg/max/stddev = 0.09/0.020/0.039/0.11 ms
```

Since the ping is just for the local host, the round-trip time should be pretty fast. Now, create a pipe to handle all ICMP packets, and place a delay of 10 ms in the pipe:

```
# ipfw add pipe 1 icmp from any to any
# ipfw pipe 1 config delay 10 ms
# ping localhost
PING localhost (127.0.0.1): 56 data bytes
64 bytes from 127.0.0.1: icmp_seq=0 ttl=255 time=39.752ms
64 bytes from 127.0.0.1: icmp_seq=1 ttl=255 time=39.991ms
64 bytes from 127.0.0.1: icmp_seq=2 ttl=255 time=39.991ms
64 bytes from 127.0.0.1: icmp_seq=3 ttl=255 time=39.991ms

--- localhost ping statistics ---
4 packets transmitted, 4 packets received, 0% packet loss
round-trip min/avg/max/stddev = 39.752/39.931/39.991/0.103 ms
```

Wow. Now the ping times are close to 40 ms. Instead of adding the 10-ms delay, dummynet added a 40-ms delay to the data stream. How did that happen? The answer is in the way dummynet handles traffic.

The dummynet rule created did not specify which packets would be handled, so both incoming and outgoing packets were subjected to the 10-ms delay. That automatically doubled the delay from 10 ms to 20 ms for each packet. Not only does the ping program send out one packet, it also must receive one packet (the ping return packet), requiring two packets to pass through the firewall. Since each packet is subject to the 20-ms delay, now you have two 20-ms delays to wait for, or a total of 40 ms of delays. This is demonstrated in Figure 14.4.

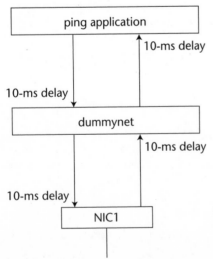

Figure 14.4   Running a ping session through dummynet.

To test this theory, you can create a new dummynet emulation, this time placing a delay only on outbound packets:

```
#ipfw flush
#ipfw add pipe 1 icmp from any to any out
#ipfw pipe 1 delay 10 ms
```

Now, watch the ping delays generated. Sure enough, the delay is now reduced to just 20 ms (remember, you are still dealing with two ICMP packets—thus the double delay).

Setting Network Bandwidths

You can also easily test dummynet emulation on the session bandwidth. Try creating a half-duplex dummynet pipe that emulates a 56-Kbps modem link, and then test a Telnet session on it:

```
#ipfw flush
#ipfw add pipe 1 ip from any to any
#ipfw pipe 1 config bw 56Kbit/s delay 100 ms
```

This configuration creates a single pipe through dummynet handling all IP traffic, and assigns it a 56-Kbps bandwidth. Not only is the bandwidth limited, but an additional delay is added, emulating various network devices that may have to handle the packets along the network path.

After creating the pipe, you can Telnet to either the local host or a remote host on the network. You should notice that the Telnet session is not smooth. Due to the way Telnet behaves (each single character entered must be echoed by the remote host), it is very susceptible to network delays. The additional delay and bandwidth limitation now affect the behavior of the Telnet session. It now behaves just as if you were dialing in on a 56-Kbps modem link. Now maybe you have an idea of how your dial-in customers feel.

Summary

The dummynet application demonstrates the use of common techniques in network emulation. A simple FreeBSD system can be used in a test network environment to emulate the behavior of different types of networks and network devices.

Dummynet can be used to emulate different types of network links from 56-Kbps lines to full-duplex 100-Mbps Fast Ethernet connections. It can also emulate network delays, drops, and errors associated with network devices such as switches and routers.

Dummynet uses the FreeBSD ipfw firewall software. The firewall software must be configured into the FreeBSD kernel to intercept packets as they traverse the system kernel between the network interface card(s) and the operating system. By intercepting all packets, the firewall software can inject delays and errors into the data streams before they get to their destination.

The next chapter discusses the NIST Net network emulator. This application provides network emulation functions similar to those offered by dummynet, but in a slightly different environment, using a different type of interface.

NIST Net

This chapter discusses another network emulation package, NIST Net. The NIST Net application provides network emulation functions on Linux workstations and servers. You can use NIST Net to emulate network problems such as packet loss, delays, bandwidth limitations, and drops. This chapter describes the NIST Net application, how to install it on your Linux system, and how to use it to emulate different types of network environments on your test network.

The NIST Net application was developed (not surprisingly) at the U.S. National Institute of Standards and Technology (NIST), by the Internetworking Technology Group, as a method to test the network dynamics of IP networks. Since it incorporates network emulation techniques, it performs equally well emulating various types of network scenarios.

What Is NIST Net?

The NIST Net application consists of five different parts:

- A Linux kernel module that intercepts network packets
- A command-line tool to add, remove, and modify network emulation rules

- A graphical X Windows tool to add, remove, and modify network emulation rules

- A Linux kernel module and application to monitor rule behavior and statistics

- A Linux kernel module to intercept network packets and redirect them to an alternate location

This section describes each of these pieces, and discusses how they work together to make the NIST Net application a full-featured network emulation tool.

NIST Net Emulations

The NIST Net application is a robust emulator that provides several different types of network emulation. These emulation types can be combined to emulate an entire network environment within the single test box. The different types of emulations supported are:

- Bandwidth limitation
- Packet delay
- Packet reordering
- Packet loss
- Packet duplication
- Packet diversion

The following sections describe each of these emulation features, and how they are implemented within NIST Net.

Bandwidth Limitation

NIST Net allows you to configure the Linux kernel to limit network traffic to a set bandwidth, emulating different types of network links. After you specify the desired bandwidth in bytes per second, NIST Net throttles the incoming packet stream to control the number of bytes passed through the kernel.

If the incoming packet stream is less than the desired bandwidth limitation, no packet delays are performed (at least, not from the bandwidth limiter; a separate packet delay may still be used). If the incoming packet stream exceeds the desired bandwidth limitation, NIST Net delays the packets to match the appropriate output speed.

For calculating the packet stream bandwidth, the current packet is not taken into account. This presents a slight problem, in that there are different ways to send the packet stream within the time limit. NIST Net gives you three options:

- The data is sent at the start of the time period.
- The data is sent in the middle of the time period.
- The data is sent at the end of the time period.

Depending on the rate of the data passing through NIST Net, the different options may produce different results.

Packet Delay

NIST Net can inject three different types of delay into the packet stream:

- A fixed delay
- A variable delay, controlled by the user
- A distributed delay, changing the delay values according to packet traffic

With three different types of packet delays available, NIST Net allows you to configure your emulation to match many different types of network scenarios. NIST Net contains a default distribution delay that modifies packet delay based on a mathematical distribution table. The variable delay provides a method for you to define a new distribution table to load into the NIST Net kernel module.

Packet Reordering

NIST Net also provides packet-reordering emulation. Packet reordering often is a result of multipath networks (usually WANs that use packet switching), where packets sent via different paths arrive at the destination at different times.

This is emulated in NIST Net by dividing the packet stream into separate streams, and injecting different delay values into each stream. If the difference between the injected delays is large enough, one stream should arrive significantly earlier than the other stream. This provides a simple packet-reordering algorithm, whereby a set number of packets arrive out of order at the destination.

Packet Loss

NIST Net provides two different methods for packet loss:

- Uniform percentage of dropped packets
- Traffic-dependent packet drop

The traffic-dependent packet drop method uses the derivative random drop (DRD) method of dropping packets from the incoming packet stream. DRD is a modification of the random early drop (RED) method discussed in Chapter 13, "Measuring Application Performance." While it still incorporates the functionality of RED (the ability to drop more packets from busy packet streams than from slower packet streams), it provides a simpler mechanism to determine which packets should be dropped.

Packet Duplication

A nice feature that NIST Net incorporates is the ability to duplicate packets within the data stream. The duplication value is set as a percentage of packets within the stream. By duplicating a percentage of packets, you can observe how the application (or network device) handles random duplicate data packets within the data stream. This feature allows you to emulate retransmitted packets within the network.

Packet Diversion

Another interesting feature of NIST Net is the ability to divert packets from the data stream to an alternate network address and port. Some type of network application must then capture the diverted packets. Since the diverted packets can be sent to another network address, the application does not have to reside on the same device as NIST Net.

By diverting packets, you can easily monitor the amount and types of packets traversing the kernel. The diverting software allows you to specify what IP sessions to divert by source and destination addresses, as well as source and destination port numbers. This enables you to monitor specific network application traffic on the device.

The NIST Net Kernel Module

Like dummynet, NIST Net must intercept network packets as they traverse the operating system kernel. While dummynet has to be compiled into the FreeBSD kernel to operate, NIST Net takes advantage of the modular Linux kernel.

From Linux kernel version 2.2 on, one nice feature of the Linux kernel is that it has been designed to be modular. The kernel consists of two separate parts:

- Core features that are compiled into the kernel to provide the basic functionality of the system
- Kernel modules that can be loaded and unloaded at will

Many Linux kernel functions have been moved to modular programs that can be loaded and unloaded from the core kernel at any time during the system operation. This helps prevent the kernel bloat of the past, when all system drivers had to be compiled into the kernel at once. Providing kernel modules allows the core kernel to be modified with only the modules that are required for a particular system.

The NIST Net application is installed as a kernel module, and can be inserted or removed at any time from the running Linux system, without adversely affecting the operation of the system. The insmod program is used to install the NIST Net modules. The insmod command line looks like:

```
insmod [-fhkLmnpqrsSvVxXyY] [-e persist_name] [-o module_name]
[-O blob_name] [-P prefix] module [symbol=value...]
```

As you can see from the command line, there are lots of options for the insmod program. Table 15.1 shows the options that are available.

Table 15.1   insmod Command-Line Options

OPTION	DESCRIPTION
-f	Force the module to load even if the kernel version does not match.
-k	Set the auto-clean flag on the module, allowing the module to be removed when it is not in use.
-L	Set a lock to prevent simultaneous loads of the module.
-m	Display a load map of the module.
-n	Go through the steps of loading the module without actually loading it.
-p	Probe the module to determine if it would successfully load.
-q	Quiet mode, do not print a list of unresolved symbols.
-r	Install non-root modules.
-s	Redirect all output to the syslog instead of the terminal.
-S	Force the module to have kallsyms debugging data.
-v	Use verbose mode.
-x	Do not export the module's external symbols.
-X	Export the module's external symbols.
-y	Do not add ksymoops debugging data.

(continued)

Table 15.1 *(continued)*

OPTION	DESCRIPTION
-Y	Add ksymoops debugging data.
-o	Specifically provide the module name.
-O	Specify the binary object name used for the module.
-P	Specify a prefix to use for the module, such as a version name.
-e	Specify any persistent data used by the module.

Under normal conditions, the NIST Net module can be installed using insmod without any additional command-line parameters. The output from the insmod program shows the location of the module file used:

```
# insmod nistnet
Using /lib/modules/2.4.3-20mdk/misc/nistnet.o
#
```

If you need to remove the NIST Net module, you can use the rmmod command:

```
rmmod [ -aehrsvV] module
```

Just like the insmod program, rmmod uses several different command-line options to modify its behavior. Table 15.2 shows the command-line options that are available.

Again, under normal conditions, the NIST Net module can be removed using rmmod without any additional command-line parameters.

Table 15.2 rmmod Command-Line Options

OPTION	DESCRIPTION
-a	Remove all modules (usually not a good idea).
-e	Save persistent data for the module, without unloading it.
-r	Remove a module stack.
-s	Redirect all output to the syslog.
-v	Use verbose mode.
-V	Display the version of rmmod.

The NIST Net Configuration Tools

After the NIST Net module is loaded into the kernel, you must control the way it handles network traffic. This is done using two separate tools:

- cnistnet (a command-line text-based interface)
- xnistnet (an X Windows graphical interface)

Each of these tools can be used to turn the NIST Net network emulation on and off, add, modify, and remove rules, and obtain statistics about running rules.

Unlike dummynet, NIST Net provides the ability to turn the network emulation on and off without having to remove the rules. You can easily move back and forth between normal and network-emulation operations:

```
# cnistnet -d
# ping localhost
PING localhost.localdomain (127.0.0.1) from 127.0.0.1 : 56(84) bytes of
data.
64 bytes from localhost.localdomain (127.0.0.1): icmp_seq=0 ttl=255
time=111 usec
64 bytes from localhost.localdomain (127.0.0.1): icmp_seq=1 ttl=255
time=60 usec
64 bytes from localhost.localdomain (127.0.0.1): icmp_seq=2 ttl=255
time=58 usec
64 bytes from localhost.localdomain (127.0.0.1): icmp_seq=3 ttl=255
time=44 usec
--- localhost.localdomain ping statistics ---
4 packets transmitted, 4 packets received, 0% packet loss
round-trip min/avg/max/mdev = 0.044/0.068/0.111/0.026 ms
# cnistnet -u
# ping localhost
PING localhost.localdomain (127.0.0.1) from 127.0.0.1 : 56(84) bytes of
data.
64 bytes from localhost.localdomain (127.0.0.1): icmp_seq=0 ttl=255
time=100.122 msec
64 bytes from localhost.localdomain (127.0.0.1): icmp_seq=1 ttl=255
time=100.055 msec
64 bytes from localhost.localdomain (127.0.0.1): icmp_seq=2 ttl=255
time=100.149 msec
64 bytes from localhost.localdomain (127.0.0.1): icmp_seq=3 ttl=255
time=100.099 msec

--- localhost.localdomain ping statistics ---
4 packets transmitted, 4 packets received, 0% packet loss
round-trip min/avg/max/mdev = 100.055/100.106/100.149/0.226 ms
#
```

In this example, a rule is used to delay packets to and from the local host by 100 ms. When NIST Net is turned off (using the -d option), the ping results are about 68 microseconds. After NIST Net is turned on (using the -u option), the ping results are about 100 milliseconds. The emulation rule can be enabled or disabled at will, providing great flexibility when testing the network emulation.

> **WARNING** One important thing to remember about NIST Net is that, unlike dummynet, the NIST Net emulation only affects one direction of the packet stream. Thus, when you specify a delay value, such as 100 ms, that value is not doubled for the emulation, as it was in dummynet.

The cnistnet tool handles rules based on the source and destination addresses within the rule. Different rules can be used to affect the behavior of packet traffic between different endpoints on the network (including the local host). Source and destination addresses can be specified in numeric or host-name format, and host or network format. A TCP or UDP port number can also be added to the source or destination address to indicate a specific network application. A few examples would be:

```
192.168.1.1 192.168.1.6 (all IP traffic between the hosts)
192.168.1.0 192.168.5.0 (all IP traffic between the networks)
0.0.0.0 192.168.1.6:80 (all HTTP traffic going to host 192.168.1.6)
shadrach.ipsnet1.net 0.0.0.0 (all IP traffic from host shadrach)
```

After you define the source and destination addresses, the specific network emulation values are specified, such as bandwidth, delays, and loss (see the *Using NIST Net* section).

The xnistnet tool provides the same functionality as the cnistnet tool, except in a graphical environment. Figure 15.1 shows a sample xnistnet window.

You can define the source and destination addresses using the same format options as with cnistnet in the appropriate text boxes. Each network emulation value can also be set within the appropriate text box on the xnistnet window.

The NIST Net Optional Tools

Besides the basic network emulation functions, NIST Net also provides two add-on modules and related programs. This section describes the additional modules and their associated programs.

> **WARNING** Only one add-on module can be active at a time, so care must be taken when using the add-on modules.

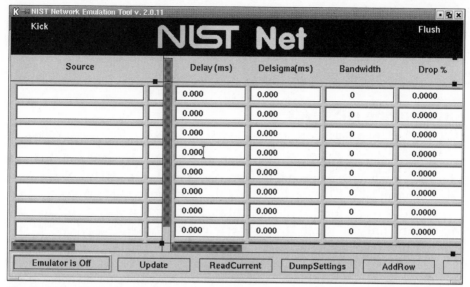

Figure 15.1   The xnistnet window.

mungebox

The mungebox application allows you to watch the statistics of the NIST Net emulation, separately from the NIST Net module. The mungebox application uses its own module, mungemod, which creates its own device, /dev/munge-box, which interfaces with the NIST Net module. This allows the mungebox program to access information from the NIST Net emulator. The mungebox program is used to provide statistical information about the performance of the NIST Net module.

The mungebox application is important not so much for what it does, but more for what it demonstrates. The mungebox application demonstrates how to write applications that interface with NIST Net to extract information from the NIST Net module.

nistspy

The nistspy application also interfaces with the NIST Net module. The spy-mod module is used to create a device (/dev/spymod) that redirects traffic from NIST Net to a user-specified destination.

This provides a method to watch network traffic in real time from a separate network address (the destination can be specified as a hostname or IP address, and a TCP port number). By redirecting all traffic to an alternate destination, you can set up a monitor application to watch all of the network traffic defined in the NIST Net rules.

Downloading and Installing NIST Net

This section describes how to obtain the NIST Net application, and install it on your Linux system.

Downloading NIST Net

The NIST Net main Web page is located at http://snad.ncsl.nist.gov/itg/nistnet. This page contains information about NIST Net, as well as links to an installation guide Web page, and instructions on how to use NIST Net.

To download NIST Net, you must go to the installation guide Web page, and access the download form Web page (http://snad.ncsl.nist.gov/itg/nistnet/requestform.html). Although NIST Net is free software, NIST requires that you fill out a simple questionnaire before being able to download the software. The questionnaire only asks a few questions (such as your company or organization name, your area of interest, and an email address). After answering the questions, you are taken to a download area where you can download the latest version of NIST Net (at the time of this writing, it is version 2.0.12).

The NIST Net application is distributed in source code. You must compile the source code to produce the NIST Net modules and application programs. The distribution file is in the standard compressed tar format (nistnet.2.0.12 .tar.gz). You must uncompress and untar the distribution into a working directory. The command:

```
tar -zxvf nistnet.2.0.12.tar.gz
```

creates the working directory nistnet, and places all of the source code files in a directory structure beneath it.

Compiling NIST Net

Unfortunately, the NIST Net application requires quite a few different things to be present on the system before you can successfully compile the programs. The two main things that must be present are:

- The system kernel source files
- The X Windows development files

Each of these presents its own set of problems when you are trying to prepare the system for NIST Net.

Getting the Required Files

Although NIST Net does not require you to recompile the Linux kernel, you must have the kernel source files installed on your system. This allows the NIST Net application to compile with the appropriate header file information for the kernel.

Most Linux distributions include the kernel source files as an add-on package. My Mandrake 8.0 Linux system uses the Linux version 2.4.3 kernel, included in the kernel-source RPM package on the secondary CD-ROM contained in the package. Unfortunately, you cannot just install the kernel-source RPM package by itself. I had to load quite a few additional RPM packages before I could load the kernel source. The packages I had to load on my system were:

- bison-1.28-8mdk.i586.rpm
- byacc-1.9-9mdk.i586.rpm
- db3-devel-3.1.171mdk.i586.rpm
- egcs-1.1.2-44mdk.i586.rpm
- egcs-cpp-1.1.2-44mdk.i586.rpm
- flex-2.5.4a-14mdk.i586.rpm
- libncurses5-devel-5.2-12mdk.i586.rpm (some Linux systems call this ncurses-devel)

Each of these RPM packages must be installed using the rpm program:

```
# rpm -Uvh bison-1.28-8mdk.i586.rpm
```

After all of the packages are installed, you can install the actual kernel-source package (kernel-source-2.4.3-20mdk.i586.rpm on my system).

Besides the standard kernel source files, you must also have the current kernel configuration files available for NIST Net. These are the files used to determine which drivers are loaded in the current kernel, and how they are loaded. Many Linux systems include these files by default (they were installed by default on my Mandrake 8.0 Linux sytem). If they are not included, or are not configured for the current kernel, you must recreate them manually.

This is done by changing to the /usr/src/linux directory, and running the make command with either the config or menuconfig option (the menuconfig option provides simpler menu options for installing kernel drivers).

WARNING When recreating the kernel configuration files, make sure that you include all of the drivers required for your system.

After the configuration files are created, you must run the make program again with the dep option.

Once the kernel-source package is installed, you must also install an X Windows development library. There are several different X Windows libraries that are used in the Linux world. My Mandrake 8.0 Linux uses the XPM X Windows library, which is included in the libxpm4-devel-3.4k-16mdk.i586.rpm distribution RPM package. The NIST Net Web page indicates that it can also be used with the Athena Xaw, Xaw3d, and neXtaw libraries.

Compiling the Source Code

After installing all of the required libraries and kernel files, you are ready to start compiling the actual NIST Net application. The nistnet working directory contains the standard configure script, which is used to check the system for the necessary files, and to create the makefile used to compile the program.

Before running the configure script, you can view the Config file located in the nistnet directory. There are a few options (such as the bandwidth delay handling options) that can be modified and set to the values you require for your network emulation environment.

When running the configure script, it will ask you a couple of questions:

```
$ ./configure
Kernel headers found at /lib/modules/2.4.3-20mdk/build/include/linux
Add explicit congestion notification (ECN) support [yes]?
Add class/type of service (COS) support [no]?
```

The first thing the configure script does is search for the kernel source files. If they are not found on the system, an error message is displayed, and the configure script stops. After finding the kernel source files, the configure script asks if you want to use explicit congestion notification (ECN) support. This uses the TCP ECN feature to notify network devices when the network (or in this case, the network emulation) is getting overloaded. If the TCP device supports ECN, it should automatically start throttling packets to help reduce the congestion. ECN support will be included by default if you hit the Enter key for the question.

The second question asks if you want to include IP class of service (CoS) support. This includes the standard IP Type of Service (ToS) as well as the newer CoS protocol used to prioritize packets within the IP packet stream. If you need to emulate networks that support CoS applications (such as streaming audio or video), you should include CoS support in the NIST Net emulation.

After the configure script finishes, you are ready to compile the NIST Net application. One makefile is used to compile all of the kernel modules and application programs associated with NIST Net. From the nistnet directory, just run the make and make install programs (you will have to be the root user to run the make install program). This installs the NIST Net kernel modules in a common location in a subdirectory under the /lib/modules directory, where the system modules are stored. On my system, they are located in the directory:

```
/lib/modules/2.4.3-20mdk/misc
```

The module names are:

- mungemod.o (the mungebox module)
- nistnet.o (the main NIST Net module)
- spymod.o (the nistspy module)

The command-line executable files (cnistnet, mungebox, and nistspy) are placed in the /usr/local/bin directory, while the xnistnet X Windows application is placed in the X Windows application directory (/usr/X11R6/bin on my system).

NOTE NIST Net also includes an additional executable file, hitbox, which is now obsolete, but still provided for backwards compatibility. Use the cnistnet program instead.

Loading NIST Net

Before you can start NIST Net, you must first load the nistnet kernel module. This can be done directly, using the insmod program, or you can use the Load.Nistnet script file located in the NIST Net working directory. One nice feature of using the Load.Nistnet script is that it attempts to protect the enhanced real-time clock (RTC) character device driver.

Unfortunately, NIST Net conflicts with the RTC driver on Linux systems. To avoid this, the Load.NistNet script attempts to unload the rtc module from the kernel before loading the NIST Net module. If this is not done, the rtc module will not function properly, even after the NIST Net module is unloaded.

There is one caveat to this. Many Linux systems (including my Mandrake distribution) load the RTC driver as part of the core kernel drivers, and not as a module. If this is the case, you cannot unload the RTC module before installing NIST Net. You will see this if you use the Load.Nistnet script:

```
# ./Load.Nistnet
rmmod: module rtc is not loaded
Couldn't find rtc module - /dev/rtc will be mostly
unusable after running nistnet.  Sorry about that....
To prevent this message, recompile rtc
```

```
(Enhanced Real Time Clock Support, under
character devices) as a module.
Using /lib/modules/2.4.3-20mdk/misc/nistnet.o
nistnet module installed
#
```

As the message states, you should rebuild the Linux kernel (using the make menuconfig described in the *Compiling NIST Net* section earlier), and specify that the RTC driver be loaded as a module. Within the menuconfig menus, the RTC support will appear under the character devices section. Select M (for module) from the menuconfig options. After you do this, the RTC support is contained in the rtc module, which can be loaded and unloaded as necessary.

When the NIST Net module has been installed, the device /dev/nistnet should be available on the system. Now you are ready to test out the NIST Net installation.

Using NIST Net

This section describes the methods that are used to configure NIST Net to emulate different network environments. Most of the scenarios are similar to the way the dummynet system was configured, creating separate rules for each emulation scenario.

Using cnistnet

The cnistnet tool uses command-line options to add, modify, and remove emulation rules, as well as show statistics about the rules. Table 15.3 shows the command-line options available for cnistnet.

Table 15.3   cnistnet Command-Line Options

OPTION	DESCRIPTION
-a	Adds a new rule definition
-d	Disables the NIST Net rules
-D n	Turn on debugging with level n (1 = minimum, 9 = maximum)
-F	Flushes the NIST Net emulation queues
-G	Shows global statistics
-K	Kickstarts the clock
-r	Removes a rule definition

Table 15.3 *(continued)*

OPTION	DESCRIPTION
-R	Displays the current rule table (add -n to show address in numeric format)
-s	Displays the current statistics for each rule
-S	Constantly displays the current statistics for each rule
-u	Disables the NIST Net rules
-U	Turns off debugging

The -a, -r, -s, and -S options all specify a source and destination address pair to uniquely define the rule. The format of the source and destination addresses is:

```
-a src[:port[.protocol]] dst[:port[.protocol]] [cos]
```

The first two options listed are the source and destination addresses the rule applies to. The addresses are specified using the format:

```
address[:port[.protocol]]
```

The address can be specified using a hostname, a numeric host IP address value, or a network IP address value. If the address specified is a network, traffic from any host on that network will be affected by the rule.

By default, the rule will apply to all IP packets from (or to) the specified address. You can also specify an optional port number, to further define the traffic (such as port 80 for HTTP traffic). By default, the port number will apply to both TCP and UDP ports. You can further define the protocol if necessary (using tcp or udp).

After the source and destination addresses are specified, the Class of Service (CoS) value may be entered, if you are using a specific CoS for the rule (and CoS support was enabled when you compiled NIST Net).

When adding a new rule, you must specify the add new keywords after the destination address. Next, a list of emulation options that are desired for the rule must be specified. Each emulation option uses a special command-line option. These options are shown in Table 15.4.

Table 15.4 cnistnet New Rule Options

OPTION	DESCRIPTION
—bandwidth	Specifies the bandwidth limitation (in bytes per second)
—delay	Specifies the delay (in milliseconds)

(continued)

Table 15.4 *(continued)*

OPTION	DESCRIPTION
—drop	Specifies the drop percentage
—drd	Specifies the DRD minimum and maximum values
—dup	Specifies the duplicate packet percentage

For example, to specify a rule for the local host that limits the bandwidth to 7,000 bytes/second, adds a 100-millisecond delay, drops 3 percent of the packets, and duplicates 5 percent of the packets, you would use the following command:

```
# cnistnet -a localhost localhost add new --bandwidth 7000 --delay 100 -
-drop 3 --dup 5
addnistnet: localhost:0 to localhost:0 (prot 0 cos add),
            delay 100.000000 (sigma 0.000000 corr 0.000000),
            bandwidth 7000, drop 3.000000 (corr 0.000000),
            dup 5.000000 (corr 0.000000),
            drdmin 0, drdmax 0, drdcongest 0
#
```

When the command is executed, NIST Net returns the status of the request. The complete rule is displayed, along with any error messages that may result (for instance, if the NIST Net module is not loaded).

You can display the active rules at any time by using the -R option:

```
# cnistnet -R
cnistnet -a localhost.localdomain localhost.localdomain --delay 100.000
--drop 2.9999 --dup 5.0003 --bandwidth 7000
#
```

Notice that the rule is displayed exactly as it would be typed on the command line. There is a reason for this. When the NIST Net module is unloaded (either manually, or due to a reboot), all of the entered rules are lost. If you are using a complicated emulation with lots of rules, it can be tedious having to reload all of the rules every time the system is rebooted.

Instead, you can redirect the output of the -R command option to a file, and turn the file into an executable script:

```
# cnistnet -R > rules.nist
# chmod 700 rules.nist
```

Now, after the rules are flushed from the module, all you need to do is run the rule script file to automatically replace all of the rules with a single command.

After loading the rules, you can start NIST Net using the -u command-line option. After a while, you can observe the statistics, using either the -s (for one sample) or -S (for continuous sampling) option:

```
# cnistnet -s localhost localhost
statnistnet: localhost -> localhost (0)
n_drops rand_drops drd_drops  mem_drops  drd_ecns   dups   last packet
size  qsize bandwidth  total bytes
  2            2         0          0          0      9  1041531601.109551
56      0       140         6608
#
```

When specifying the -s and -S options, remember to specify the source and destination addresses that identify the rule you want to monitor. This output shows that indeed some packets have been dropped and duplicated on the emulator.

Besides the fixed values for packet delay, drops, and duplicates, you can also define distributions for variable delays, drops, and duplicates. The distribution information is added as an additional value with the original information, separated with a forward slash.

To specify a delay distribution, you must specify the mean value as the fixed delay entry, and the standard deviation as a second value:

```
# cnistnet -a localhost localhost add new —delay 100 2.12
```

This rule defines a mean delay of 100 ms, with a 2.12-ms standard deviation. To also incorporate a correlation value, you must use the forward slash:

```
# cnistnet -a localhost localhost add new —delay 100 2.12/0.95
```

The drop and duplication correlation values can also be defined with their fixed percentage values, in the same way:

```
# cnistnet -a localhost localhost add new —drop 5.0/0.65 —dup 2.0/0.76
```

Using xnistnet

The xnistnet program provides the same functionality as the cnistnet program, but in an easier-to-view graphical form. When you start the xnistnet program, a blank form appears (unless there are already rules configured in the running NIST Net module. This is shown in Figure 15.2.

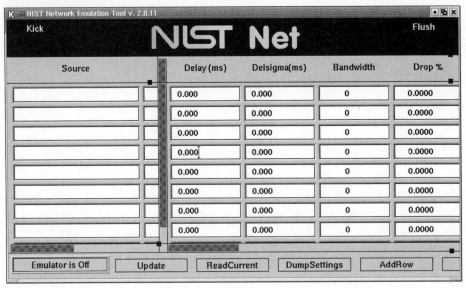

Figure 15.2 Blank xnistnet form.

Within the xnistnet form, you can scroll across the window panes for the addresses and rule definitions, by clicking on the scroll bar on the bottom. What may not be obvious, however, is the way it scrolls. If you click the left mouse button on the scroll bar, the window shifts to the left. To get the window to scroll back to the right, you must click the right mouse button.

Creating Rules

The left-hand xnistnet window provides text boxes for the source and destination addresses that the rule applies to, and for the CoS value, as well as a button to click if you want to remove an existing rule from the emulator.

As with cnistnet, you can enter the source and destination values either as hostnames or IP addresses, along with an optional port number and protocol name. Figure 15.3 shows the localhost values entered into the address area, and the individual emulation values set for the rule.

After the rule emulation values have been configured, you must click the Update button to activate the rule on the emulator. If the NIST Net emulator is not enabled, you must click the Emulator On button to enable the emulator. When the emulator is running, the button name changes to Emulator Off. You can click that button to disable the NIST Net emulator.

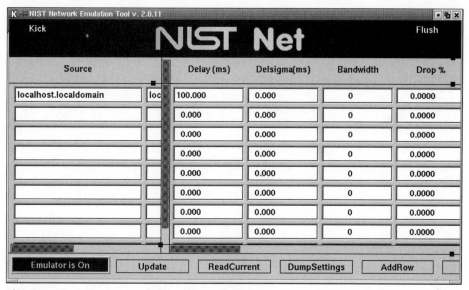

Figure 15.3   xnistnet emulation rule text boxes.

Modifying Rules

The right-hand xnistnet window provides text boxes both for the emulation rule values and rule statistics output. This provides a method to easily view the rule statistics in real time. The first set of text boxes shows the current emulator values for the rule. The emulator values are:

- Delay (in milliseconds)
- Delay standard deviation (in milliseconds)
- Bandwidth (in bytes per second)
- Drop (in percentage of packets per data stream)
- Duplicate (in percentage of packets per data stream)
- DRDmin (the minimum packet queue, in packets)
- DRDmax (the maximum packet queue, in packets)

After the emulation rule values, the emulation statistical information is displayed, also using text boxes. The values displayed are:

- The running average bandwidth value (in bytes per second) passing through the rule
- The total number of dropped packets resulting from the rule

- The total number of duplicated packets resulting from the rule
- The time the last packet was processed by the rule (in milliseconds)
- The size of the last packet processed by the rule (in bytes)
- The number of packets in the rule queue waiting to be processed
- The total number of bytes processed by the rule

These values are shown in Figure 15.4.

The emulation statistical values are updated continuously, as long as the emulator is enabled, and the xnistnet application is running. This provides a handy way to monitor the activity on all of the rules from one place.

Summary

This chapter discussed the NIST Net network emulation package. NIST Net provides a way to emulate different network environments from a Linux system using standard network connections and kernel packet processing. Since NIST Net can be used on any Linux system, it provides an inexpensive method to emulate networks in test environments.

The NIST Net application is installed as a Linux kernel module. Since it is a kernel module, it can be loaded and unloaded at any time, without affecting the operating system. This feature enables you to experiment with the network emulation features without adversely affecting any other applications using the system.

Figure 15.4   xnistnet emulation statistical values.

NIST Net uses both a command-line program and an X Windows program to allow you to define and customize network emulation features. NIST Net provides emulation for bandwidth limitation, packet delays, packet drops, and packet duplication. Each of these features can be defined in rules that apply to specific network and/or host addresses, allowing you to configure several different rules for different network situations.

The next chapter describes a slightly different approach to network emulation. The Network Traffic Generator application provides a method for actually generating different types of network traffic on a test network, providing an environment that can emulate different types of cross-traffic on a production network.

## CHAPTER 16

Network Traffic Generator

This chapter describes a different method of simulating network traffic on a test network. The Network Traffic Generator application allows a single Unix workstation or server to emulate network traffic generated by multiple network workstations. You can use this technique to emulate production network traffic on test networks. The first part of this chapter explains the concept of a network traffic generator. A description of the Network Traffic Generator application follows, with instructions for installing and using it.

As described in Chapter 13, "Measuring Application Performance," testing network applications on a test network does not necessarily provide accurate results. The test network does not properly duplicate the network environment present in normal production network traffic. To duplicate the production network environment, you must inject cross-traffic on the test network that emulates normal production data. The Network Traffic Generator application can be used to generate different types of network traffic, in varying quantities, from a single network host. This section describes the Network Traffic Generator application.

What Is Network Traffic Generator?

Robert Sandilands developed the Network Traffic Generator application primarily as a method for creating sample network traffic to test network equipment. It also performs well as a generator of sample network traffic on test networks, emulating production traffic. This section describes how Network Traffic Generator works, and the different program pieces that are involved in using it.

How Network Traffic Generator Works

The Network Traffic Generator application was designed to be a modular application, providing a way for programmers to expand its functionality by creating additional modules. The modules are divided into four categories:

- The core module
- The protocol module
- The payload module
- The reply module

Figure 16.1 demonstrates how these modules fit together.
The following sections describe each of the different modules.

The Core Modules

The core modules provide the basic functionality for the application. They define whether the Network Traffic Generator application will behave as a client device or as a server device.

The server module listens for incoming network connection attempts, and services them according to the configuration of the protocol and reply modules. One server module can service multiple client connections. As each new connection is received, a new instance of the server module is spawned to handle the individual client connection. Currently, the only server module provided is the basic module, which can handle packets of any size up to 100 Kbytes. After the server accepts the client connection, it processes incoming packets from the client, and responds in a manner appropriate to the specified response module.

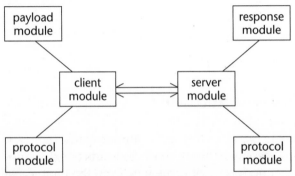

Figure 16.1   The Network Traffic Generator model.

The client module attempts to connect to a remote server device using a specified protocol module. The number of clients used is specified in the client module. Currently, the only client module available is the fixed module, which provides a fixed number of client instances to handle the specified client connections. Each client handles a single connection to the server.

The Protocol Modules

The protocol modules define the network protocol used to communicate between the client and the server. Obviously, both must be using the same protocol to properly communicate.

Different protocol modules can produce different types of network traffic. Currently, Network Traffic Generator provides two protocol modules:

- tcp
- udp

The tcp module provides connection-oriented communications between the client and server. Each TCP connection must be established using the standard TCP SYN-ACK handshake method, and each connection must be closed using the FIN-ACK method. Creating connections for each test session produces more network overhead for the test. Besides the normal TCP overhead, TCP connections also must account for each packet transmitted between the hosts, resulting in the possibility of packet retransmissions and duplicate packets.

The udp module provides connectionless communications between the client and server. Since the communication is connectionless, it is possible to have packet loss within the data stream. The udp module does not account for packet loss, so any dropped packets are not detected or retransmitted.

The Payload Modules

The payload modules define how the client transmits data to the server. There are currently three different payload modules available:

- fixed
- increasing
- random

The fixed payload module provides a data payload of a fixed size for each test packet. The size of the payload is specified when the client module is started, and must be at least 8 bytes. Currently, the maximum payload size supported by Network Traffic Generator is 100 Kbytes.

The increasing payload module increases the size of the sent packets during the length of the communication session. The payload size starts out at a specified size, and increments by a specified amount either until the end of the session, or until it reaches a specified maximum value, or 100 Kbytes. The number of times each size packet is sent can also be specified when the client starts.

The random payload module selects a randomly sized data payload for each packet in the communication session. The minimum and maximum values can be specified when the client starts. The number of times each size of packet is sent can also be specified.

The Response Modules

The way the server module responds to client packets is controlled in the response module. Currently there are two response modules available:

- ack
- echo

The ack response module instructs the server to respond to each data packet received from the client with a simple 8-byte acknowledgment packet. This response is used for both TCP and UDP protocols.

The echo response module instructs the server to respond to each data packet received from the client with the contents of the original data packet received.

WARNING Using the echo response module should double the network bandwidth used by Network Traffic Generator, as each data packet is sent twice on the network (once from the client to the server, and again from the server back to the client).

The Network Traffic Generator Programs

The Network Traffic Generator application uses two separate programs to perform the traffic generating. This section describes the two programs, and explains how they are used to create the artificial network traffic on the test network.

Command-Line Interface

The Network Traffic Generator application incorporates command-line interface programs to control the server and client programs.

The trafserver program is the server side of the Network Traffic Generator application. It listens for incoming connection attempts from the client program, and handles each connection as a separate instance.

The trafclient program is the client side of the Network Traffic Generator application. It is used to send packets to the server program from a remote device on the network. There can be multiple client programs connecting to the same server program, as demonstrated in Figure 16.2.

The test network can contain multiple server and client programs running on separate devices on the network. A single client device can emulate multiple production clients, so only one client is required to emulate production traffic on a single subnet. If you want to emulate traffic on several subnets, you can set up a single client device on each subnet, and have them emulate multiple production clients sending data to a single host server. By forcing the clients to connect to servers on other subnets, you can also test network devices, such as routers or switches, for any loading problems.

X Windows Interface

The Network Traffic Generator application also includes an X Windows interface version of the command-line programs. The xtrafserver and xtrafclient programs provide a graphical interface to the trafserver and trafclient programs. The values that are normally entered as command-line options are instead entered as text box values on the X Windows interface.

NOTE The X Windows interface programs require the Kylix Linux libraries to compile and run. Installing these libraries is covered in the *Downloading and Installing the Package* section.

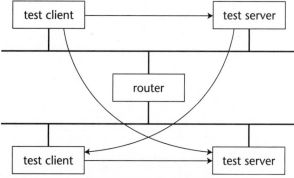

Figure 16.2   The Network Traffic Generator server and client programs.

Generating Network Traffic

The advantage of using the Network Traffic Generator application is its ability to emulate different types and quantities of network traffic from a single client device. This enables the network administrator to inject network traffic patterns in test networks while testing network applications.

Depending on the type of network traffic present on your production network, you will want to emulate different forms of traffic. The most common forms of traffic seen on production networks are:

- Bulk data transfers
- Client/server transactions
- Connectionless communication

This section describes these different types of network traffic, and explains how the Network Traffic Generator emulates them.

Bulk Data Transfers

Bulk data transfers are often used in networks to transfer data files from one network device to another. Whether the operation is performed by a standard FTP file transfer, or by copying a file to a network file server drive, the format of the network traffic is similar: one device sends large packets of data to another device, which acknowledges the packets with a small ACK packet. Of course, this process is repeated many times during the course of the file transfer, as demonstrated in Figure 16.3.

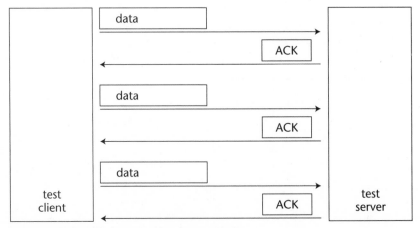

Figure 16.3 Bulk data transfer characteristics.

Since the bulk data transfer must use guaranteed packet delivery, almost all data transfer methods use a connection-oriented protocol, such as TCP. This ensures that the data packets sent to the remote device are received error-free and in the proper order. Of course, the connection-oriented protocols also can produce packet retransmissions, which will cause additional network load.

During the course of the bulk data transfer, network utilization often reaches peak levels, as the data stream is sent to the remote device. This produces network degradation for the duration of the data transfer.

The bulk data transfer environment is emulated in Network Traffic Generator using the payload module. You can set the payload for each data packet to any size (currently from 8 bytes to 100,000 bytes). The packet size you select should match the block size used in the data transfer method you are emulating. Many network file systems use 4,000-byte block sizes to transfer data.

The response module used should be the ack module. This module just sends a simple 8-byte acknowledgment packet back to the sending device, without duplicating the actual data transferred.

Client/Server Transactions

Client/server transactions are common in networks that use database systems such as Oracle or Microsoft SQL Server. The client application sends short database requests to the server, which processes each request and sends a larger data stream back in response to the query. This characteristic is demonstrated in Figure 16.4.

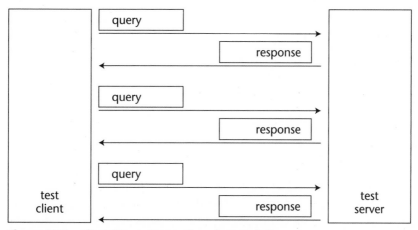

Figure 16.4   Client/Server transaction characteristics.

In many ways, the client/server transaction produces the opposite traffic pattern from the bulk data transfer pattern. The client sends smaller query packets (usually less than 1,000 bytes) to the server, which in turn sends larger response packets containing data back to the client. The response packets are usually not a set size, but can be a random amount of data, depending on the query results.

While the server response packets are larger than the client query packets, they are usually smaller than the bulk data transfer packets, as the returned data query is usually limited in size.

Connectionless Communication

Connectionless communication network patterns are not often found in production networks, except when there are managed network devices. Managed network devices use the SNMP protocol to communicate with configuration devices (as described in Chapter 3, "Network Device Utilization").

Most connectionless communication is performed using the UDP protocol. Since the transactions are connectionless, there is no guarantee that the packets will arrive at the intended destination. At times of high network utilization, connectionless sessions are often plagued with high packet loss rates, resulting in an increase of packet retransmissions (which of course just adds to the network utilization problem).

Downloading and Installing the Package

The Network Traffic Generator application can be downloaded as a source code distribution file to compile on your Unix system. This section describes the steps to download, compile, and install Network Traffic Generator.

Downloading

The main Web site for Network Traffic Generator is located at:

```
http://galileo.spaceports.com/~rsandila/traffic.html
```

This page contains links to the Network Traffic Generator download page, located at the SourceForge Web site. Currently, there are two supported versions of Network Traffic Generator. The older version is called traffic, and contains code that is copyrighted by Robert Sandilands' former employer, Secure Worx South Africa (Pty) Ltd. The newer version, called newtraffic, is a completely new package, solely developed, released, and maintained by Sandilands.

WARNING The really confusing part of the situation is that the newtraffic distribution file is called traffic, which is the same as the old distribution file name. Make sure you download from the newtraffic-source area on SourceForge.

At the time of this writing, the current version of traffic is 0.1.3, and it is available in three different distribution formats:

- A compressed and tarred source code distribution: traffic-0.1.3.tgz
- An RPM packaged source code file: traffic-0.1.3.-2mdk.src.rpm
- A zipped distribution file: traffic-0.1.3.zip

Any one of the source code distribution files can be used to create the working directory, called traffic-0.1.3. All of the source code files are placed in the working directory.

Before Compiling

Before you can compile the traffic-0.1.3 file, you must first make sure you have all the necessary pieces on your system. Specifically, there are two different packages that you must make sure you have installed:

- fastdep
- Kylix libraries

fastdep

Traffic uses the fastdep application, created by Bart Vanhauwaert, which is a fast dependency generator for C and C++ programs. If your Unix distribution does not install fastdep by default, it may be included as an additional package in your distribution.

If it is not included in your Unix distribution, you can download the source code (or binary files for Linux) from the fastdep Web site, located at:

```
http://www.irule.be/bvh/c++/fastdep/
```

The Web site contains the source code distribution as fastdep.tar.gz, or a binary Mandrake Linux distribution file as fastdep-0.14-1.i586.rpm. If you download the binary rpm distribution, you can install it using the standard RPM package installer program.

If you download the source code, you must uncompress it into a working directory (fastdep-0.14 at the time of this writing), and use the configure and make programs to compile it.

> **WARNING** Both fastdep and traffic use C++ code. You must ensure that you have a proper C++ compiler (such as the GNU g++ package) installed on your system.

Kylix Libraries

If you plan on using the X Windows graphical interface program xtrafserver or xtrafclient, you must have the Kylix libraries and runtime installed on your Linux system.

Kylix is a Borland compiler product for the Linux environment. Applications created using Kylix must have the Kylix runtime libraries installed on the Linux system to operate. Applications that include Kylix function calls must have the Kylix compiler libraries installed to compile properly on the system.

In the case of traffic, both the Kylix compiler libraries and runtime libraries must be installed on the Linux system for traffic to compile and run. The Kylix libraries are freely available for download from the Kylix library Web site, kylixlibs, also maintained on the SourceForge Web site:

```
http://kylixlibs.sourceforge.net/index.html
```

The Kylixlibs project maintains packages for Red Hat, Mandrake, and Debian Linux distributions. The list of library files that must be downloaded is:

- kylixlibs3-borqt
- kylixlibs3-runtime
- kylixlibs3-borstlctrl
- kylixlibs3-unwind
- kylixlibs3-qt

Each of these files has a unique filename for the specific Linux distributions. Download the library set appropriate for your distribution, and use the distribution package installer program to install them.

> **WARNING** The Kylix libraries require the Xfree86 version 4.1 or newer libraries. My old Mandrake 8.0 system only had version 4.0.3 libraries, and had to be upgraded. If you are planning to use the X Windows traffic programs, it is probably easier to install a newer Linux installation package, preferably one of the ones that has Kylix library support.

Compiling and Installing

After the kylixlib packages are installed, you are ready to compile traffic on your system. You must be in the working directory (traffic-0.1.3) to compile the package.

The distribution uses the autoconf program to create the configure script, so the first step is to run autoconf from the working directory. This creates the standard configure script, which can then be run to prepare for compiling the application. If you want to include the xtrafserver and xtrafclient programs, you must use the --with-kylix command-line option with the configure command:

```
$ ./configure --with-kylix
```

As usual, the configure script checks the system for software dependencies, and creates an appropriate makefile. After the makefile is created, you use the make program to compile the source code and create the executable programs, and the install option of the make program to install the executable files in a common location. For most Unix distributions, the trafserver and trafclient programs are placed in the /usr/local/bin directory. For these programs to work, they must have access to each of the module libraries used by Network Traffic Generator. These module libraries are stored in a separate location from the executable programs. On my Linux system, they were stored in /usr/local/lib/traffic. Table 16.1 lists the library files that were installed.

Table 16.1   Network Traffic Generator Library Files

LIBRARY	USED BY	DESCRIPTION
client_fixed.so	trafclient	The fixed client module
payload_fixed.so	trafclient	The fixed-size payload module
payload_increasing.so	trafclient	The increasing size payload module
payload_random.so	trafclient	The random size payload module
protocol_tcp.so	trafclient and trafserver	The TCP protocol module
protocol_udp.so	trafclient and trafserver	The UDP protocol module
reply_ack.so	trafserver	The acknowledgment reply module
reply_echo.so	trafserver	The echo reply module
server_basic.so	trafserver	The basic server module

Using Network Traffic Generator

After the executable and library files are installed, you can start using Network Traffic Generator to emulate traffic on your test network. This section describes the different features of the trafclient and trafserver programs, along with some instructions on how to set up a test environment for network application testing.

WARNING The Network Traffic Generator application is intended to generate network traffic on test networks. Using it on a production network will impede the flow of production network traffic.

Command-Line Options

The trafclient and trafserver command-line programs both require options to configure the client and server modules. This first section describes the command-line options required to configure Network Traffic Generator to generate specific types of network traffic.

Server

The trafserver program must know which server and reply modules to use, along with the specific protocols and ports used for the test traffic. All of these variables must be configured on the command line when starting trafserver. The format of the trafserver command line is:

```
trafserver -sn servermode -rn replymod [-L librarypath] protocol port ...
```

The first two options on the command line define the server and reply modules used for the test server. At the time of this writing, there is only one server module available, the basic module. There are two possible reply modules, ack and echo. As mentioned earlier in the *How Network Traffic Generator Works* section, the ack module returns a simple acknowledgment packet to the client, while the echo module returns the entire client packet.

After specifying the server and reply modules, you can optionally define the location of the traffic library files. If you have followed the standard install procedures, this should not be necessary.

The final options to define are the protocol modules and port numbers used. You can define multiple protocol and port pairs, up to the length limitation of the command line. The trafserver program will listen for incoming connection attempts for the protocol defined on the port numbers defined.

A sample trafserver session would look like this:

```
$ trafserver -sn basic -rn ack tcp 9050 udp 9050
trafserver Starting
Initializing Reply
Initializing Protocols
Initializing Servers
Starting servers. Press ENTER to end.
```

This command starts two server sessions, one listening on TCP port 9050, and a second one listening on UDP port 9050. Both servers will use the basic server module, along with the ack reply module. The trafserver program will block the terminal that it is started on, until you press the Enter key to stop the servers.

WARNING Unix ports 0 through 1023 are restricted to the root user. If you select port numbers above 1023, you do not have to be the root user to use trafserver.

Client

The trafclient program also needs information to contact the server program and send test packets. As with the trafserver program, trafclient gets the required information from the command-line options. The format of the trafclient command line is more complex, as there are more modules to have to define values for.

There are three categories of options that you must configure on the command line:

- The client module options
- The protocol module options
- The payload module options

The client module options are shown in Table 16.2.

Table 16.2   trafclient Client Module Options

OPTION	DESCRIPTION
-cn	Defines the client module name (currently, only fixed is available)
-cmin	Defines the minimum number of client connections
-cmax	Defines the maximum number of client connections

(continued)

Table 16.2 *(continued)*

OPTION	DESCRIPTION
-cinc	Defines the increment value of client connections
-ctim	Defines the time the client will send packets
-n	Defines the number of client sessions created

For the fixed client module, only the -cmax and -n options are available. It is best to match the -cmax and -n values, so a separate client session can be created for each session used in the test. The protocol module options are shown in Table 16.3

The destination protocol, address, and port values must match the values used on the remote server. Finally, the payload module options must be defined. These are shown in Table 16.4.

Different payload modules require different options. The fixed payload module only uses the -pmax option to define the fixed payload size. All packets in the test will use the same number of bytes. The increasing payload module uses the -pmin, -increment, and -time options to set the minimum packet size (-pmin), the number of packets of that size that will be sent (-time), and the number of bytes the packets will increase by (-increment). Here are some sample payload options:

- **-pn fixed -pmax 100** sends fixed packets of 100 bytes.

- **-pn increasing -pmin 10 -pmax 100 -increment 10** sends one packet of 10 btyes, then one packet of 20 bytes, and so on up to a 100-byte packet.

- **-pn random -pmin 10 -pmax 100 -time 10** sends 10 packets of a random size between 10 and 100 bytes, then sends 10 more packets of a random size, and so on until stopped.

Table 16.3 trafclient Protocol Module Options

OPTION	DESCRIPTION
-dn	Defines the protocol module name (currently either tcp or udp)
-da	Defines the destination address of the remote server
-dp	Defines the destination port number of the remote server connection

Table 16.4 trafclient Payload Module Options

OPTION	DESCRIPTION
-pn	Defines the payload module name (fixed, increasing, or random)
-pmin	Defines the minimum number of bytes in the payload
-pmax	Defines the maximum number of bytes in the payload
-increment	Defines the increment value used to increase the payload size
-time	Defines the number of packets to send at a specific size

A sample complete trafclient session should look like this:

```
$ trafclient -cn fixed -cmax 100 -n 100  -da 192.168.1.6 -dp
9050 -dn tcp -pn fixed -pmax 100
trafclient Starting
Initializing Payloads
Initializing Protocols
Starting clients. Press ENTER to end.
```

When the client is started, it attempts to connect to the remote server defined, establishes the defined number of sessions (100 in this example), and begins the packet transfers according to the defined protocol and payload values. To stop the clients, you must press the Enter key.

WARNING Network Traffic Generator continuously transmits packets from the client to the server—there is no dead time. Configuring lots of clients will put a continual load on the network. This may or may not be what you want. Use caution when performing the tests.

Setting Up a Test

Now that you have functional server and client hosts, the trick is to determine how to best use them to emulate a production network. Two things to take into consideration when using a test network are (1) where the test client and servers are placed in the test network, and (2) the type of network traffic they are configured to emulate. This section discusses some pitfalls to watch out for when using Network Traffic Generator in a test network environment.

Test Host Placement

In networks that are divided by routers or switches, you must be careful to strategically place the client devices on the network to load the appropriate network links. Figure 16.5 shows a sample test network environment.

The central switch in the test network controls the traffic flow between the devices. Placing the traffic generator server and client on separate ports on the switch will provide extra load for the switch, but will have no impact on the network application server and clients. This scenario does not accurately depict a production network environment.

A better solution for test networks is to use shared network hubs, along with multiple traffic-generating clients and servers. This scenario is shown in Figure 16.6.

In this test network, each segment from the router contains both network application clients and Network Traffic Generator clients. The Network Traffic Generator servers are located both on the same segment as the network application server, and on an alternate segment. This configuration helps produce varying traffic load on different segments that will directly affect the network application clients and server.

Test Host Configuration

After determining the proper location for the test hosts, you must determine what type of network traffic they should emulate. As mentioned earlier, in the *Generating Network Traffic* section, there are basically three types of network traffic that can be generated by Network Traffic Generator:

- Bulk data transfer
- Client/Server transactions
- Connectionless communication

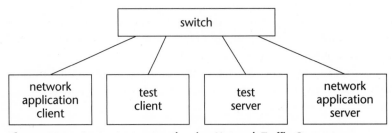

Figure 16.5   A poor test network using Network Traffic Generator.

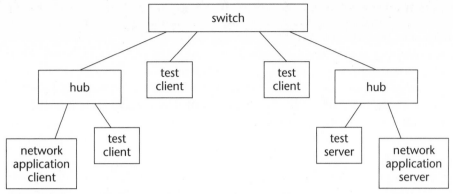

Figure 16.6 A better test network using Network Traffic Generator.

The different network traffic types are emulated using the protocol and payload settings on trafclient, and the reply settings on trafserver. For both bulk data and client/server emulation transfers, use the ack server module. This accurately emulates the one-sided data transfer feature. The payload module can be varied, depending on the type of traffic emulated. For bulk data traffic, you should use a fixed payload type, as data is usually transferred in set blocks. For client/server transactions, it is best to use the random payload module.

It is also best to utilize different clients implementing different protocol, payload, and reply settings on the same network to emulate different types of network traffic on the production network.

Watching the Test Traffic

As you have noticed from the sample trafserver and trafclient sessions, no information about the actual traffic is presented by Network Traffic Generator. All it does is produce the network traffic; it does not indicate anything about the response times or network load present during the test.

To obtain this information, you will have to turn to the network performance tools presented in Part II of this book. One of the easiest tools to use in this scenario is the tcptrace tool, which can read captured tcpdump or Win-Dump files and display the IP session statistics.

For the sample session, I used a 10-client TCP session using the ack server module, and random payloads from 100 bytes to 1,000 bytes. This was generated by means of the following command line:

```
trafclient -cn fixed -cmax 10 -n 10 -pn random -pmin 100 -pmax 1000 -da
192.168.1.6 -dp 9050 -dn tcp
```

Before the client started, I started tcpdump on the server device, capturing all packets destined to TCP port 9050, and storing them in a capture file:

```
# tcpdump tcp port 9050 -w test.cap
```

After allowing the client to run for a few minutes, I stopped the client and server, and also stopped the tcpdump program. The resulting capture file can be analyzed by the tcptrace application:

```
$ tcptrace test.cap
1 arg remaining, starting with 'test.cap'
Ostermann's tcptrace -- version 6.2.0 -- Fri Jul 26, 2002

29420 packets seen, 29420 TCP packets traced
elapsed wallclock time: 0:00:00.883518, 33298 pkts/sec analyzed
trace file elapsed time: 0:00:13.088615
TCP connection info:
1: 192.168.1.1:2267 - 192.168.1.6:9050 (a2b) 1544> 1543< (complete)
2: 192.168.1.1:2268 - 192.168.1.6:9050 (c2d) 1528> 1527< (complete)
3: 192.168.1.1:2269 - 192.168.1.6:9050 (e2f) 1434> 1434< (complete)
4: 192.168.1.1:2270 - 192.168.1.6:9050 (g2h) 1469> 1469< (complete)
5: 192.168.1.1:2271 - 192.168.1.6:9050 (i2j) 1439> 1439< (complete)
6: 192.168.1.1:2272 - 192.168.1.6:9050 (k2l) 1517> 1517< (complete)
7: 192.168.1.1:2273 - 192.168.1.6:9050 (m2n) 1474> 1474< (complete)
8: 192.168.1.1:2274 - 192.168.1.6:9050 (o2p) 1445> 1445< (complete)
9: 192.168.1.1:2275 - 192.168.1.6:9050 (q2r) 1475> 1475< (complete)
10: 192.168.1.1:2276 - 192.168.1.6:9050 (s2t) 1386> 1386< (complete)
$
```

As expected, 10 separate client sessions between the two hosts were captured. You can use the -l option to analyze one specific session to see the packet statistics:

```
$ tcptrace -o3 -l test.cap
1 arg remaining, starting with 'test.cap'
Ostermann's tcptrace -- version 6.2.0 -- Fri Jul 26, 2002

29420 packets seen, 29420 TCP packets traced
elapsed wallclock time: 0:00:00.359822, 81762 pkts/sec analyzed
trace file elapsed time: 0:00:13.088615
TCP connection info:
10 TCP connections traced:
================================
TCP connection 3:
        host e:        192.168.1.1:2269
        host f:        192.168.1.6:9050
        complete conn: yes
        first packet:  Thu Jan  9 15:15:38.474352 2003
        last packet:   Thu Jan  9 15:15:51.558120 2003
```

```
        elapsed time:  0:00:13.083767
        total packets: 2868
        filename:      test.cap
    e->f:                                   f->e:
        total packets:          1434            total packets:          1434
        ack pkts sent:          1433            ack pkts sent:          1434
        pure acks sent:            3            pure acks sent:            3
        sack pkts sent:            0            sack pkts sent:            0
        max sack blks/ack:         0            max sack blks/ack:         0
        unique bytes sent:    790451            unique bytes sent:     11432
        actual data pkts:       1429            actual data pkts:       1429
        actual data bytes:    790451            actual data bytes:     11432
        rexmt data pkts:           0            rexmt data pkts:           0
        rexmt data bytes:          0            rexmt data bytes:          0
        zwnd probe pkts:           0            zwnd probe pkts:           0
        zwnd probe bytes:          0            zwnd probe bytes:          0
        outoforder pkts:           0            outoforder pkts:           0
        pushed data pkts:       1429            pushed data pkts:       1429
        SYN/FIN pkts sent:       1/1            SYN/FIN pkts sent:       1/1
        req 1323 ws/ts:          Y/Y            req 1323 ws/ts:          Y/Y
        adv wind scale:            0            adv wind scale:            0
        req sack:                  Y            req sack:                  Y
        sacks sent:                0            sacks sent:                0
        urgent data pkts:     0 pkts            urgent data pkts:     0 pkts
        urgent data bytes:   0 bytes            urgent data bytes:   0 bytes
        mss requested:    1460 bytes            mss requested:    1460 bytes
        max segm size:     999 bytes            max segm size:       8 bytes
        min segm size:     100 bytes            min segm size:       8 bytes
        avg segm size:     553 bytes            avg segm size:       7 bytes
        max win adv:      5840 bytes            max win adv:     34560 bytes
        min win adv:      5840 bytes            min win adv:      5792 bytes
        zero win adv:        0 times            zero win adv:        0 times
        avg win adv:      5840 bytes            avg win adv:     34271 bytes
        initial window:   804 bytes            initial window:      8 bytes
        initial window:     1 pkts             initial window:      1 pkts
        ttl stream length:790451 bytes         ttl stream length:11432
bytes
        missed data:         0 bytes           missed data:               0
bytes
        truncated data: 747581 bytes           truncated data:            0
bytes
        truncated packets: 1429 pkts           truncated packets:         0
pkts
        data xmit time:  11.140 secs           data xmit time:   11.108
secs
        idletime max:      1919.6 ms           idletime max:         1881.8
ms
        throughput:       60415 Bps            throughput:              874
Bps
$
```

This produces lots of information about the packets involved with the test traffic. Two interesting statistics to note are the max and min segment (packet) sizes:

```
max segm size:      999 bytes

min segm size:      100 bytes
```

Just as I had specified, the maximum packet size in the session was just under 1,000 bytes, and the minimum packet size was 100 bytes.

Summary

This chapter described the Network Traffic Generator application, which is used to generate network traffic on test networks. The traffic generated can emulate different types of network applications, such as bulk data transfers and client/server transactions.

The Network Traffic Generator application uses a modular approach to implementing the different types of network traffic. The modules define how the client and server functions operate—that is, how the server responds to client packets (for instance, echoing them back or simply acknowledging them) and how the client module sends packets to the server (for instance, the size of the packet data).

There can be multiple Network Traffic Generator clients communicating with a single server host. You should use enough client devices on the network to accurately emulate production network traffic on the test network. The layout of the test network is crucial to the operation of the test network traffic. Using routers and switches can often segment generated traffic away from the network application traffic, nullifying the test traffic. Placing test clients on the same network segments as the network application clients, and the test server on the same segment as the network application server will produce optimal results, placing network traffic on the same network path as the test application.

The next chapter introduces the ns application. The ns application performs network simulation, modeling network behavior mathematically, and displaying the expected results.

This chapter introduces the Network Simulator (ns) application, which is used to simulate network behavior using C++ and OTcl programs. Network simulators perform all of the network simulations in software. No actual packets are used in the simulation. Even the data packets supplied to the simulator are simulated. This chapter first describes the Network Simulator application, and explains how it simulates different network objects. Instructions for downloading and installing the software follow (this is definitely one of the more complicated packages presented in this book). Finally, some examples of network simulation using ns are presented, showing how to model basic network environments using ns, and how to interpret the resulting data.

The Network Simulator package was developed at the University of California Berkeley as a method to simulate network behavior without having to actually use a test network. This allows network administrators to play "What if?" games, by easily creating different network environments to test network application performance. This section describes the Network Simulator application, and explains how it is designed to simulate networks.

What Is ns?

The Network Simulator application consists of a single program, ns (not to be confused with the application package name). The ns program reads a network model, defined as an OTcl program, either from a command-line interface or from a program file, and executes it. The OTcl program defines the desired network elements being simulated, the input data used in the network simulation, and the data to produce as output.

> **NOTE** The OTcl language is an extension to the Tcl/Tk language, and is used for object-oriented programming. It was developed at MIT and released to the public to support object-oriented programming in Tcl.

The ns program by itself just produces trace files that show the behavior of the network model during the simulation. For the average network administrator, this is not too useful. To help analyze the simulation output, there are two companion programs that can be used with ns. The following section describes the ns application programs, and explains how they are used to completely model and analyze a network.

Network Simulator Programs

The Network Simulator application itself consists of a main program used to run the network simulation, and some support programs used to view and interpret the simulation and results. This section describes the parts included in the Network Simulator application.

ns

The ns program is the meat of the Network Simulator application. It is used to run the network simulation defined in a supplied OTcl program. While the network simulation program is run, the ns program provides two types of output mechanisms:

- A trace file that records each individual packet as it is processed in the simulator
- A monitor file that records packet statistics and counts as packet streams are processed in the simulator

The trace file includes information used to track the progress of each simulated packet as it traverses nodes in the network. There are two formats of trace files, one used for ns, and another used for the nam program, discussed in the next section.

The monitor file can be used to plot network utilization, packet drops, and other network features after the simulation is complete. The xgraph application is used to plot information stored in the monitor file.

In order to process the output information, the Network Simulator package includes two other programs, which are discussed next.

nam

The Network Animator (nam) program was also developed at the University of California Berkeley, and is used to read the output of the ns program, and graphically display the results of the simulation. Each node and link in the simulation is defined in the output file, and displayed in the graphical model, as shown in Figure 17.1.

The nam program has the ability to step through the ns output file and recreate the network simulation in graphical format. As each network application transmits data on the simulated network, nam displays the packets as they travel along the links from node to node.

With the nam program you can change the speed of the simulation, as well as stop and start the simulation at any point during the simulator time period. These controls allow you to zoom in on a specific event within the simulation and observe the behavior of the network devices being simulated.

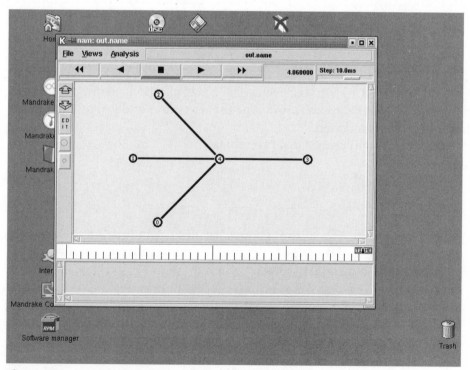

Figure 17.1   Sample Network Simulator simulation output.

xgraph

The xgraph application, also developed at the University of California Berkeley is used to display the monitor data files in a graphical format. Much like the gnuplot and xplot applications, this application uses the X Windows environment to graph the monitor data files against the timeline generated during the network simulation.

Network Model Elements

Each network element must be modeled within the simulation, including network devices, network links, network protocols used, and network applications. Each network element is defined in ns using C++ classes. The characteristics and behaviors of each element are configured into the class, and used within the Tcl program.

Network Nodes

The basic building blocks of a network model are the end nodes and the links that connect them. Network Simulator models nodes in two separate forms:

- **Unicast node.** Sends data to only one remote node at a time (the default behavior)
- **Multicast node.** Sends data to multiple remote nodes at one time

Nodes are used to connect protocols and applications as they send data between the nodes. Each node provides either a source or destination point for the application simulation.

Nodes are created using the set command:

```
set n0 [new Simulator node]

set n1 [new Simulator node]
```

These lines create two separate nodes, labeled n0 and n1. As each node is created, it is assigned a unique identifier in the simulator. The node ID is shown as each command is entered:

```
% set n0 [new Simulator node]
_o4
% set n1 [new Simulator node]
_o11
%
```

The node ID is used internally to identify the node, while the OTcl program references the node using the node label.

Network Links

Just as in the real network, nodes are connected together with links. The links provide a way to inject delays, bandwidth limitations, errors, and packet loss between nodes. There are two basic types of links provided in the simulation:

- **Simplex links.** Provide only one-way data passage
- **Duplex links.** Provide two-way data passage

These links represent point-to-point connections, such as those between routers, and between a LAN switch and a network device. When creating the link, you must specify some parameters that define how the link behaves in the simulation. The formats of the link commands are:

```
new Simulator simplex-link node1 node2 bw delay queuetype
new Simulator duplex-link node1 node2 bw delay queuetype
```

The parameters used to define the link are:

- *node1* The starting point of the link (order is important for simplex links)
- *node2* The ending point of the link (again, order is important for simplex links)
- *bw* The bandwidth limitation of the link, specified as a value and units (such as 10 Mb)
- *delay* The delay injected into the link, specified as a value and unit (such as 100 ms)
- *queuetype* The queuing model the link uses to queue packets

The simulator provides several types of queuing methods to handle packets as they traverse the link. The available queuing methods are DropTail (a FIFO method), FQ (fair queuing), SFQ (stochastic fair queuing), RED (random early detection), and DRR (deficit round-robin queuing).

Some sample link definitions:

```
% new Simulator duplex-link $n0 $n1 10Mb 100ms DropTail
_o18
% new Simulator simplex-link $n2 $n3 10Mb 100ms RED
_o25
% new Simulator duplex-link $n1 $n2 56Kb 400ms SFQ
_o32
%
```

As you can see in the examples, as each network link is created, it is assigned a unique link ID for the simulator. Unlike nodes, links are not assigned labels, as they are not referenced within the OTcl program.

While network link models work fine for point-to-point connections, they do not accurately simulate multipoint connections, such as shared LAN environments. For this, Network Simulator has a special model class.

> **NOTE** Not all LAN devices must be modeled using the ns LAN models. For example, a switch device provides multiple point-to-point connections. Each switch connection can be modeled using a duplex-link model.

The make-lan method uses a list of nodes that are connected together in a single shared LAN environment. The bandwidth of the LAN, along with the delay, queue type, and channel type are defined in the creation of the LAN:

```
new Simulator make-lan "$n0 $n1 $n2 $n3" 10Mb 10ms LL Queue/DropTail
Mac/Csma/Cd
```

This LAN definition creates a four-node 10-Mb Ethernet LAN. After the LAN is created, the nodes within the LAN can be assigned agents and protocols, just as with point-to-point links.

Network Agents

The agent models represent endpoints where network packets are created and consumed. These models reflect the protocols that are used in the network, and the way the individual protocols transmit data across the network.

There are lots of different agents that can be used to represent different types of protocols (and different behavior within protocols). The main agents that are used in network simulations are:

- **TCP** models a TCP sending device (sends a packet and waits for an acknowledgement).
- **UDP** models a UDP sending device (sends packets without waiting for acknowledgments).
- **TCPSink** models a TCP receiving device (sends a small acknowledgment for each packet received).
- **NULL** models a UDP receiving device (accepts packets but takes no action).
- **LossMonitor** is a special model that keeps packet statistics on accepted and lost packets.

As you can probably tell, two separate agents simulate a single network connection model. The agent pair represents the sending device and the receiving device in the connection session. Each agent must be assigned to a node in the model, and only one agent instance can be used with another agent instance (two remote senders cannot communication with a single receiver; two receivers must be assigned to the node).

To assign agents to nodes, you must use the attach-agent command. The sequence looks like:

```
set udp0 [new Agent/UDP]
new Simulator attach-agent $n0 $udp0

set null0 [new Agent/Null]
new Simulator attach-agent $n1 $null0
```

After the two agent objects are defined and attached to nodes, you can create a connection between them using the connect command:

```
new Simulator connect $udp0 $null0
```

This creates the link between the UDP sender model and the NULL receiver model. After the agent connection is created, you can use it to pass application data between nodes.

Network Applications

The application models simulate data traffic on the network. Just as in network emulation, different types of network applications require different types of simulations. Network Simulator provides for several application models, as well as allowing you to create your own using C++ classes.

There are three main application class models used:

- **Application/Traffic** generates artificial traffic patterns.
- **Application/Telnet** generates traffic simulating a normal Telnet session.
- **Application/FTP** generates traffic simulating a normal FTP session.

The Telnet and FTP applications produce data streams that you should be familiar with. The Telnet application sends short bursts of short packets, simulating a remote terminal sending characters to a remote Telnet server. The server in turn sends a long burst of packets, simulating a response from the server. The time between sessions is random, simulating work being done on the client end before sending data. The FTP application simulates the sending of long data packets to the remote node, and the remote node sending a short acknowledgment packet in return.

Both the Telnet and FTP applications must be attached to a TCP agent to operate properly (they both require acknowledgments from the remote node). The commands to do this are:

```
set ftp1 [new Application/FTP]
$ftp1 attach-agent $tcp0

set telnet1 [new Application/Telnet]
$telnet1 attach-agent $tcp1
```

The Traffic application consists of four separate subapplications:

- Traffic/Exponential
- Traffic/Pareto
- Traffic/CBR
- Traffic/Trace

The Exponential traffic application generates network traffic in on-and-off cycles. During an on cycle, traffic is sent at a constant bit rate to the receiver. During the off cycle, no traffic is generated. The time between the on and off periods is determined by an exponential distribution. You can set the average burst and idle times, the rate used to send the packets, and the packet size for the application. The commands to do this would be:

```
set exp1 [new Application/Traffic/Exponential]
$exp1 set packetSize_ 500
$exp1 set burst_time 500ms
$exp1 set idle_time_ 500ms
$exp1 set rate_ 200k
$exp1 attach-agent $udp0
```

The Pareto traffic application also generates network traffic in on-and-off cycles, but uses a Pareto distribution. It includes a shape_ parameter that allows you to define the shape parameter used :

```
set par1 [new Application/Traffic/Pareto]
$par1 set packet_Size_ 500
$par1 set burst_time_ 500ms
$par1 set idle_time_ 500ms
$par1 set rate_ 200k
$par1 set shape_ 1.75
$par1 attach-agent $udp0
```

The CBR traffic application generates packets continually at a constant bit rate. The packet size, bit rate, interval between packets, and maximum number of packets to send can all be specified for the CBR application:

```
set cbr1 [new Application/Traffic/CBR]
$cbr1 set packetSize_ 500
$cbr1 set rate_ 200k
$cbr1 interval_ 50ms
$cbr1 maxpkts_ 2000
```

The Trace application is different in that it generates traffic based on data contained in a trace file. After the application is created, the trace file used must be assigned to the new object:

```
set tfile [new Tracefile]
$tfile filename trace.out
set tr1 [new Application/Traffic/Trace]
$tr1 attach-tracefile $tfile
```

The trace file format consists of multiple text lines, each containing two 32-bit fields. The first field defines, in microseconds, the time until the next packet will be generated. The second field defines the size in bytes of the next packet.

After the applications are defined, you must define when they are started and stopped in the simulation. The at command is used to define these values. Time within the simulation is defined in seconds, and can be specified as a floating-point value. An example of defining an application would be:

```
new Simulation at 1.0 "$ftp1 start"

new Simulation at 3.75 "$ftp1 stop"
```

This defines the starting and stopping times for the application defined by the ftp1 label. The FTP application will start 1 second after the start of the simulation, and stop 3.75 seconds into the simulation.

ns Modeling Language

All of the network elements are combined in a single OTcl program to produce the desired network environment model. The assigned label for the element (prefixed with a dollar sign, as in shell script programming) references elements within the program. You can also use labels to create shortcuts, such as when using the new Simulator tag seen in all of the commands.

Besides the simulation elements, you can also define procedures that combine commands into a single function. This is most commonly done when referencing the closing commands to end the simulation.

The easiest way to demonstrate a Network Simulator model is to show a simple example:

```
set ns [new Simulator]
set nf [open out.nam w]
$ns namtrace-all $nf

set n0 [$ns node]
set n1 [$ns node]

$ns duplex-link $n0 $n1 10Mb 10ms DropTail
```

```
set tcp1 [new Agent/TCP]
$tcp1 attach-agent $n0

set sink1 [new Agent/TCPSink]
$sink1 attach-agent $n1

$ns connect $tcp1 $sink1

set ftp1 [new Agent/FTP]
$ftp1 attach-agent $tcp1

proc finish {} {
    global ns nf
    close $nf
    exec nam $nf &
    exit 0
}

$ns at 1.0 "$ftp1 start"
$ns at 3.5 "$ftp stop"
$ns at 4.0 "finish"

$ns run
```

You should recognize most of the commands used in this model. The first two commands are new, but easily understood. The first command creates a label to use for the pesky new Simulator tag. This enables you to use the label instead of having to type the full tag all the time. The second command creates an output file for the results from the simulation, and assigns a label to the file-name. The output file is created in nam format, allowing the nam program to interpret the output and draw the simulation.

Next, two nodes are defined, along with a duplex link that connects them. After that, a TCP agent is created and assigned to one node, and then a TCPSink agent is created on the other node. The two agents are connected together to provide a data path for the application, using the connect command. An FTP application is then defined, and attached to the TCP agent. Finally, a procedure called finish is created, which closes the output file that was defined and runs the nam program to examine the output file.

At the end of the program, the application start and stop times are defined, along with the time the finish procedure is started. Finally, the run command is used to start the simulation.

Downloading and Installing ns

As mentioned at the start of this chapter, the Network Simulator application is one of the most complex applications covered in this book. It requires lots of different packages to operate on the Unix system. Fortunately, there is a handy package provided that includes all of the necessary programs.

Downloading

The Network Simulator Web site, located at http://www.isi.edu/nsnam/ns/, contains links to many different ns resources, including the download page. From the download page you can download different versions and packages for ns. At the time of this writing, the most current version of ns is available at the URL:

```
http://www.isi.edu/nsnam/dist/ns-src-2.1b9a.tar.gz
```

This download is just for the ns application. If you want to download the package that provides all of the applications necessary to run ns, download the file:

```
http://www.isi.edu/nsnam/dist/ns-allinone-2.1b9a.tar.gz
```

The ns-allinone package contains the applications shown in Table 17.1.

Table 17.1   ns-allinone Package Contents

PACKAGE	DESCRIPTION
Tcl version 8.3.2	Required
Tk version 8.3.2	Required
OTcl version 1.0a8	Required
ns version 2.1b9a	Required
nam version 1.0a11a	Optional (used to display ns output)
xgraph version 12	Optional (used to display monitor files)
cweb version 3.4g	Optional (used for documenting programs)
SGB version 1.0	Optional (Stanford GraphBase application for describing graphs)
gt-itm version 1.1	Optional (used with SGB to graphically create ns model files)
sgb2ns version 1.1	Optional (used to convert gt-itm SGB files to ns OTcl files)
zlib version 1.1.3	Optional (used for nam)

That's a lot of packages included in one distribution file. Some of the packages included in the allinone distribution are optional. If do not want to download the allinone package (the distribution file is over 48 Mb in size), you can download the required packages separately, from their respective download Web sites, but I recommend just biting the bullet and downloading the allinone distribution.

After downloading the distribution file, you can uncompress it into a working directory using the standard tar command. The working directory created is ns-allinone-2.1b9a.

Compiling and Installing

The allinone distribution package includes a shell script that can be run to compile all of the included packages at once. The install script should be run from the working directory. Be prepared for a long compile session, as each individual package is configured and compiled. When the install is complete, all of the executable files are located in the bin subdirectory within the working directory. You can copy these files to a standard location on your system for easier access.

Validating the Installation

You can validate the ns installation using the validate script, located in the ns-2.1b9a subdirectory of the allinone working directory. The validate script is used to test the ns installation using test OTcl scripts that produce known output results. The validation tests will run for quite a long time, but should all produce positive results.

NOTE If you have downloaded the required ns pieces individually and cannot get the validate test to work, consider downloading the allinone package and manually installing the pieces you want. Each of the individual pieces is dependent on specific release versions of other pieces.

Performing a Network Simulation

Now that the ns application environment is installed, you are ready to begin modeling and simulating a network environment. This section describes the events necessary to simulate a network, and to analyze the output from the simulation.

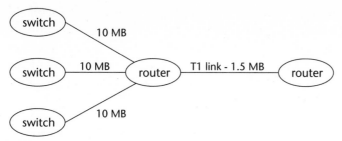

Figure 17.2   Test network configuration.

Creating the Simulation Model

The first step, obviously, is to determine the network you want to simulate, and to create the OTcl program that models the network. For this example, we will construct a simple switched network environment, with multiple switches connected to a router, sending data to a remote router. The network layout is shown in Figure 17.2.

This network shows clients connected to three network switches connected to a single router with a T1 link to another router. The network model will simulate the network switches and clients as an individual node producing traffic to the router. Obviously, the bottleneck in this network will be the T1 line connecting the two routers together. The point of the simulation is that it allows you to watch network traffic as it traverses the T1 link.

To help you watch the traffic on the network, the simulator will use a constant bit rate source from each switch to the server. In a real-world network simulation, you could use the FTP or Telnet application source to watch the type of network traffic that generates the worst conditions for the T1 link.

The OTcl program created to model the network is shown in Figure 17.3.

```
set ns [new Simulator]
set nf [open out.nam w]
set f1 [open out1.tr w]
set f2 [open out2.tr w]
set f3 [open out3.tr w]
set f4 [open outtot.tr w]
$ns namtrace-all $nf

$ns color 1 Blue
$ns color 2 Red
$ns color 3 Green

set n0 [$ns node]
```

Figure 17.3   The test.tcl model program. *(continued)*

```
set n1 [$ns node]
set n2 [$ns node]
set n3 [$ns node]
set n4 [$ns node]

$ns duplex-link $n0 $n3 10Mb 20ms DropTail
$ns duplex-link $n1 $n3 10Mb 20ms DropTail
$ns duplex-link $n2 $n3 10Mb 20ms DropTail
$ns duplex-link $n3 $n4 1.5Mb 200ms SFQ
$ns duplex-link-op $n3 $n4 queuePos 0.5

set udp0 [new Agent/UDP]
$ns attach-agent $n0 $udp0
$udp0 set class_ 1
set udp1 [new Agent/UDP]
$ns attach-agent $n1 $udp1
$udp1 set class_ 2
set udp2 [new Agent/UDP]
$ns attach-agent $n2 $udp2
$udp2 set class_ 3

set sink0 [new Agent/LossMonitor]
$ns attach-agent $n4 $sink0
set sink1 [new Agent/LossMonitor]
$ns attach-agent $n4 $sink1
set sink2 [new Agent/LossMonitor]
$ns attach-agent $n4 $sink2

$ns connect $udp0 $sink0
$ns connect $udp1 $sink1
$ns connect $udp2 $sink2

set cbr0 [new Application/Traffic/CBR]
$cbr0 set packetSize_ 500
$cbr0 set rate_ 750k
$cbr0 attach-agent $udp0
set cbr1 [new Application/Traffic/CBR]
$cbr1 set packetSize_ 500
$cbr1 set rate_ 750k
$cbr1 attach-agent $udp1
set cbr2 [new Application/Traffic/CBR]
$cbr2 set packetSize_ 500
$cbr2 set rate_ 750k
$cbr2 attach-agent $udp2

proc record {} {
        global sink0 sink1 sink2 f1 f2 f3 f4
        set ns [Simulator instance]
```

Figure 17.3 *(continued)*

```
        set time 0.1
        set bw0 [$sink0 set bytes_]
        set bw1 [$sink1 set bytes_]
        set bw2 [$sink2 set bytes_]
        set now [$ns now]
        puts $f1 "$now [expr $bw0/$time*8/1500000]"
        puts $f2 "$now [expr $bw1/$time*8/1500000]"
        puts $f3 "$now [expr $bw2/$time*8/1500000]"
        puts $f4 "$now [expr ($bw0+$bw1+$bw2)/$time*8/1500000]"
        $sink0 set bytes_ 0
        $sink1 set bytes_ 0
        $sink2 set bytes_ 0
        $ns at [expr $now+$time] "record"
}

proc finish {} {
        global ns nf f1 f2 f3 f4
        $ns flush-trace
        close $nf
        close $f1
        close $f2
        close $f3
        close $f4
        exit 0
}

$ns at 0.0 "record"
$ns at 0.5 "$cbr0 start"
$ns at 1.0 "$cbr1 start"
$ns at 2.0 "$cbr2 start"
$ns at 3.5 "$cbr0 stop"
$ns at 3.75 "$cbr1 stop"
$ns at 4.0 "$cbr2 stop"
$ns at 5.5 "finish"

$ns run
```

Figure 17.3 *(continued)*

This model creates five nodes (one for each switch, and one for each router). A 10-Mb point-to-point link is created for each switch to the router, and a 1.5-Mb point-to-point link is used for the connection between the two routers. The queuing method defined for the router link emulates the stochastic fair queuing method used by the router. The duplex-link-op command:

```
$ns duplex-link-op $n3 $n4 queuePos 0.5
```

is used to monitor the queue for the link between the two routers (the T1 link). This will graphically display how packets are queued in the router, and when (or if) any packets are dropped.

Each of the switch nodes is assigned a UDP agent, and the remote router is assigned three LossMonitor agents (remember, each agent can only process one remote agent). The LossMonitor agent will allow you to monitor the bytes received during the simulated packet streams.

To generate data, the CBR application is used, providing a constant bit stream (set at 750 Kb per second) from each of the hubs to send to the router.

Four separate monitor files are created, called f1, f2, f3, and f4. Data is added to each file using the record procedure. The LossMonitor application value bytes_ is used to extract the number of bytes received by the server over a set time period. The value is used to calculate a bandwidth value for each stream, and total all of the streams together. After the calculation, the bytes_values are reset to zero, to start over. The record procedure is started at the beginning of the simulation, and kicks itself off every tenth of a second.

A closing procedure (called finish) is created to stop the trace and cleanly close all of the output files. This procedure can also be used to automatically start the nam or xgraph program, but for now just have it exit the simulation so you can run the nam and xgraph programs manually.

After the procedures, the schedulers are defined, indicating when each application will start sending data, and when they will stop. This simulation ramps up the data by starting each hub's traffic separately from the others, and letting it run concurrently with the other hub traffic. Obviously, three links, each running at a data rate of 750 Kbps, will overrun the 1.5-Mbps T1 link, but that is the point of this simulation.

> **NOTE** After getting the hang of manually creating the OTcl model program, try the gt-itm program. It allows you to graphically design the model, and then produces a file that can be converted to an ns OTcl program using the sgb2ns program (also included in the allinone distribution).

Running the Simulation

After saving the OTcl program in a file (called test.tcl for this example), you can start the network simulation and allow it to run:

```
$ ns test.tcl
```

If all goes well, the simulation should be completed and should create the desired output files. If any errors occur in processing the model file, they are displayed:

```
$ ns test.tcl
can't read "odp0": no such variable
    while executing
"$ns attach-agent $n0 $odp0"
    (file "test.tcl" line 31)
$
```

This example should produce five separate output files:

```
$ ls -al out*
-rw-r--r--    1 rich      rich       1281048 Jan 16 18:47 out.nam
-rw-r--r--    1 rich      rich          1715 Jan 16 18:47 out1.tr
-rw-r--r--    1 rich      rich          1667 Jan 16 18:47 out2.tr
-rw-r--r--    1 rich      rich          1555 Jan 16 18:47 out3.tr
-rw-r--r--    1 rich      rich          1766 Jan 16 18:47 outtot.tr
$
```

The out.nam file contains the simulation information necessary for nam to display the network simulation. The nam file contains lines for each object and event in the simulation. A partial listing of the out.nam file looks like:

```
V -t * -v 1.0a5 -a 0
A -t * -n 1 -p 0 -o 0xffffffff -c 31 -a 1
A -t * -h 1 -m 2147483647 -s 0
c -t * -i 1 -n Blue
c -t * -i 2 -n Red
c -t * -i 3 -n Green
n -t * -a 4 -s 4 -S UP -v circle -c black -i black
n -t * -a 0 -s 0 -S UP -v circle -c black -i black
n -t * -a 1 -s 1 -S UP -v circle -c black -i black
n -t * -a 2 -s 2 -S UP -v circle -c black -i black
n -t * -a 3 -s 3 -S UP -v circle -c black -i black
l -t * -s 0 -d 3 -S UP -r 10000000 -D 0.02 -c black -o right-up
l -t * -s 1 -d 3 -S UP -r 10000000 -D 0.02 -c black -o right
l -t * -s 2 -d 3 -S UP -r 10000000 -D 0.02 -c black -o right-down
l -t * -s 3 -d 4 -S UP -r 10000000 -D 0.02 -c black -o left
q -t * -s 4 -d 3 -a 0.5
q -t * -s 3 -d 4 -a 0.5
+ -t 0.5 -s 0 -d 3 -p cbr -e 500 -c 1 -i 0 -a 1 -x {0.0 4.0 0 -------
null}
- -t 0.5 -s 0 -d 3 -p cbr -e 500 -c 1 -i 0 -a 1 -x {0.0 4.0 0 -------
null}
h -t 0.5 -s 0 -d 3 -p cbr -e 500 -c 1 -i 0 -a 1 -x {0.0 4.0 -1 -------
null}
```

The first character in the output file identifies the type of event the record represents. Table 17.2 shows the different types of records that can be present.

Table 17.2 The nam Trace File First Character

CHARACTER	DESCRIPTION
V	Defines the nam version required to process the trace file
w	Defines a wireless node
A	Defines hierarchical address information
c	Defines the color used to represent the object
n	Defines a node
l	Defines a network link
q	Defines a queue
+	Defines when a packet enters the network queue
-	Defines when a packet leaves the network queue
h	Defines a network hop for the packet
r	Defines that the packet was received by the final destination
a	Defines an agent

Each record type uses its own parameters to define the information represented by the record. The -s parameter is used to identify the source information, and the -d parameter is used to define the destination information.

The monitor files produce the output defined in the record process, the time of the monitor sample, and the bandwidth value for the link.

Using nam

After the namtrace output file is created, you can use the nam program to process it:

```
$ nam out.nam
```

The nam program reads the namtrace file, and generates the simulation layout. The nodes and links are displayed on the graph, showing the basic network layout. You can click the Re-layout button to rearrange the layout to your liking. The timeline at the bottom shows the simulation time, and the pointer shows where in the simulation nam is currently showing. The step slider allows you to set the speed that the simulation runs at.

When you click the play button (the right arrow button) the simulation starts. Colored blocks traversing the network indicate simulated data packets sent by the nodes. The length of a block depicts the size of the packet relative to the speed of the link. For example, the 500-byte data blocks used in this example appear larger when they traverse the T1 link than when they traverse the 10-Mb link.

As the simulation runs, at some point node 3 must queue packets. The queued packets are displayed as a line above the node, as shown in Figure 17.4.

As the simulation continues, the node queue fills up, and packets must be dropped. Blocks falling off the queue to the bottom of the display indicate this. Since each data stream is represented as a different color, you can see that the stochastic fair queuing algorithm is working—an equal number of data from each stream is dropped.

You can experiment with different settings in the OTcl model program and see the results in the nam display. Changing the speeds of the network links and the rate of the CBR streams can have dramatic effects on the simulation.

Using xgraph

The monitor trace files can be displayed using the xgraph program. You can either display each monitor trace file individually, or all of them on a single graph:

```
$ xgraph out1.tr out2.tr out3.tr outtot.tr
```

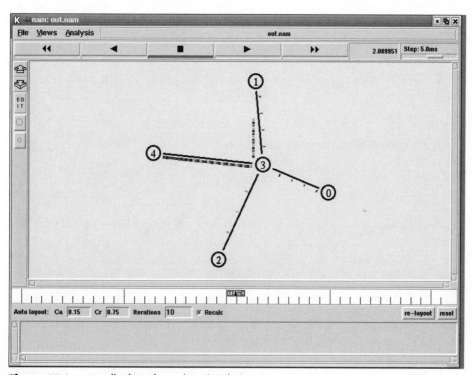

Figure 17.4   nam display of running simulation.

The output from the xgraph program is shown in Figure 17.5.

Three of the graphs show the bandwidth of the T1 line for each individual data stream. The total bandwidth is also shown on the graph. Notice how as the bandwidth hits 100 percent, the individual data streams are throttled back due to the packet drops from the router queue. You can use this technique to plot any of the variables from the LossMonitor agent.

Summary

The Network Simulator application is used to programmatically simulate a network environment. This allows you to observe network device behavior without having to construct the actual network.

Each element in the network environment is modeled using a C++ routine. This includes network device nodes, such as hubs, switches, and routers, as well as network links. Different elements display different characteristics, such as packet delays, packet loss, and packet processing. The simulation models account for the different characteristics within the C++ code.

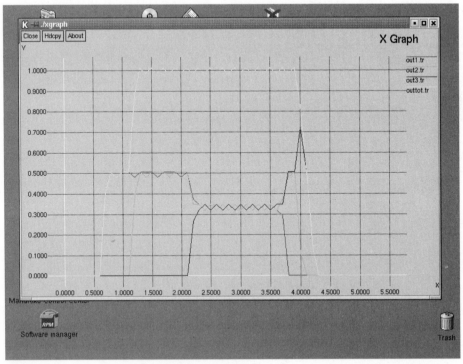

Figure 17.5 xgraph display of monitor trace files.

Network Simulator then uses the OTcl programming language, developed at MIT, to allow the network administrator to easily create model files defining how the individual network elements are configured. Using the OTcl language, the network administrator does not need to know the C++ modeling language used by the Network Simulator application.

After the model is created, it is run from the command-line ns program. The ns program steps through the model, injecting data packets into the network as defined in the network model program. Network output is sent to several different files used both to trace the network activity and to monitor network events.

The output files produced by ns can be examined using the nam and xgraph applications. The nam program reads the ns trace file output and graphically simulates the network configuration and events. This provides a real-time graphical display of the simulation behavior. The xgraph program is used to graph the network monitor events, showing network utilization and packet-loss statistics.

The next chapter presents the Scalable Simulation Framework (SSF) application. The SSFNet application uses SSF to provide another programmatic simulation for networks, using either the C++ or Java language. There are many different implementations of the SSFNet application available, both open source and commercial. Chapter 18 discusses the open source versions of SSFNet that can be used to simulate network environments.

SSFNet

This chapter presents the SSFNet application, another network simulation package. SSFNet uses the Scalable Simulation Framework (the SSF part), a standard simulation language, to implement simulation models of various network elements and traffic (the Net part). First, this chapter discusses the role of SSF in network modeling, and explains how SSFNet uses SSF to model network elements. Next, a discussion of how to install SSFNet and use it to model simple network environments is presented.

There are two popular implementations of SSF available for network administrators to use for network simulation:

- The Dartmouth SSF package (DaSSF)
- Renesys Corporation's Raceway package (SSFNet)

Both packages use SSF classes to implement network models for simulating large-scale network behavior. The DaSSF package uses C++ classes to model devices, links, and events, while SSFNet uses Java classes. Due to the simplicity of the SSFNet package (and Java), it was used for the examples in this chapter.

NOTE While the core SSF classes are open source, the Renesys implementation of SSF is done using proprietary software. The SSFNet implementation requires a license from Renesys corporation. However, SSFNet is free for students, faculty, and staff members of educational institutions, as well as for U.S. government employees (there is also a 30-day free trial available to commercial users). The concepts explained in this chapter regarding network modeling using SSF also apply to the DaSSF package, which is freely available to all.

What Is SSF?

SSF is used to model discrete event simulation. A set of application programming interfaces (APIs) is created in a common language to provide object-oriented models for elements used in the simulation. Once the models are created, they can be used in any type of simulation that requires those types of elements. There are five base classes used to define the SSF environment:

- Entities
- Processes
- Events
- In Channels
- Out Channels

Each of these base classes is described in the following sections.

Entities

The term entity, within SSF, refers to objects that can own processes and channels. Each entity within the SSF model can be aligned (or connected with) other entities.

An entity is the base object, which is allowed to send and receive data within the network simulation. Entities can be monitored to observe how much data the model processes, and how that data is processed.

Processes

Entities contain processes, which control the information generated and requested by the entities. Processes owned by different entity groups may execute concurrently in the simulation. A fairness policy is implemented that prevents any one process from being executed twice within the same simulation time.

Processes are controlled by process states, which indicate the execution state the process is in. The execution state indicates whether a process is ready to be run, or if it is suspended, waiting for a resource. The scheduling procedure within SSF schedules processes as they become available to run. Processes that are suspended waiting for a specific simulation time are given higher priority than processes suspended waiting for resources.

Events

The simulation is controlled by a series of events that occur during the course of the simulation. The simulation events are configured to simulate data traffic, and the way entities handle data traffic.

Events may be saved and released as they are processed. This enables monitoring of the events as the simulation progresses. Events may also use aliasing to create pointers to events.

In Channels

In Channels are used to receive data within the SSF simulation for the entity. Each In Channel is mapped to zero or more Out Channels to create a communication channel between entities. Entities receive events from the In Channels and process the events.

Out Channels

Out Channels are used in an entity to send data to other entities within the SSF simulation. Each Out Channel is mapped to zero or more In Channels to create a communication channel between entities. Once the entity processes the events, any data produced from the event can be forwarded via the Out Channel to other entities.

What Is SSFNet?

The SSFNet application package contains a complete Java implementation of the SSF engine, along with complete Java models of network devices, links, and protocols. This section describes SSFNet, and explains how it is used to model a network environment.

Libraries

The SSFNet package contains the SSF libraries within Java .jar files. The .jar files contain the Java class files for each simulation model. The two main packages are SSF.OS and SSF.Net.

The SSF.OS package is used to model the host and protocol characteristics within the framework. The main classes contained within the SSF.OS package are:

- **ProtocolGraph**, which defines protocols used for hosts
- **ProtocolSession**, which defines the communication method used for the protocol
- **ProtocolMessage**, which defines the packet used in the ProtocolSession carrying simulated data

Individual protocol models (such as SSF.OS.IP, SSF.OS.TCP, and SSF.OS.UDP) are contained within the SSF.OS package. Each protocol model defines the characteristics of a different type of network communication type (such as connectionless traffic for UDP models, and connection-oriented traffic for TCP models).

The SSF.Net package also contains classes for modeling network objects, including devices, interfaces, links, and routers. The main classes contained within the SSF.Net package are:

- **Net**, which defines the network configuration
- **Host**, which defines host endpoints on the network
- **Router**, which defines network interconnection devices
- **NIC**, which defines network interfaces for hosts and routers
- **Link**, which defines connections between hosts and router interfaces

Each of these elements is defined in the simulation configuration file using a special modeling language.

Domain Modeling Language (DML)

Networks are modeled within SSF using DML. The DML program specifies the network devices, links, and protocols used within the simulation, using a simplified language notation rather than forcing network modelers to program in the SSF implementation language (usually C++ or Java).

The DML specification provides a standard format for defining elements within the model. The format contains DML expressions, which are lists of space-separated key and value pairs.

Each value is encapsulated with brackets, indicating the start and end of the value:

```
key [ value ]
```

Different keys can be separated with spaces or carriage returns:

```
key1 [value1] key2 [value2]
key3 [value3]
```

There may also be definitions of keys within value descriptions:

```
key1 [ key2 [value2] ]
```

This section describes the elements used to create a DML definition for a network.

Networks

Individual networks are defined using the Net tag. The network definition includes the hosts, links, routers, and protocols necessary to complete the simulation. Each network must be assigned a unique network ID value, which is used to identify hosts within the network. An unidentified top-level network must be defined to represent the entire simulation network. It looks something like this:

```
Net [
    # definitions for common network attributes
    Net [ id 1
        # definitions for network 1 hosts
    ]
    net [ id 2
        # definitions for network 2 hosts
    ]
]
```

This definition defines a network simulation of two separate networks. Each network is configured by the attributes defined within its value sections. For creating duplicate networks, the id_range attribute can be used instead of the id attribute:

```
Net [id_range [from 1 to 5]
    # definitions for all the networks
]
```

This creates five separate networks, each with common configurations, such as hosts and links (as you will see in the *Hosts* section, hosts are addressed by network ID as well as host ID, so having duplicate host IDs on separate networks is OK).

There are attributes used in the top-level Net definition to define network-wide features necessary to control the behavior of the simulation. They are:

- frequency
- randomstream
- traffic

The frequency attribute is used to define the clock tick increment within the simulation. The frequency of the overall network must be set to a value equal to or higher than the fastest link speed used in the network definition (see the *Links* section).

```
Net [
     frequency 100000000
]
```

This defines a 100-Mb clock increment for the overall network, and assumes that the fastest link in the network is 100 Mb.

The randomstream attribute is used to define how random numbers are generated for data streams within the simulation. The format of the random-stream attribute is:

```
randomstream [
   generator generatorname
   stream streamname
   reproducibility_level instancetype
]
```

The generator value defines the type of random number generator used for the simulation. There are three values that can be used:

- **MersenneTwister** is the strongest uniform pseudo-random number generator available.
- **Ranlux** is an advanced pseudo-random number generator based on the RCARRY algorithm.
- **Java** is the standard Java Random() function.

The stream value defines a string to seed the random number generator. The reproducibility_level value defines how many instances of the random number generator will be produced within the simulator. This defines how entities acquire random numbers, and whether the random number generator instances are shared between entities. The possible values for this are:

- **timeline.** All entities share the same random number generator in sequence.
- **host.** All random numbers required within a host definition share the same random number generator.

- **protocol.** All random numbers required within a protocol definition share the same random number generator.

- **distribution.** Every random number request from all entities has its own independent random number generator.

The traffic attribute defines the traffic patterns generated within the simulation. Hosts are configured as clients and servers within the simulation, and the traffic attribute defines which clients communicate with which servers. The pattern key is used to define the client and server addresses:

```
traffic [
    pattern [
        client clientaddr
        servers [ nhi serveraddr port portaddr]
    ]
]
```

The *clientaddr* and *serveraddr* values define specific hosts defined within the simulation. The simulation client ID references the client used for the traffic pattern. One traffic pattern defines the connection for a single client. Multiple pattern keys can be defined for a single traffic attribute.

There may be more than one servers value defined for the client. Each servers value defines the address of a server (including the interface value), as well as a port number used for the connection. An example of this would be:

```
traffic [
    pattern [
        client 1
        servers [nhi 3(0) port 1600 ]
        servers [nhi 4(0) port 1600 ]
    ]
    pattern [
        client 2
        servers [nhi 5(0) port 1600 ]
    ]
]
```

Hosts

Within the network definition, hosts define endpoints that contain client or server objects to send and receive traffic on the network. The host attribute is defined as:

```
host [
    id idvalue
    interface [
        # interface definitions
```

```
        ]
    graph [
        # protocols defined for the host
    ]
]
```

Hosts are identified by both the network ID and host ID numbers, separated with a colon. Thus, host 1:3 identifies host 3 on network 1.

Interfaces on a host (yes, there can be more than one) are identified with the interface attribute. Attributes for the interface are:

```
interface [
    id value
    bitrate speed
    latency delay
    buffer size
    flaky prob
    queue queuename
    tcpdump dumpfile
]
```

A unique id value must be specified for the interface on the host. A specific interface on the host is referenced by the interface number within parentheses—the address 3(0) references interface 0 on host 3. The speed of the interface is defined by the bitrate attribute (in bits per second). The latency attribute allows you to define a delay value for the interface if necessary.

Some more exotic attributes include setting the buffer size (in bytes) of the interface, setting a packet drop probability (using flaky) setting a queuing method (the default is dropTailQueue), and defining a tcpdump file to send all the simulated packet traffic to.

The graph attribute is used to ProtocolGraph objects supported by the host. Individual protocol definitions are described later in the *Protocols* section.

Links

After defining networks and hosts, you will want to connect the hosts within the network together. This is done using the link attribute. Each of the host interfaces connected together on the same link are defined using the attach attribute, along with a delay value (in seconds) set for the entire link:

```
link [attach 1(0) attach 2(0) attach 3(0) delay 0.005]
```

This definition connects three host interfaces together in a single link, and assigns a delay of 5 ms to the link. A simple network configuration would look like:

```
Net [
    frequency 100000000
    host [
        id 1
        interface [id 0 bitrate 10000000 latency 0.001]
    ]
    host [
        id 2
        interface [id 0 bitrate 10000000 latency 0.001]
    ]
    link [attach 1(0) attach 2(0) delay 0.005]
]
```

Of course, this simple network definition doesn't do anything yet, but it shows the basics for defining hosts and links within the network. Next it's time to define a router, which allows communication between hosts on different networks.

Routers

The router attribute is used to simulate a router device connected between networks. The format of the router attribute is:

```
router [
    id value
    interface [
        # interface definition
    ]
    graph [
        # protocol definitions
    ]
    route [
        # detailed router definitions
    ]
]
```

As with hosts, routers are addressed by a specific router ID value (they must be unique on each network, including host addresses), and one or more interface ID values. The interface definitions are the same as used for the host attribute.

The graph attribute is used to specify the protocols used by the router (as described in the *Protocols* section, next). The route attribute is used to specify additional router attributes that modify the behavior of the router. The most common route attribute is dest. It is used to define a default interface for network traffic to be forwarded to, if it is not found in the routing table:

```
router [
    id 1
    interface [id_range [from 0 to 5] bitrate 10000000 buffer 8000]
    route [dest default interface 0]
]
```

In this sample configuration, the default route path is interface 0 on the router. Any packets entering the router that do not have a specific destination defined in one of the other interfaces will be automatically forwarded to interface 0.

Protocols

Host and router entities must know how to communicate on the simulated network. Configuring different protocol layers within the device ensures this. Each protocol necessary for communication must be defined in the graph attribute, using the ProtocolSession attribute. Protocols are defined in top-down order.

The ProtocolSession protocols are contained in the SSF.OS class. Different SSF implementations contain different sets of protocols. Table 18.1 lists the protocols that are available in the SSF.Net package.

The session is defined using the format:

```
ProtocolSession [
    name protname use class
    # additional attributes
]
```

Table 18.1   SSFNet Protocols

PROTOCOL	DESCRIPTION
IP	The base-level IP support
TCP.tcpSessionMaster	TCP session support
UDP.udpSessionMaster	UDP session support
Socket.socketMaster	Socket programming interface
TCP.test.tcpClient	TCP client device
TCP.test.tcpServer	TCP server device
OSPF.sOSPF	OSPF routing protocol
BGP4.BGPSession	BGP4 routing protocol

Each protocol type can be defined by additional attributes that are specified within the ProtocolSession. Each protocol type has its own set of attributes that are used to control the behavior of the protocol. The tcpClient protocol type defines the characteristics of a standard TCP client device. It uses these attributes:

- **start_time** defines when the client should start sending packets.
- **start_window** defines a window of time from the start_time when the client can start sending packets.
- **show_report** determines if output information should be produced when a packet is sent.
- **debug** determines if debug information should be produced.
- **file_size** sets the amount of data that will be transferred.
- **request_size** sets the size of the response packets.

A sample configuration would look like:

```
host [
    id 1
    interface [id 0 bitrate 10000000 latency 0.005]
    graph [
        ProtocolSession [name TCPServer use SSF.OS.TCP.test.tcpServer]
        ProtocolSession [
            name TCPClient use SSF.OS.TCP.test.tcpClient
            start_time 1.0
            start_window 1.0
            file_size 50000000
            request_size 10
        ]
        ProtocolSession [name socket use SSF.OS.Socket.socketMaster]
        ProtocolSession [name tcp use SSF.OS.TCP.sessionMaster]
        ProtocolSession [name ip use SSF.OS.IP]
    ]
]
```

This example specifies both a client and server session on the same host; thus, this host can be used as both a client and a server in the simulation.

Downloading and Installing SSFNet

As mentioned in the chapter introduction, there are a few different SSF implementations available to simulate network operations. The Renesys corporation implements SSF technology in the SSFNet package a collection of Java libraries. The SSFNet package includes the standard open source SSF classes, as well as additional proprietary kernel and support libraries used for SSF and DML.

Since SSFNet is implemented as a set of Java libraries (.jar files), it can be used on any platform that supports Java. This means that you can run SSFNet simulations on both your Unix hosts and your Windows workstations. This section describes how to download and install the SSF.Net package for either environment.

> **NOTE** The SSFNet Java libraries require that either the Java runtime environment (JRE) or Software Development Kit, Standard Edition (J2SE) be installed on the system. The current version of these is 1.4.1, patch 01, which is available on the Sun Java Web site (http://java.sun.com).

Downloading

The main SSFNet Web page is supported by the SSF project, and is located at www.ssfnet.org. It contains documentation and tutorials on using SSFNet to simulate network behavior. There are also links to places to download SSF implementations.

The SSFNet distribution is supported by Renesys on its own Web site. You must connect to a registration Web page to register for downloading the software. At the time of this writing, the current version of SSFNet is 1.4, and the registration page is located at:

```
http://www.renesys.com/cgi-bin/raceway1.4
```

The registration page requests that you fill out a simple form, and then emails you a pass phrase and URL to download the actual software.

> **NOTE** Corporate users of SSFNet can download a 30-day trial copy of SSFNet. This is the full working version without any limitations. License fees are used to support development of SSFNet.

The download file is a gnuzipped tar file: ssfnet_raceway[1].tar.gz.

Installing

After downloading the distribution file, you must uncompress and unpack it into a directory. The distribution file contains both the source code for SSFNet and the precompiled Java libraries, so it is ready for installation. If you want to unpack the distribution into a permanent directory, you can use the -C option of the tar command:

```
tar -zxvf ssfnet_raceway[1].tar.gz -C /usr/local
```

This command creates the directory /usr/local/ssfnet, and places all of the library and source code files there.

Creating a Development Environment

Since the SSFNet classes are contained in Java libraries, they must be available for the Java runtime environment to locate when executing SSFNet simulations. This requires you to set up environment variables on the system to point to the location of the jar files, as well as the Java runtime files.

In order to run the java command-line program from any location on your system, you should add the location of the java file to the PATH environment variable. On my Linux system, it is located in the directory /usr/java/j2sdk1.4.1_01/bin. This location will vary, depending on your system installation, and whether you loaded the JRE or J2SE Java package.

On Unix systems, the PATH environment variable can be modified from the profile file in your $HOME directory. On my Mandrake system, this is actually .bash_profile. On some Unix systems it is called just .profile. You do not want to replace the existing PATH variable, but add the new path to it:

```
export PATH=$PATH:/usr/java/j2sdk1.4.1_01/bin
```

On Windows systems, the PATH environment variable is modified from the System Properties dialog box. This can be reached by either selecting Start, Settings, Control Panel from the Start menu, then selecting the System icon, or by right-clicking on the My Computer desktop icon, then selecting the Properties menu item. Windows NT, 2000, and XP all allow you to set environment variables for the currently logged-in user, or system-wide variables if you have Administrator privileges. The new path for the java executable file should be appended to the existing PATH environment variable.

After setting the PATH environment variable, you must set the CLASSPATH environment variable, for Java to find the SSFNet Java classes. There are five paths that must be added to the CLASSPATH:

- /usr/local/ssfnet/lib/raceway.jar (the Renesys SSFNet libraries)
- /usr/local/ssfnet/lib/ssfnet.jar (the standard SSF.Net libraries)
- /usr/local/ssfnet/lib/cernlite.jar (the random number generators)
- /usr/local/ssfnet/lib/regexp.jar (the utilities library package)
- /usr/local/ssfnet/src/ (the source code top-level directory)

Again, you can add these values to the existing CLASSPATH environment variable in the .profile (or .bash_profile) file in the $HOME directory:

```
export CLASSPATH=$CLASSPATH:/usr/local/ssfnet/lib/raceway.jar:
/usr/local/ssfnet/lib/ssfnet.jar:/usr/local/ssfnet/lib/cernlite.jar:
/usr/local/ssfnet/lib/regexp.jar:/usr/local/ssfnet/src/
```

The Windows version of the CLASSPATH can also be set from the System Properties dialog box, as with the PATH environment variable.

After setting the PATH and CLASSPATH environment, you must log out and log back in to acquire the new settings. You can test to see if they are set by trying to run SSFNet without specifying a DML file:

```
$ java SSF.Net.Net
------------------------------------------------------------------
|         Raceway SSF 1.1b01 (15 March 2002)
|         (c)2000,2001,2002 Renesys Corporation
|
|         ??
|
------------------------------------------------------------------
Syntax: Net [-check]
            [-dump]
            [-relax]
            [-ip a.b.c.d/m]
            maxtime dmlfile1 [ dmlfile2 [...dmlfileN]]]

 -check: schema-check the input DML file(s) first
 -dump: dump NHI/CIDR/IP address tables, but don't actually run the
model
 -relax: fail to enforce strict rules about CIDR/IP attributes
 -ip addr: allocate IP addresses from the given block (default:
0.0.0.0/0)
$
```

This shows that both the Java executable file and the SSFNet library files are accessible from the working directory.

Using SSFNet

Now that you have SSFNet installed, it is time to create a test model and observe how it is simulated within the SSFNet environment. This section walks through the process of creating a network model, and watching the output from SSFNet as it is simulated.

Creating a Model

For this exercise, you will create a simple network model containing three clients located on a 10-MB LAN, along with a router. The router connects to another router at 1.5 Mb (simulating a T1 link). Connected to the remote router is a server device. Figure 18.1 shows a diagram of this configuration.

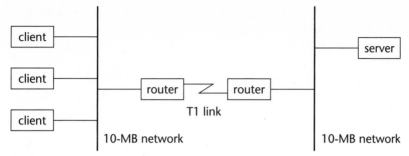

Figure 18.1   Sample network configuration.

The sample network is set to emulate all three clients sending traffic to the remote server at a constant rate. This should overrun the T1 line, which will limit the throughput to the server. The DML code used to simulate this network is shown in Figure 18.2.

```
Net [
    frequency 10000000

    randomstream [
        generator "MersenneTwister"
        stream "stream1"
        reproducibility_level "timeline"
    ]

    traffic [
        pattern [
            client 1
            servers [nhi 4(0) port 1600]
        ]
        pattern [
            client 2
            servers [nhi 4(0) port 1600]
        ]

        pattern [
            client 3
            servers [nhi 4(0) port 1600]
        ]

    ]

    host [
        idrange [from 1 to 3]
        interface [id 0 bitrate 10000000]
```

Figure 18.2   DML model of sample network. *(continued)*

```
                nhi_route [dest default interface 0 next_hop 10(0)]
                graph [
                    ProtocolSession [
                        name TCPclient use SSF.OS.TCP.test.tcpClient
                        start_time 1.0
                        start_window 1.0
                        file_size 1000000
                        request_size 10
                        show_report true
                    ]
                    ProtocolSession [name socket use
SSF.OS.Socket.socketMaster]
                    ProtocolSession [name tcp use SSF.OS.TCP.tcpSessionMaster
                        tcpinit[
                            show_report true
                        ]
                    ]
                    ProtocolSession [name ip use SSF.OS.IP]
                ]
            ]

        host [
            id 4
            interface [id 0 bitrate 10000000 tcpdump test.dmp]
            nhi_route [dest default interface 0 next_hop 11(0)]
            graph [
                ProtocolSession [
                    name TCPServer use SSF.OS.TCP.test.tcpServer
                    port 1600
                    request_size 10
                    show_report true
                ]
                ProtocolSession [name socket use
SSF.OS.Socket.socketMaster]
                ProtocolSession [name tcp use SSF.OS.TCP.tcpSessionMaster
                    tcpinit[
                        show_report true
                    ]
                ]
                ProtocolSession [name ip use SSF.OS.IP]
            ]
        ]

        router [
            idrange [from 10 to 11]
            interface [id 0 bitrate 10000000]
            interface [id 1 bitrate 1500000]
            graph [ProtocolSession [name ip use SSF.OS.IP]]
```

Figure 18.2 *(continued)*

```
        route [dest default interface 1]
    ]


    link [attach 1(0) attach 2(0) attach 3(0) attach 10(0)]
    link [attach 11(0) attach 4(0)]
    link [attach 10(1) attach 11(1)]
]
```

Figure 18.2   *(continued)*

Most of the lines in this model are straightforward. First, the network definition defines the simulation frequency at 10000000 (as this is the fastest link
rate), a randomstream is defined for the entire simulation, and the traffic patterns are defined. Three separate patterns are defined, one from each client to
the host.

Next, the three client hosts are defined. This is different from what you have
seen earlier, as all three hosts are defined in a single host attribute. The idrange
attribute is used to specify all three hosts at once. Each of the hosts has a single
network interface, set for 10 Mb, along with the tcpClient protocol and necessary subprotocols. The tcpClient protocol has additional attributes defined,
such as the size of the file to transfer (1 Mb). The show_report attribute is used
to output information from each client as it starts the file transfer.

The nhi_route attribute is similar to the route attribute described in the
Routers section. Since the model does not specify IP addresses, the route path
for each host must be specified. The nhi_route attribute allows you to specify
the default interface to use, along with the address of the device that will forward packets to the next network:

```
nhi_route [dest default interface 0 next_hop 10(0)]
```

The server host is defined next. When the interface is defined, an additional
attribute is included:

```
interface [id 0 bitrate 10000000 tcpdump test.dmp]
```

The tcpdump subattribute is used to tell SSFNet to record all of the simulated packets sent and received on this interface to a file in tcpdump format.
This allows you to use tcpdump and tcptrace to analyze the simulation traffic
(as will be discussed in the *Interpreting the Results* section). The tcpServer protocol is defined for the server, specifying the show_result subattribute to display the events during the simulation.

The routers are defined in a single router attribute section. Each router has
two interfaces, a 10-Mb connection to the networks, and a 1.5-Mb interface to
simulate the T1 connection. The routers must simulate the IP protocol so they
can forward IP packets between the networks.

Finally, the links connecting the devices are defined. The first link definition defines the LAN connection between the three client hosts and the first router. The second link definition defines the LAN connection between the server host and the second router. The final link definition defines the T1 connection between the two routers.

Running the Simulation

After creating the DML model, you can run it through the SSFNet simulator, using the java command line, along with the SSF.Net.Net base class. The format of the SSFNet line is:

```
java SSF.Net.Net time modelname
```

where *time* defines the amount of time (in seconds) you want the simulation to run, and *modelname* defines the DML file you want to use in the simulation.

Running the simulation produces the following results:

```
$ java SSF.Net.Net 100 test.dml
---------------------------------------------------------------------
|        Raceway SSF 1.1b01 (15 March 2002)
|        (c)2000,2001,2002 Renesys Corporation
|
|        ??
|
---------------------------------------------------------------------

CIDR            IP Block           b16              NHI
--              0.0.0.0/27         0x00000000
0               0.0.0.0/29         0x00000000       1(0)  2(0)  3(0)  10(0)
1               0.0.0.12/30        0x0000000c       11(0)  4(0)
2               0.0.0.8/30         0x00000008       10(1)  11(1)


NHI Addr             CIDR Level          IP Address Block      % util
--                   --                  0.0.0.0/27            56.25


**                   Using specified 100.0ns clock resolution

--- Phase I: construct table of routers and hosts

--- Phase II: connect Point-To-Point links

--- Phase III: add static routes
## Net config: 6 routers and hosts
## Elapsed time: 0.725 seconds
** Running for 1000000000 clock ticks (== 100.0 seconds sim time)
1.0897069 TCP host 3 src={0.0.0.3:10001} dest={0.0.0.14:1600}  Active
Open
1.0902842 TCP host 4 src={0.0.0.14:1600} dest={0.0.0.3:10001} SYN recvd
```

```
1.9199429 TCP host 2 src={0.0.0.2:10001} dest={0.0.0.14:1600}  Active
Open
1.9204565 TCP host 1 src={0.0.0.1:10001} dest={0.0.0.14:1600}  Active
Open
1.9205202 TCP host 4 src={0.0.0.14:1600} dest={0.0.0.2:10001} SYN recvd
1.9210338 TCP host 4 src={0.0.0.14:1600} dest={0.0.0.1:10001} SYN recvd
15.1613078 [ sid 1 start 1.0897069 ] TCPclient 3 srv 4(0) rcvd 1000000B
at 568.52kbps - read() SUCCESS
15.1613078 TCP host 3 src={0.0.0.3:10001} dest={0.0.0.14:1600}Active
Close
15.1618851 TCP host 4 src={0.0.0.14:1600} dest={0.0.0.3:10001}Active
Close
15.1618851 TCP host 4 src={0.0.0.14:1600}dest={0.0.0.3:10001}Passive
Close
17.7129151 [ sid 1 start 1.9199429 ] TCPclient 2 srv 4(0) rcvd 1000000B
at 506.554kbps - read() SUCCESS
17.7129151 TCP host 2 src={0.0.0.2:10001} dest={0.0.0.14:1600}Active
Close
17.7134924 TCP host 4 src={0.0.0.14:1600} dest={0.0.0.2:10001}Active
Close
17.7134924 TCP host 4 src={0.0.0.14:1600}dest={0.0.0.2:10001}Passive
Close
17.721875 [ sid 1 start 1.9204565 ] TCPclient 1 srv 4(0) rcvd 1000000B
at 506.283kbps - read() SUCCESS
17.721875 TCP host 1 src={0.0.0.1:10001} dest={0.0.0.14:1600} Active
Close
17.7224523 TCP host 4 src={0.0.0.14:1600} dest={0.0.0.1:10001}Active
Close
17.7224523 TCP host 4 src={0.0.0.14:1600}dest={0.0.0.1:10001}Passive
Close
-----------------------------------------------------------------------
| 1 timelines, 5 barriers, 24171 events, 3374 ms, 8 Kevt/s
-----------------------------------------------------------------------
$
```

The simulation is allowed to run for 100 seconds, although, as seen in the output, it only took slightly less than 18 seconds for it to complete the data transfers. After the opening banner, SSFNet lists the networks that it identified in the DML file. Since no IP addresses were defined, SSFNet shows the assigned address ranges for each network.

Next, SSFNet uses three phases to interpret and run the model. If any errors are encountered during the individual phases, a Java runtime error will be produced.

WARNING Unfortunately, the Java runtime errors produced by SSFNet are not self-explanatory. Often lots of guessing and digging are required to determine what part of the DML file produced the error. Often, starting out simple and building parts of the network allows you to isolate what piece causes a particular Java error message.

After the three phases are complete, the output generated from any show-report attributes is displayed as the simulation runs. As seen in this example, each of the clients displays when the TCP connection is started, when the data is transferred, and when the connection is closed. Likewise, the server host also indicates its progress during the simulation. This feature enables you to watch the network connections, and determine if things are progressing the way you intended them to progress.

After the simulation is complete, you can analyze any dump files that were created from the hosts.

Interpreting the Results

When the tcpdump attribute is used on an interface, a complete tcpdump formatted dump file is created with the simulation packets. As SSFNet creates actual IP packets, you can analyze the produced dump file using both the tcpdump program and the tcptrace program, described in Chapter 10, "tcptrace."

In this example, the server host creates the tcpdump file test.dmp, containing all of the packets received and sent by the host (host number 4 in this example). You can perform a quick analysis of the traffic using the default tcptrace command:

```
$ tcptrace test.dmp
1 arg remaining, starting with 'test.dmp'
Ostermann's tcptrace -- version 6.2.0 -- Fri Jul 26, 2002

5883 packets seen, 5883 TCP packets traced
elapsed wallclock time: 0:00:05.239794, 1122 pkts/sec analyzed
trace file elapsed time: 0:00:16.633536
TCP connection info:
  1: 0.0.0.3:10001 - 0.0.0.14:1600 (a2b)   981>  980<  (complete)
  2: 0.0.0.2:10001 - 0.0.0.14:1600 (c2d)   981>  980<  (complete)
  3: 0.0.0.1:10001 - 0.0.0.14:1600 (e2f)   981>  980<  (complete)
$
```

As expected, three separate connection sessions were observed, one for each client host sending the data file to the server host. Note how SSFNet assigned a unique IP address to each of the hosts in the simulation, even though they were not specifically configured in the DML model.

As with any tcpdump dump file, you can use the tcptrace -l and -o options to observe the details for a single session:

```
tcptrace -l -o1 test.dmp
```

This command produces the detailed results of the first client's network traffic. You can observe the network behavior as the client sent the 1-Mb data file to the server.

You can also use the tcptrace graphical features to graph the network behavior during the simulation. The command:

```
tcptrace -G -o1 test.dmp
```

generates several important graphs showing the network behavior of the simulated data transfer. Figure 18.3 shows the standard throughput graph generated from the data.

As seen from the figure, the throughput dramatically drops off as all of the data transfers from the clients kick in. Figure 18.4 shows the round-trip time (RTT) graph of the data transfer.

The round-trip time indicates that, as expected, the T1 link between the client and host has slowed things down considerably.

After observing the basic network simulation results, you can modify the model to observe different types of data transfers. Instead of defining all three clients in one host attribute, you can create three separate host attributes—each one transferring different types and sizes of data—and even define different start times for each.

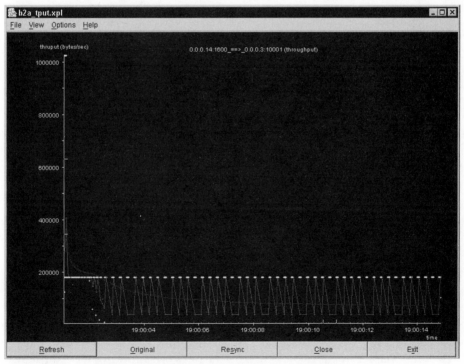

Figure 18.3 Throughput of simulated data transfer from client 1.

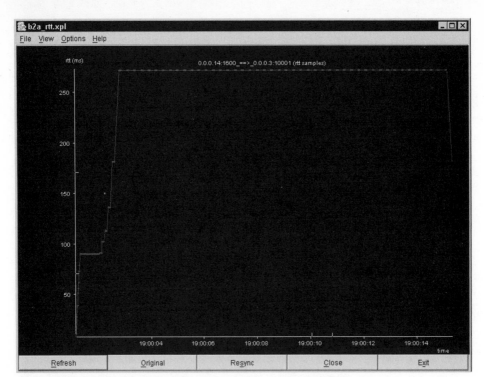

Figure 18.4 Round-trip time of data transfer from client 1.

Summary

The Scalable Simulation Framework (SSF) provides a robust modeling environment for simulating entities, events, and processes in different types of situations. The SSFNet application uses SSF to model network behavior, modeling network devices, links, and protocols.

SSFNet uses Java to create class models for hosts, routers, network links, and protocols that can be combined together to simulate a large network environment. Once the network model is defined, simulations can be performed showing how each network device and link will perform given different network conditions.

SSFNet has the ability to create standard tcpdump dump files containing the network traffic generated by the network simulation. The dump files can then be analyzed using tcpdump and tcptrace to observe how the simulated network handled the data traffic.

The final chapter in this book wraps up the network application performance section by presenting a sample production network environment and test application. Each of the network application performance tools presented in this section is used to simulate and emulate the production environment, and the test results will be compared against the real-world network performance.

## CHAPTER 19

Comparing Application Performance Tools

Now that you have a whole suite of network application performance tools available for use, it would be a good idea to see a specific example of how each one can be used within a production application environment. This chapter wraps up the book by presenting a sample production network and application, and walking through the use of simulation and emulation tools to see what type of application performance to expect.

The whole purpose of network emulation and simulation is to observe network behavior without affecting the actual production network. Part III of this book presented several tools that can be used to either emulate or simulate a production network in a controlled environment, allowing you to test network application performance. The first section of this chapter explains how to create network models to accurately emulate or simulate network application performance.

Modeling the Production Environment

The first step to network emulation or simulation is to produce an accurate model of the production network. Sometimes this can be a difficult task. In these days of complicated switches, routers, and client devices, tracing the end-to-end path between two network endpoints is not easy.

It is usually best to simplify the network model as much as possible. If there are lots of components between the network endpoints, often simply modeling the bottleneck points is enough for the model to make an accurate estimate of network performance. If you have several 100-Mb switches connected together, passing data off to a router connected with a T1 link to the Internet, a model of traffic to and from the Internet does not need to include all of the switch devices. The network performance will be most affected by the performance of the router, with minimal effect from the switches. To model this network you can create a detailed model of the router behavior, and model the switches as just additional delay in the network.

The Production Network

This chapter demonstrates how to emulate and simulate a common network problem—connecting customers to applications on remote servers. Often network applications are tested in test environments in which all workstations and servers are local. However, in the production network environment, remote offices are often connected to the network to access the application. The network shown in Figure 19.1 contains several layers of hubs, switches, and routers between the client and server within a corporate network environment.

This figure shows a typical production network configuration. In this example there are two separate corporate buildings, each containing customer workstations and a local server. Workstations on customers' desktops are connected to a shared hub in a wiring closet. The hubs for each floor are connected to a switch, which in turn is connected via a high-speed link to a central core switch and router. Each switch in the building operates on a separate VLAN, maximizing network performance. The servers are directly connected to the central switch, also to maximize performance.

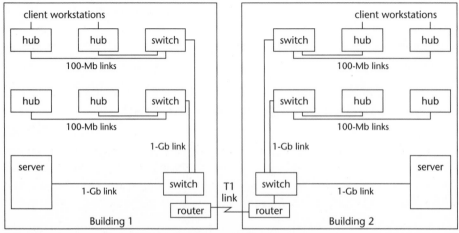

Figure 19.1 Complicated production network environment.

The two buildings are connected via a T1 link, using routers connected to the central switches. Customers can connect to the server in either building to access applications and data. However, if a network application is fielded on a single server, customers located in the remote building must traverse the T1 link to access the application. This is where the bottleneck occurs, and where network modeling must be done to observe just how much slower the application's performance will be for those customers.

Modeling the Network

Instead of trying to model the entire corporate network environment, you can break the network down into a series of black-box components, each with specific behavioral characteristics. Figure 19.2 shows a simplified model of the complicated network.

The simplified network consists of two separate switch networks, connected via a T1 link (using routers). Each switch network connects endpoint devices to a common node, representing the internal building network. This node will introduce a small amount of delay into the data path, but does not adversely affect the network traffic too much. Since the bottleneck on the internal network is the 100-Mb links from the workstations to the hubs, the link from the device nodes to the switch node is set to 100 Mb. The network bottleneck produced by the T1 link is modeled using both router endpoints and a 1.5-Mb link.

NOTE This model assumes that the local switches will not experience overloading with normal network traffic. If this occurs in your network, you will want to also model the queue behavior within the switches and determine how that affects the network application performance.

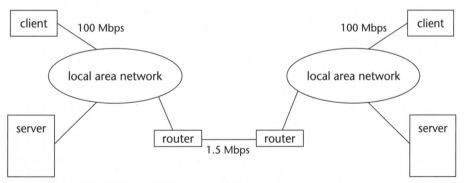

Figure 19.2 Simplified model of the production network.

The point of these tests is to determine the response times that should be expected when a customer accesses a network application on a remote server, and when the customer accesses the same application on a local server. This should provide a good benchmark to determine how the T1 link affects the performance of the network application.

For the purposes of this example, let's assume that the network application is a client/server-based application. The customer workstation sends small query packets to the server, and receives larger response packets containing the query information. A 10-Mb data file size will be used to model the amount of data returned by the server from multiple client queries. This should produce a large enough data sample to determine the effect of the T1 link on the network application.

NOTE With the client/server model, you can perform the data transfer in either direction, as the same results should apply to both directions of data travel.

Using ns

The first simulation generated uses the ns application. For the ns simulation, a model must be created, using the OTcl language, that accurately simulates both the network environment and the network application data traffic pattern. This section explains how to create a model, run the simulation, and interpret the results.

Building the Model

The ns OTcl model must include nodes to simulate the network environment model shown in Figure 19.2. Each node must be defined, along with the links connecting the nodes, and the protocols used to transfer the data. A diagram of the ns model is shown in Figure 19.3.

The ns network model uses nodes to represent each of the network devices in the simplified network model. Each link must be defined to represent the bandwidth and delay present in the production system.

Since ns only produces trace files of the simulation, to determine the amount of time required to transfer 10 Mb of data between the client devices and the server, you must process the data in the trace file. To produce the trace file, you must configure the trace feature to track the data packets as they are sent and accepted by the devices.

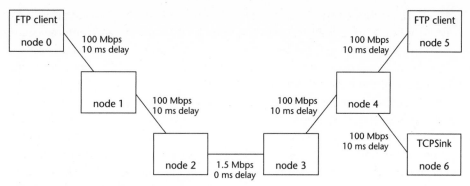

Figure 19.3 ns network model diagram.

The resulting OTcl model is shown in Figure 19.4.

```
set ns [new Simulator]
set nf [open out.nam w]
set nf2 [open out.tr w]
$ns namtrace-all $nf
$ns trace-all $nf2

$ns color 1 Blue
$ns color 2 Red

set n0 [$ns node]
set n1 [$ns node]
set n2 [$ns node]
set n3 [$ns node]
set n4 [$ns node]
set n5 [$ns node]
set n6 [$ns node]

$ns duplex-link $n0 $n1 100Mb 10ms DropTail
$ns duplex-link $n1 $n2 100Mb 10ms DropTail
$ns duplex-link $n2 $n3 1.5Mb 0ms SFQ
$ns duplex-link $n4 $n3 100Mb 10ms DropTail
$ns duplex-link $n5 $n4 100Mb 10ms DropTail
$ns duplex-link $n6 $n4 100Mb 10ms DropTail

$ns duplex-link-op $n2 $n3 queuePos 0.5

set tcp0 [new Agent/TCP]
$ns attach-agent $n0 $tcp0
$tcp0 set class_ 1

set ftp1 [new Application/FTP]
```

Figure 19.4 Network model for the ns simulation. *(continued)*

```
$ftp1 attach-agent $tcp0

set tcp1 [new Agent/TCP]
$ns attach-agent $n5 $tcp1
$tcp1 set class_ 2

set ftp2 [new Application/FTP]
$ftp2 attach-agent $tcp1

set sink1 [new Agent/TCPSink]
$ns attach-agent $n6 $sink1

set sink2 [new Agent/TCPSink]
$ns attach-agent $n6 $sink2

$ns connect $tcp0 $sink1
$ns connect $tcp1 $sink2

proc finish {} {
        global ns nf nf2
        $ns flush-trace
        close $nf
        close $nf2
        exit
}

$ns at 1.0 "$ftp1 start"
$ns at 1.0 "$ftp2 start"
$ns at 3.0 "$ftp2 stop"
$ns at 60.0 "$ftp1 stop"
$ns at 70.0 "finish"

$ns run
```

Figure 19.4   *(continued)*

The simulation model defines six nodes, and connects them using the appropriate network link speeds and delays. Each of the Ethernet links has a 10-ms delay added, to model the delay induced by the switch devices in the network. One node on each network is configured to be an FTP client using the FTP application model, while a single end node is configured to be the FTP server using the TCPSink agent model. This configuration allows a constant data transfer between the client nodes and the server node.

Running the Model

After creating and saving the simulation model, you can run it using the ns command-line program:

```
$ ns test.tcl
```

Depending on the speed of your Unix host, the simulation may run for a few seconds, then finish. After it finishes, you should see two files: out.nam and out.tr. The out.nam file contains the network simulation data for the nam animator program. The out.tr file contains the network simulation regarding the raw data transfers.

You can observe the network in action by using the nam program with the out.nam file:

```
$nam out.nam
```

This starts the nam application, and loads the data from the out.nam file. You may want to click the Relayout button a few times, until the network layout suits your taste. Figure 19.5 shows the basic layout of the network simulation, along with packets as they are being processed.

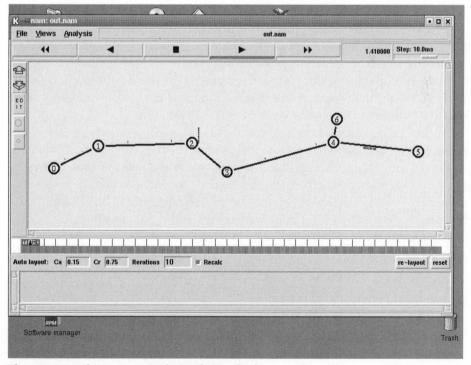

Figure 19.5   The nam network simulation display.

You can watch the queue status of the router devices as packets are passed from the remote client to the server device.

Interpreting the Results

After the ns simulation is run, you can analyze the out.tr file to observe the data transfers. A sample of the out.tr contents looks like:

```
+ 1 0 1 tcp 40 ------- 1 0.0 6.0 0 0
- 1 0 1 tcp 40 ------- 1 0.0 6.0 0 0
+ 1 5 4 tcp 40 ------- 2 5.0 6.1 0 1
- 1 5 4 tcp 40 ------- 2 5.0 6.1 0 1
r 1.010003 0 1 tcp 40 ------- 1 0.0 6.0 0 0
+ 1.010003 1 2 tcp 40 ------- 1 0.0 6.0 0 0
- 1.010003 1 2 tcp 40 ------- 1 0.0 6.0 0 0
r 1.010003 5 4 tcp 40 ------- 2 5.0 6.1 0 1
+ 1.010003 4 6 tcp 40 ------- 2 5.0 6.1 0 1
- 1.010003 4 6 tcp 40 ------- 2 5.0 6.1 0 1
r 1.010006 4 6 tcp 40 ------- 2 5.0 6.1 0 1
```

The trace file shows the status of each simulated packet at any given time in the simulation. The format of the trace file is:

```
event time src dst pkttype pktsize flags fid srcaddr dstaddr seqnum pktid
```

The event field defines the status of the packet record. A plus sign indicates that the packet has been placed in the queue for the associated source and destination node link. A minus sign indicates that the packet has been removed from the link queue, while a letter *r* indicates that the destination node has received the packet. You can use this information to monitor the amount of data that is received by each node in the simulation.

The goal of this simulation was to watch how long it would take each client to send 10 Mb of data to the server. You can use the trace file to watch the data packets as they are received within the network, and count the data. To ensure that you are tracking data from the right client, you need to choose two points in the network that are unique to the individual client data paths. Monitoring data received by node 4 from node 3 ensures that it is data received from client 0, while monitoring data received by host 4 from node 5 ensures it is from client 5.

You can write a simple shell script to create an output file containing the time field and the sum of the packet size field for specific source and destination nodes. A sample would look like this:

```
cat out.tr | grep ^r | grep "3 4 tcp 1040" | awk '{old = old + $6;
printf("%f\t%d\n", $2, old)}' > out.34
```

This script scans the trace file, looking for received packets (the ^r part) from host 3 to host 4 (the 3 4 part) that contain data (the 1040 part). That information is fed into an awk script, which sums the packet sizes, and prints the time and the packet size sum value. The result is redirected to an output file. The result of the output file looks like:

```
$ head out.34
1.096288          1040
1.101835          2080
1.162349          3120
1.167940          4160
1.173487          5200
1.179034          6240
1.228499          7280
1.234046          8320
1.239593          9360
1.245139          10400
$
```

By changing the host numbers in the shell script, you can produce a similar file for the data between hosts 5 and 4, showing the local client data path. Now, you can use the xgraph program to chart both data lines and observe the data streams, as shown in Figure 19.6.

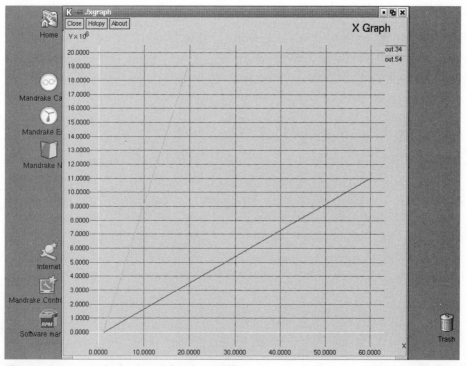

Figure 19.6 xgraph display of the data traffic.

As seen in the xgraph display, both of the data streams start at 1 second into the simulation. The data stream from client 5 to the server reached 10 Mb at about 11 seconds into the simulation, while the data stream from client 0 to the server reached the 10-Mb data mark at about 55 seconds. This indicates that the remote client transfer took about 54 seconds, while the local client transfer took about 10 seconds.

Performing additional analysis of the trace output, you can compare the individual times for each data stream. It took on average 6 ms for one data packet to traverse the network from the remote client to the server, while it took less than 1 ms for the same data to traverse the local network from the local client. A 5-ms difference does not seem like a long time, but, as seen in this example, when large amounts of data are traversing the network, it adds up to a large overall performance delay.

Using SSFNet

Next up is the SSFNet model. To simulate the model network, you must create a DML program defining the network devices and links, along with the protocols used. This section describes the steps necessary to build an SSFNet model and observe the results.

Building the Model

The SSFNet DML model must define the pertinent devices and links to simulate from the production network. Figure 19.7 shows the SSFNet model used to simulate the sample network.

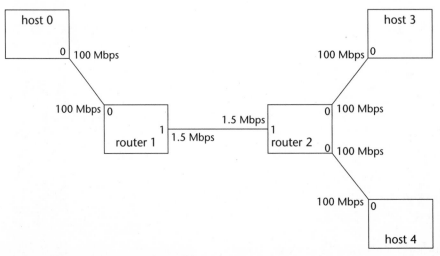

Figure 19.7 SSFNet network model.

The SSFNet network model uses the Ethernet LAN modeling feature to simulate the speed and delay present in the internal switch network within the buildings. This greatly simplifies the model. Each device must also have the proper interfaces configured (shown by the small numbers on the nodes) to represent the link speeds in the model. Figure 19.8 shows the resulting DML model code.

```
Net [
    frequency 1000000000

    randomstream [
        generator "MersenneTwister"
        stream "stream1"
        reproducibility_level "timeline"
    ]

    traffic [
        pattern [
            client 0
            servers [nhi 4(0) port 1600]
        ]
      pattern [
          client 3
          servers [nhi 4(0) port 1600]
      ]
    ]

    host [
        id 0
        interface [id 0 bitrate 10000000]
        route [dest default interface 0]
        graph [
            ProtocolSession [
                name TCPclient use SSF.OS.TCP.test.tcpClient
                start_time 1.0
                start_window 1.0
                file_size 10000000
                request_size 40
                show_report true
            ]
            ProtocolSession [name socket use SSF.OS.Socket.socketMaster]
            ProtocolSession [name tcp use SSF.OS.TCP.tcpSessionMaster
                tcpinit[
                    show_report true
                ]
            ]
            ProtocolSession [name ip use SSF.OS.IP]
```

Figure 19.8 SSFNet DML model. *(continued)*

```
            ]
    ]

    host [
        id 3
     interface [id 0 bitrate 100000000]
     nhi_route [dest default interface 0 next_hop 2(0)]
     graph [
         ProtocolSession [
             name tcpClient use SSF.OS.TCP.test.tcpClient
             start_time 1.0
             start_window 1.0
             file_size 10000000
             request_size 40
             show_report true
         ]
         ProtocolSession [name socket use SSF.OS.Socket.socketMaster]
         ProtocolSession [name tcp use SSF.OS.TCP.tcpSessionMaster
             tcpinit [
                 show_report true
             ]
         ]
         ProtocolSession [name ip use SSF.OS.IP]
     ]
    ]

    host [
        id 4
        interface [id 0 bitrate 100000000 tcpdump test7.dmp]
        nhi_route [dest default interface 0 next_hop 2(0)]
        graph [
            ProtocolSession [
                name TCPServer use SSF.OS.TCP.test.tcpServer
                port 1600
                request_size 10
                show_report true
            ]
            ProtocolSession [name socket use SSF.OS.Socket.socketMaster]
            ProtocolSession [name tcp use SSF.OS.TCP.tcpSessionMaster
                tcpinit[
                    show_report true
```

Figure 19.8 *(continued)*

```
            ]
        ]
        ProtocolSession [name ip use SSF.OS.IP]
      ]
   ]

   router [
       id 1
    interface [id 0 bitrate 100000000]
    interface [id 1 bitrate 1500000]
    graph [ProtocolSession [name ip use SSF.OS.IP]]
    route [dest default interface 1]
    ]
    router [
       id 2
    interface [id 0 bitrate 100000000]
    interface [id 1 bitrate 1500000]
    graph [ProtocolSession [name ip use SSF.OS.IP]]
    route [dest default interface 1]
    ]

    link [attach 0(0) attach 1(0) delay 0.010]
    link [attach 1(1) attach 2(1)]
    link [attach 2(0) attach 3(0) attach 4(0) delay 0.010]
]
```

Figure 19.8 *(continued)*

Hosts 0 and 3 are configured as TCP client devices, capable of sending a 10-Mb file using standard TCP. Host 4 is configured as a TCP server device, accepting the 10-Mb file stream from the clients, and returning an acknowledgment packet. Two router devices are configured to simulate the T1 link within the production network. Since no IP addresses are assigned to the simulation, default routes are specified for each device on the network. Both of the local networks are modeled using a single LAN connecting the devices, and a 10-ms delay period.

Running the Model

The SSFNet model is run using the java command-line interpreter, along with the SSF.Net.Net base class used in the Raceway SSFNet system. Since each of the client devices and the server device use the show_report feature, you can observe the start and end of the data streams. The output looks like:

```
$ java SSF.Net.Net 100 test.dml
------------------------------------------------------------------
|       Raceway SSF 1.1b01 (15 March 2002)
```

```
|        (c)2000,2001,2002 Renesys Corporation
|
|          ??
|
-----------------------------------------------------------------------

CIDR          IP Block           b16            NHI
--            0.0.0.0/27         0x00000000
0             0.0.0.12/30        0x0000000c     0(0)  1(0)
1             0.0.0.8/30         0x00000008     1(1)  2(1)
2             0.0.0.0/29         0x00000000     2(0)  3(0)  4(0)


NHI Addr              CIDR Level          IP Address Block     % util
--                    --                  0.0.0.0/27           56.25


**               Using specified 1.0ns clock resolution

--- Phase I: construct table of routers and hosts

--- Phase II: connect Point-To-Point links

--- Phase III: add static routes
## Net config: 5 routers and hosts
## Elapsed time: 0.667 seconds
** Running for 100000000000 clock ticks (== 100.0 seconds sim time)
1.919942997 TCP host 3 src={0.0.0.2:10001} dest={0.0.0.3:1600} Active
Open
1.920456578 TCP host 0 src={0.0.0.13:10001}dest={0.0.0.3:1600} Active
Open
1.930046197 TCP host 4 src={0.0.0.3:1600} dest={0.0.0.2:10001} SYN recvd
1.941005111 TCP host 4 src={0.0.0.3:1600} dest={0.0.0.13:10001} SYN
recvd
14.39844274 [ sid 1 start 1.919942997 ] tcpClient 3 srv 4(0) rcvd
10000000B at 6411.027kbps - read() SUCCESS
14.39844274 TCP host 3 src={0.0.0.2:10001} dest={0.0.0.3:1600} Active
Close
14.40854594 TCP host 4 src={0.0.0.3:1600} dest={0.0.0.2:10001} Active
Close
14.40854594 TCP host 4 src={0.0.0.3:1600} dest={0.0.0.2:10001} Passive
Close
57.521336685 [ sid 1 start 1.920456578 ] TCPclient 0 srv 4(0) rcvd
10000000B at 1438.826kbps - read() SUCCESS
57.521336685 TCP host 0 src={0.0.0.13:10001} dest={0.0.0.3:1600} Active
Close
57.541885218 TCP host 4 src={0.0.0.3:1600} dest={0.0.0.13:10001} Active
Close
57.541885218 TCP host 4 src={0.0.0.3:1600} dest={0.0.0.13:10001} Passive
Close
-----------------------------------------------------------------------
| 1 timelines, 5 barriers, 117752 events, 7450 ms, 17 Kevt/s
-----------------------------------------------------------------------
$
```

By analyzing the output from the simulation, you can see the start and stop times for each data stream. The next step is to analyze this information to see how the data transfers performed.

Interpreting the Results

From the output data produced by SSFNet, you can determine the time it took for each individual data transfer. For the slow link from host 0 to host 4, the transfer started at about 1.92 seconds in the simulation, and finished at about 57.52 seconds, for a total transfer time of about 55.6 seconds, very close to what the ns test predicted.

For the local file transfer, the transfer again started at about 1.92 seconds in the simulation, and finished at about 14.4 seconds, for a total transfer time of about 12.5 seconds. The ns prediction for this value was a little less close, but still in the same ballpark. Remember, the point of the simulation is to compare the two transfer times, which in both cases, so far, indicate that remote clients will observe a significant decrease in performance when running the network application.

Using dummynet

The first network emulator package to test is the dummynet application. This is used to create a test network environment on a FreeBSD system that can emulate the actual production network. This section explains how to create the dummyet network emulation, and how to observe network application behavior within the test network.

Building the Emulation Environment

Since the dummynet application intercepts packets at the kernel level of the FreeBSD system, you can configure dummynet to affect data traffic either between two installed network cards, or from the local system to the network card or to itself. For this test, I will configure dummynet to intercept packets between itself and a remote device on the test network. The test network application will be an FTP session from the local machine to the remote test host.

Dummynet builds rules that affect network traffic as it traverses the system kernel. A single rule will define the total network behavior between the two endpoints. You must incorporate all network delays and bandwidth limitations within the single rule.

WARNING Remember that dummynet affects the network traffic both when it enters the kernel and as it leaves the kernel, so any delays configured must be cut in half.

Since dummynet uses the ipfw program, you must clear out any existing rules that may affect the test, and then enter the rules necessary to create the emulation rule:

```
# ipfw flush
Are you sure [yn] y
# ipfw add pipe 1 tcp from 192.168.1.1 to 192.168.1.6
# ipfw add pipe 2 tcp from 192.168.1.6 to 192.168.1.6
# ipfw pipe 1 config bw 1.5Mb/s delay 10ms
# ipfw pipe 2 config bw 1.5Mb/s delay 10ms
```

The first command clears any existing rules in the ipfw table. The second command creates a pipe used for all TCP traffic originating from the local host IP address to the specific IP address of the remote test host. The next command creates a second pipe handling traffic in the opposite direction.

After the two pipes are created, they can be configured for the appropriate network bandwidth limitation and delay time. These create an emulation environment for the T1 router and incorporate a network delay representing the delay found on the local network switches. After the first emulation is complete, you must remove these rules, using the flush option, and create two new rules using the 100-Mbps link speed to emulate the local client test.

Running the Emulation

After creating the first set of emulation rules, you can begin a simple network application test by starting an FTP session between the test hosts and sending a 10-Mb file to represent the data stream between the hosts. First, you must create a sample 10-Mb file to use.

I like to echo a string of a known size to a file, then ping-pong copy the file to another file until the size is appropriate:

```
$ echo 01234567890123456789901234 > test
$ cat test > test1
$ cat test1 >> test
$ cat test >> test1
  .

  .
$ ls -al test
-rw-r--r--    1 rich     rich     10000000 Jan 28 15:39 test
$
```

This example creates a 25-byte file, and continually concatenates it onto a work file until the file size is 10 Mb. When the test file is complete, you are ready to start the FTP session:

```
$ ftp 192.168.1.6
Connected to 192.168.1.6.
220 ProFTPD 1.2.2rc1 Server (ProFTPD Default Installation)
Name (192.168.1.6:rich): rich
331 Password required for rich.
Password:
230 User rich logged in.
Remote system type is UNIX.
Using binary mode to transfer files.
ftp> put test
local: test remote: test
200 PORT command successful.
150 Opening BINARY mode data connection for test.
226 Transfer complete.
10000000 bytes sent in 56.3 secs (1.8e+02 Kbytes/sec)
ftp>
```

As seen in the FTP session output, it took 56.3 seconds to transfer the 10-Mb file between the two hosts. This is consistent with the data seen in the network simulations. Next, flush the existing rules, and add the rules to emulate the 100-Mbps link speed:

```
# ipfw pipe 1 config bw 100Mb/s delay 10ms
```

Again, send the sample file via FTP, and watch the results. This time the FTP output shows the total transfer time for the 10-Mb file as 11 seconds. Both of these values are right in line with the results seen in the network simulations.

Using NIST Net

The next network emulation package to test is the NIST Net application. This application allows you to emulate the production network on a Linux system. This section explains how to create the NIST Net model, and how to observe network application behavior within the test network.

Building the Emulation Environment

Like dummynet, NIST Net can be used as either a bridge device between separate network segments, a router device between different subnetworks, or a standalone emulator, affecting only traffic within the local loopback address. In both the bridging and routing scenarios, you must have two network cards in your Linux system, and configure the system for either bridging or routing. You can configure the NIST Net module to affect only specific packets for specific IP addresses, port numbers, and protocols.

For this example, I configured NIST Net to affect all IP network between the local host device and a specific remote IP address connected via a 100-Mb hub on a test network. No external traffic will be present to taint the test samples. For the network application, I will FTP a 10-Mb file to emulate the client/server transactions for 10 Mb of data.

With NIST Net, you must emulate all the production network characteristics within a single model command line. This forces you to determine the end-to-end bandwidth limitations, as well as any delays, packet drops, and retransmissions. As with the dummynet model, the NIST Net model defines the bottleneck speed along the network path, and incorporates any network delays that are present. For this emulation, I will use a 1.5-Mbps bottleneck speed to represent the T1 line limitation for the remote client, and a 100-Mbps bottleneck speed for the local client. The remote click will use a 20-ms delay representing both sets of local switches in the network path, while the local client will use a single 10-ms delay.

> **WARNING** Remember that NIST Net specifies the network bandwidth value as bytes per second, not bits per second. You must divide the network speed by 8 to use the correct speed emulation.

The commands used to start and configure NIST Net for the first test are:

```
# Load.Nistnet
# cnistnet -a 192.168.1.6 192.168.1.1 add new --bandwidth 187500 --delay
20
# cnistnet -a 192.168.1.1 192.168.1.6 add new --bandwidth 187500 --delay
20
# cnistnet -u
```

The first command loads the NIST Net kernel module. You should receive a confirmation message indicating that the module loaded properly (it has been omitted from this output). The second command defines the NIST Net rule used to limit the bandwidth to 1.5 Mbps (187,500 bytes per second), set a delay for 20 ms between the hosts, and of course, define the source and destination hosts for the test.

The third line creates a second rule that duplicates the settings of the first rule, but for the return direction of the connection path. Finally, the NIST Net emulation is started, using the -u command-line option.

> **WARNING** Don't forget to use the -u option to start the emulator. Without it, the configured rules will not be active and affect network traffic.

Running the Emulation

After NIST Net has been started, you can create a test file to FTP between the two test hosts. Any standard method of creating a 10-Mb file can be used.

Now that you have a test file, you can begin the emulated network transfer:

```
ftp> put test
local: test remote: test
200 PORT command successful.
150 Opening BINARY mode data connection for test.
226 Transfer complete.
10000000 bytes sent in 54.8 secs (1.8e+02 Kbytes/sec)
```

As you can see from the FTP output, the NIST Net emulator did its job, limiting the bandwidth of the file transfer so it took 54.8 seconds. Next you must change the rules to reflect a 100-Mbps bandwidth, emulating the local client connection to the server:

```
# cnistnet -a 192.168.1.1 192.168.1.6 add new —bandwidth 12500000 —delay
10
```

The results from this test indicated that the transfer took 11.5 seconds. Again, this is similar to the other emulation and simulation results.

Final Results

After running the network emulators and simulators, you now have a good idea of how the network application will perform on the actual production network. Table 19.1 recaps the results from each of the tests.

As you can see from the test results, all of the tools produce somewhat similar results for the production network. Now, it is time to watch the real network application perform on the production network, to see if the tools are accurate.

Table 19.1   Test Recap

TEST	LOCAL CLIENT TRANSFER (SEC)	REMOTE CLIENT TRANSFER (SEC)
ns	10	54
SSFNet	12.5	55.6
dummynet	11	56.3
NIST Net	11.5	54.8

Again, a simple FTP session is used to transfer a 10-Mb file between hosts on the network. The first test uses hosts separated by a T1 link, connecting two remote networks:

```
ftp> put test
local: test remote: test
200 PORT command successful.
150 Opening BINARY mode data connection for test.
226 Transfer complete.
10000000 bytes sent in 58.6 secs (1.5e+02 Kbytes/sec)
```

The actual data transfer across the T1 link took 58.6 seconds, which is consistent with the simulation and emulation results. All of the network application performance tools were close enough to the correct answer that they could be relied on to determine other network application behavior. You can also fine-tune each of the network models to more accurately represent the actual production network environment.

Summary

This section of the book presented five different scenarios for testing network application performance for a production network environment. This chapter concluded the section by comparing the tools in a common scenario.

The first step to working with network application performance tools is to properly model the production network and application data. Most production networks are complicated, and trying to model every network device would be impractical. Instead, you must determine which network devices and links are the bottlenecks, and which ones contribute to network problems such as delays, dropped packets, and packet retransmissions. After creating a simplified version of the production network, you are ready to simulate and emulate.

Both of the network simulation tools presented, ns and SSFNet, model network devices, links, and data, using configuration files. By defining only the simplified network elements in the simulation, you can easily create an accurate simulation environment that will produce data consistent with the real production network. This enables you to perform lots of "what if", easily modifying the simulation configuration by moving network devices into different locations, increasing or decreasing network link speeds, and modifying network application data that traverses the network.

The network emulation tools presented, dummynet and NIST Net, both modify data traffic as it traverses the system kernel. By placing the emulation tool between two endpoints (or between a remote endpoint and the tool host, using the tool host as the local endpoint), you can force actual network traffic to be modified by the emulation. Configuring the emulation tools is similar to configuring the network simulator models. Each emulator must have rules defined for how the data traffic flow will be affected. By limiting the bandwidth of the data flow to the network bottleneck speed, and adding delays, dropped packets, and retransmissions as necessary, you can easily emulate the production network environment within a test network.

As seen from the results, each of the network application performance tools produced results that were consistent with the actual results observed on the production network. This proves that you can indeed easily duplicate production network performance with a simplified test network environment.

This chapter concludes our walk through network performance tools. I hope you have enjoyed your experience with each of the tools, and will continue to learn and experiment in your network environment. With the advent of new network devices (and network applications), there is always something new to learn in the field of network performance. Hopefully this book has presented a good place to start, and you will continue your education in the field. The following appendix contains lots of Web resources for network performance. It is a good idea to stay in touch with the latest trends and ideas, to keep your network running smoothly. Happy networking.

Resources

One of the advantages of using open source tools is their availability on the Internet. There are scores of Web sites devoted to network performance issues and the tools used to monitor and analyze network performance. This appendix lists some of the resources that are available for each of the tools presented in this book. As with any Internet resource, the URLs provided are subject to change.

Network Monitoring Tools

- The tcpdump Web site: www.tcpdump.org
- The libpcap library: www.tcpdump.org/release/libpcap-0.7.1.tar.gz
- The winpcap library: http://winpcap.polito.it/install/default.htm
- The windump application:
  http://windump.polito.it/install.bin/alpha.WinDump.exe
- The Analyzer application: http://analyzer.polito.it/
- The Ethereal application: www.ethereal.com/distribution/

SNMP Tools

- RFC 1157 (SNMP v1): ftp://ftp.rfc-editor.org/in-notes/rfc1157.txt
- RFC 1155 (MIB): ftp://ftp.rfc-editor.org/in-notes/rfc1155.txt
- RFC 1158 (MIB-II): ftp://ftp.rfc-editor.org/in-notes/rfc1158.txt
- Net-snmp: www.net-snmp.org
- Cisco MIBs: ftp://ftp.cisco.com/pub/mibs/v1/

netperf

- The netperf Web page: www.netperf.org/netperf/NetperfPage.html
- The netperf mailing list archive: www.netperf.org/netperf/training/netperf-talk/index.html
- The netperf manual: www.netperf.org/netperf/training/netperf.ps

dbs

- The dbs Web page: http://ns1.ai3.net/products/dbs/

Iperf

- The Iperf Web page: http://dast.nlanr.net/Projects/Iperf/

Pathrate

- The Pathrate Web page: www.pathrate.org
- Pathrate tutorial: http://www.cc.gatech.edu/fac/Constantinos.Dovrolis/pathrate_tutorial.html

Nettest

- The Nettest Web page: www-itg.lbl.gov/nettest/
- OpenSSL Web page: www.openssl.org
- The pipechar application: http://www-didc.lbl.gov/pipechar/

NetLogger

- The NetLogger Web page: http://www-didc.lbl.gov/NetLogger
- The MySQL Web page: www.mysql.org
- The nl_tcpdump Web page: www.ittc.ku.edu/projects/enable/tcpdump

tcptrace

- The tcptrace Web page: http://irg.cs.ohiou.edu/software/tcptrace/index.html
- The xplot Web page: www.xplot.org

ntop

- The ntop Web page: www.ntop.org

dummynet

- The dummynet Web page: http://info.iet.unipi.it/~luigi0/ip_dummynet/
- The PicoBSD download: http://info.iet.unipi.it/~luigi/ip_dummynet/pico.000608.bin

NIST Net

- The NIST Net Web page: http://snad.ncsl.nist.gov/itg/nistnet/

Network Traffic Generator

- The traffic Web page: http://galileo.spaceports.com/~rsandila/traffic.html

ns

- The Network Simulator Web page: www.isi.edu/nsnam/ns/

SSFNet

- The SSFNet Web page: www.ssfnet.org

Index